# ASCENSION
## AND ROMANTIC
# RELATIONSHIPS

JOSHUA DAVID STONE, Ph.D.
REV. JANNA SHELLEY PARKER

# Dedication

This book is dedicated to the ascended master, Djwhał Khul, who overlighted this book and project every step of the way. I would like to honor this beloved and respected head of the Inner Plane Synthesis Ashram for his devoted service work on behalf of humanity throughout the ages.

# A Quick Note From Dr. Stone

For the sake of clarity, in terms of grammar, this book has been written from the state of consciousness of the "I" even though there are two authors. I state this here so there is no identity confusion, and to save the laborious effort of constantly having to explain and qualify identities every other sentence. I think you, my beloved readers, will find that the book reads much easier and better this way!

# ASCENSION and ROMANTIC RELATIONSHIPS

By

### Dr. Joshua David Stone

### Rev. Janna Shelley Parker

## THE EASY-TO-READ ENCYCLOPEDIA of the SPIRITUAL PATH
## ✦ Volume XIII ✦

Light Technology Publishing

Cover design by
Fay Richards

ISBN 1-891824-16-3

Published by
Light Technology Publishing
P.O. Box 3540
Flagstaff, AZ 86003
(800) 450-0985

Printed by
Sedona Color Graphics
2020 Contractors Road
Sedona, AZ 86336

# Contents

# *Preface*

As beings in the process of ascension, we are building our light and love quotients and becoming more and more telepathic. We are in greater touch with the many levels of the Spiritual Hierarchy, both planetary and cosmic. We are becoming soul-infused and, ultimately, united with our monad. Yet we are human beings in want of other human beings for community and companionship. We are in bodies, and those bodies have real and vital needs. Most of us must eat (though there are those few who do live on light). Most of us must sleep, and we all seek some kind of shelter from the elements. Almost all of us seek relationships of one kind or another, and many of us seek a romantic relationship of a deep and enduring nature.

This book on romantic relationships is written for those who are consciously on the path of ascension—those who have moved beyond the third-dimensional thinking of the bulk of humanity. And yet, some of our basic needs are quite in stride with humanity as a whole. What is being addressed within these pages is the integration of all aspects of ourselves. To be fully divine, do we not also desire to be fully human? All of us want love, almost all of us want it from our fellow human beings, and most of us want to express it within a romantic relationship.

As lightworkers we need not, nor should we, deny this part of ourselves. In fact we should learn how best to embrace this within ourselves and with our romantic partners. But we must learn how to approach it from who we are in the vaster scheme of things, viewing through the lens of our souls and monads to brighten and heighten every aspect of our romantic relationships.

For those whose calling it is to follow the life of the celibate single, that too is fine. One then commits to the divine romance between oneself and God. Thus, the focus of this book remains on romantic relationships, and specifically the romantic relationship between two lightworkers who join their lights. However, if you are a lightworker involved with a partner who is not as accelerated as you are, this book is equally for you.

# *Introduction*

The idea and inspiration to write this book came directly from Djwhal Khul. There are many books written about relationships, but most of them are written from the personality perspective, rather than from the perspective of the soul and monad. There are three levels of self-actualization: personality level, soul level and monadic level. Romantic relationships viewed from a soul and monadic level of understanding are very different from those viewed only from the personality level.

With my background as a psychotherapist and licensed marriage, family, child counselor, Djwhal Khul asked me to write this book as another important part of the whole picture. It is my humble prayer that my beloved readers will find some of my thoughts, feelings, and life experience—both clinical and personal—to be of value. This book is a manual for high level disciples, initiates and ascended beings in dealing with the teacher of all teachers: romantic relationships and parenting. It is written from the perspective of the ascended masters and the soul and monad, or Mighty I AM Presence.

Volumes in the series
**The Easy-to-Read Encyclopedia of the Spiritual Path**
by Joshua David Stone, Ph.D.
published by Light Technology

*Ascension and Romantic Relationships*

# 1

## *Finding Your Mate*

### "Seek and Ye Shall Find"

The wonderful and often-used words of Jesus/Sananda, "Seek and ye shall find," are sometimes appropriate and sometimes not when discussing romantic relationships. All too often, when one is seeking that special relationship, that perfect match "made in heaven," one finds oneself utterly bereft and alone. This leads to depression and endless worrying and wondering as to why one is alone. Is it something you have done or not done? Are you not attractive enough, not spiritual enough? This type of depressive thinking has the unfortunate result of collapsing or introverting the aura inward upon itself, taking away much of the needed radiance that ultimately works wonders in attracting a romantic relationship.

On the other hand, if you become detached and not at all focused on finding such a romance, remaining truly disinterested in finding a partner or a mate, then that too will keep a vital part of your auric field turned inward, and the necessary "vibes," so to speak, will not be there to attract anyone to you.

The best application of the axiom, "Seek and ye shall find," is to set the intent on a spiritual or a causative level, then let go and let God. Therefore, you will be planting all the necessary seeds for a romantic relationship, but you will not be constantly digging them up and thus prevent them from actually blooming.

Before proceeding, I want to clarify two things. The first is that when we address the issue of romantic relationships, if the words "him" and "her" are used when referring to a couple, it is simply because that is the most familiar and common form of relationship. It is the balance and complement of the masculine and feminine, yin and yang energies. However, this by no means excludes the romantic relationship between members of the same sex. Man has put a judgment on this, not God.

From the hierarchical point of view, there is no judgment. For each there is a particular, though often hidden, purpose in why a romantic relationship forms between members of the same sex. For all readers, then, let it be clearly stated that the romantic relationship here is for everyone equally, not only for those between a man and a woman. It is important to understand that despite outward appearances, the masculine/feminine, yin/yang elements are equally at play in same-sex relationships. Although they are obviously more subtle, nevertheless they are still a governing factor. Therefore, when him/her is used, it is simply because it is a more common and familiar term for relationships in general, but it is in no way intended to exclude partnerships between members of the same sex.

The other point is that there will be some of you who, for portions of your life or a whole lifetime, choose to remain single. You too are included in this relationship book, although admittedly some matters will be more applicable than others. However, the masculine/feminine polarity, the yin and the yang, exist within each of us. All of us must ultimately bring these to a point of balance, so there is a great deal you too can gain from reading this book.

On the most profound level, this book deals with the integration of all aspects of ourselves, on an individual as well as partnership level. Those who are single and celibate and involved in the divine romance with God can apply some of the techniques given specifically for couples. There is much in these pages that deals with intimacy, communication and respect. These are equally applicable in relationships with friends and family as well as the love relationship between oneself and God.

From a cosmic point of view, all is relationship: sun to sun, planet to star, hierarchy to humanity and humanity's relationship to the animal, vegetable and mineral·kingdoms. From a cosmic perspective, we have the divine polarity of Father/Mother God. So let us keep this in mind as we proceed.

How then shall you ask in order to receive and find your right mate? First ask God, for from the realms of causation does all manifestation come forth. Talk to God and your own higher self. Use the prayers about which so much is written in the *Beyond Ascension* book. The joy and fun of Huna prayer is that you can create your own. This type of prayer is extremely powerful, particularly in the area of manifestation. These prayers can help you attract your mate. They can be used jointly to help you as a couple to unite and bring into manifestation that which will advance your relationship in both practical matters and matters of the heart.

The next, and extremely important, thing to do is to make a list of what you want, the essence of the being you want to be deeply and romantically involved with. Be honest and specific, for vagueness only leads to unsatisfying results. Therefore, take the necessary time to explore this matter deeply. What are you looking for? What do you seek in a partner? What is most important, least important, and what fills in all of the spaces in between? It is vital that your intent be clear and precise, because that is what you are setting into motion, and that is what you will magnetize to you.

For example, if you know that you are strong in the area of homemaking or creativity but weaker in business, you may want to seek someone who will complement you. You may seek someone who does well in the business area but who is searching for a relationship that will provide the love, support and home base from which to do his/her work. Thus you will set the magnetic energies of your aura to frequencies that will magnetize the desired person to you. If a potential partner is proceeding to work in the manner you are, he or she will have been magnetizing his auric field to attract one such as yourself. In this area at least, your intent is then clear, fully stated and released to God and to the law of attraction. Thus you are playing the appropriate role of both seeker and surrenderer. You are planting the seeds, then allowing those seeds to take root and grow into a relationship.

This process should be repeated to cover the whole gamut of your preferences. It might seem like a time-consuming project, but it is well worth it. I could not begin to list the damage done by those who, in their eagerness to find a romantic relationship, completely overlooked many essentials they really wanted: We find a single parent involved with a partner who has absolutely no tolerance for children; or a gentle sensitive soul walking head-on into an abusive situation; or two people of the arts finding that neither has a clue, or desire to learn about, the practical side of life.

That is why I tell you to be clear, that you state your desired intent on all levels. This process should be as refined as possible. An example might be that you are an artist seeking a romantic relationship with another artist. But you want that prospective artist partner to have more of a worldly and monetary involvement so that you both form a functional unit while you create beautiful music together. You would read your poetry to him or her before bed; your partner would in turn have the ability to bring home the bulk of the paycheck. Another example is that of the mystic and occultist union. You would both be on a spiritual path but would function as complements of each other.

The main points here are clarity and preciseness, so that you do not find yourself adrift in a sea of disappointing romantic relationships. If your intent is specific and you hold to that vision, then you cannot help but magnetize to yourself what you have asked for.

However, it is fine to spend time getting to know different people, even getting a bit romantically involved, before you commit yourself to a relationship. It may be that the first person you attract, while fitting your intentions and the requirements of your ideal mate, is still not *the* person. Some people may function as a part of your path toward the most appropriate person for you, so don't feel that the first person you connect with is *the* person. Take things slowly and see how a relationship begins to take actual shape before you run to the altar (or a reasonable facsimile). Give yourself all the time you need to be as sure as you can before making a total commitment. You have already put the process in motion and can trust it. So take time, relax and enjoy the process, and rest assured that the results will be well worth it!

## The Four Lower Bodies

For those on the ascension path, being in the body can sometimes be an area of difficulty. For a great many of us on the path of initiation and ascension, because of the unique time in which we are living, the physical body may be the last body we consider, yet we need to consider all of them.

In past ages, and until quite recently, initiation was a much slower process in which each of the bodies was mastered and brought into alignment. Now, with acceleration happening at ever-increasing speeds, we often find ourselves at a very high level of initiation with high quotients of light and love propelling us ever forward, but with our physical, etheric, emotional and mental bodies lagging behind. When as lightworkers we enter into a romantic relationship, we must pay attention to these bodies, for much, though by no means all, of our relationships will be functioning through them. In spiritual relationships, the soul and monad will also play a great part.

The physical body must be connected to the whole of us. This process has been called "ascension as descension." As we evolve spiritually, we want to bring the energies of the soul/monad and of spirit into the body and, ultimately, into the Earth. Hence we have the ascending energies moving up through the chakra system, through the column of light, out through the top of the head and as far into the Godhead as we can consciously raise ourselves. Conversely, we have the descension of energies where we then bring these divine energies through our columns of light into our four lower bodies, grounding them into the physical and into the very Earth herself.

Because this is happening at such a high rate of speed in this cosmic day, our bodies are being forced to adjust to these highly charged frequencies. The effect on humanity can be both exhilarating and challenging. There can be fatigue and health lessons surfacing on all levels. Therefore, give yourself the time to give these bodies the necessary care and integrate the energies through relaxation, proper nutrition, supplements, some form of exercise, emotional control through the reprogramming of the subconscious via positive affirmations and a constant "holding the mind steady in the light." For detailed and specific exercises and meditations, please refer to *Soul Psychology* plus later books.

What I want to emphasize here is how the physical, etheric, emotional and mental bodies are key points of contact in a romantic relationship. They must be worked on diligently both for your own development and in preparation for a healthier connection with your prospective partner. This work needs to continue during the entire course of your relationship with your partner.

Those who feel extremely disconnected from their physical body might consider taking a hatha yoga or movement class. Basically, everyone should be doing some sort of physical exercise, even if it is simply taking a walk or stretching. For those who are physically limited, do only what you can. Remember, the path is unique for each of us, as are the lessons, so don't compare yourself either to another person or to some standard you hold in your mind. To do so is extremely destructive. Simply do the best you can with who and where you are as you move forward on the path.

This also applies to your emotional and mental aspects. If you want a romantic relationship to work, you must first begin with your relationship to yourself. (See the tools in my earlier books as well as tools that you have picked up along the way or developed yourself.) The main point is to work toward integrating and enlightening these four lower bodies with the energies of your soul and monad. You will need the whole of yourself in an effective romantic relationship, so why wait another minute?

We are all sensitive to one another and pick up on each other's energies, either consciously or unconsciously. As lightworkers, we are highly sensitive, so we will not be attracted to a grump or one who is overrun by his or her negative ego. In a like manner will we not appear attractive to another if we are filled with negativity. My best advice is to begin cleaning up now rather than later. A beautiful aura is a very attractive thing indeed. And it is an aspect that we can't dress up, but must truly make over from the inside out. There is no limit to the magnificence of a pure and radiant inner glow. Therefore, I advise you from my heart to get to work at once. The effect of clearing away negative ego patterns will have a most beneficial effect in manifesting a relationship of the highest quality.

## Your Physical Appearance

Let us take a look at the part that each of these bodies plays in a relationship. It is a fact of human nature that for almost all of us, vision is both the first and the primary way in which we relate to the world around us. For better or worse, we form an immediate impression via the visual stimulation that occurs upon first seeing a person. It is because of this that poetic phrases have been expressed such as "I was lost the moment I saw him"; "We knew as soon as our eyes met"; and "She walks in beauty as the night."

When appearance becomes the be-all and end-all, however, we function at a very unenlightened level. But to deny the fact that appearance plays an important role in both attracting and maintaining a romantic relationship would be unrealistic. We all have our particular preferences. As lightworkers, we are as vulnerable as the mass of humanity to first impressions and appearances. In fact, the more evolved we are, the more levels of appearance we are able to pick up on. We may find ourselves immediately drawn to a person's physical appearance, yet on looking more closely and deeply, we may find ourselves revolted by their auric manifestations. We should realize that as we mingle with other lightworkers in search of a romantic relationship, others are looking at *us* to see what meets their own eye.

Please bear in mind that I am not speaking of trying to fit into images and standards portrayed in the media. I am simply stating that as a race we are a visually oriented people. We should therefore take this into consideration when seeking to connect on a romantic level. We also need to realize that the physical presentation of oneself touches nearly every other aspect of human relationships as well. Therefore, rather than denying or suppressing this aspect of ourselves, we can set about doing the very best with who we are. Again, we are not trying to fit into someone else's mold or model of physical appearance. What I am talking about is the basic human condition that appreciates one who exudes confidence, good personal hygiene and a sense of honoring the form, the physical self.

For many lightworkers, during certain phases of our spiritual journeys, being in body often feels like an altogether alien concept. I have met very highly evolved souls who are so disconnected from their physical selves that they are barely in touch with their physical bodies. This is obviously not the time for a person to seek a romantic relationship—or if it is, one had better get grounded fast!

Looking at ascension as descension is a key perspective at this juncture. As lightworkers, we are rising toward the light as we are becoming light. We are equally guided to bring that light down into the physical. If we keep this in mind, then it will be easier to see the validity of honoring and taking care of our bodies. We each can be the best we can be in our physical bodies even as we strive to be so in the higher bodies. If you want to be noticed and appreciated as a physical being, you must first appreciate yourself as such, then bring that forth into manifestation the way you feel suits you best.

If comfortable jeans and new-age T-shirts or long hair and flowing dresses best express your inner self, then go that route. If you feel more confident and comfortable in a tailored look, by all means dress that way. If lots of jewelry, long earrings and massive crystals are your thing, then wear them to the hilt! What is being suggested is that you become and remain aware that what you show to the world and to prospective or current partners speaks out about you. The physical body conveys a message, even for those of us who dwell primarily in the realm of spirit. So seek to adjust your appearance to communicate what and who you are in the clearest and most confident way possible.

## Your Emotional Appearance

You are well aware that you inhabit not one body, but several. The emotional body is vital to consider, as it is very closely linked to both the physical and the mental. The emotional aura, being so closely tied to the physical, will bleed through, coloring that physical aspect of ourselves with our emotional energies. I don't care if you are a "10" in the mundane system of rating physical appearances or, more importantly, in the eyes of your partner or perspective partner, but if you have a lot of negative stuff in your emotional body, ultimately that will be seen, and it will make an otherwise attractive person less attractive.

Have you ever noticed a person who has the traditional "perfect" features or look, yet you see a sullenness or a negativity that seems to distort those otherwise-perfect features? This is because if a person is filled with hatred, anger, greed, jealousy and the like, these emotions will express themselves upon the physical form.

In the reverse situation, have you ever noticed a person with relatively plain features who appears to manifest such great inner beauty that it envelops the person, and he or she appears irresistible? Perhaps such a person is your mate. When a person is imbued with the godlike qualities of love, devotion, gentleness, compassion and joy, these permeate their entire being. These qualities take actual shape and form, so that this person seems to be an angel on Earth. There is truly no way to separate the whole of ourselves, and that is why each of the bodies needs our utmost care and attention.

## Your Mental Appearance

No discussion of one's appearance would be complete without taking into account the mental appearance. The mental body is almost as closely linked to the physical as the emotional body is, and it has an equally strong effect on it. What we think, we manifest; the thoughts we carry around with us take shape within us and manifest in our bodies.

We cannot help but build our physical bodies with thoughts. As his holiness the Lord Sai Baba has said, "The mind can create bondage or the mind can create liberation." The mind filled with ugly and debased thoughts creates an aura so filled. These thoughts seep right through into the physical vehicle, so a negative nature will find physical expression in one's face, posture and persona. I am sure you have heard people of extreme physical beauty being called ugly because of their thoughts and deeds.

By the same token, those who hold their thoughts to the good, the beautiful and the true will find those thoughts taking shape and form in their lives and bodies. One would hear it said of such a person that he or she is very beautiful. The more God-like the thoughts, the more God-like or beautiful is one's radiance.

## Summary

You have picked up this book for one of several reasons. Either you are seeking your "right partner," you are in a relationship that you want to improve, or you are wondering why you have been disappointed again and again and can't seem to hook up with the right person. So you are seeking an effective, working, wonderful romantic relationship.

What I hope you understand thus far is that first you must be right with yourself and with your connection to God before a relationship can function in a healthy manner. Your physical/etheric, emotional and mental bodies form one complete whole, and together they create both the outer and the inner appearance. You cannot disguise who you are, nor is there enough makeup in the world to cover the blemishes that reveal themselves when the emotional and mental bodies are not functioning in harmony with God's laws.

Although it is clearly stated that appearance is very important in a romantic relationship, I am not speaking about false appearance, but the appearance of the *whole* of you: the physical, emotional, mental and spiritual, which operate through the physical body. Therefore, I urge you to take a good and honest look at yourself from the perspective presented here. Your physical body is very important in actualizing a romantic relationship, but equally important are your emotional and mental bodies. Ultimately these bodies present one face and form, and each must be given its due by continually being worked on and upgraded. Then when you are either seeking a partner or desiring to improve an existing partnership, you are in the best possible shape. You will be able to call forth the best possible romantic relationship—one that is functioning at the highest level with the best possible mate.

# 2

## *Bonding Patterns*

### The Balance within Self

In a romantic relationship we are dealing with the bonding of two individuals. Each of these individuals needs to align within the four-body system as well as the higher bodies. The first relationship to be looked at is that which we have with ourselves. It makes perfect sense to do this, for it is ourselves that we are bringing to the relationship. And it is from ourselves, whether balanced or not, that we will interact and seek to bond with our partner.

For example, if we are out of sorts emotionally, overly needy or have low self-esteem, it won't really matter how giving and loving our partner is because we will not *feel* that we are loved enough. So the relationship might seem to lack a depth of loving and caring from our mate when in truth we are being loved and cared for very much. That is why it is so important first to have an awareness of our makeup and the areas that need work, then diligently work on them. While it is true that our relationships can help us see ourselves in a more positive and worthy light, if we do not work on our own issues, ultimately we will feel unsatisfied and somehow manage to sabotage the good we are receiving.

### The Balance within the Relationship

We have looked at how the balance within oneself can affect the balance within a relationship. However, this only sets the stage for an in-depth exploration of the various aspects of the dynamic of interaction within the relationship. The ways in which two people come together in partnership are infinite, so I will highlight and discuss some of the most common ones. What will be discussed is basically of a universal nature, and it is hoped that you can use these as doorways into your unique situation. In fact, some of us may be experiencing a situation from two seemingly opposite perspectives, feeling perhaps at once both victim and jailer; or the seeming *ruler* of our mate, yet the *slave* of our own weaknesses. Already you can see how vast and interwoven this subject is, so let us begin to break it down a bit.

## The Controller and the Controlled

For one reason or another, some of us need to feel ourselves in control at all times. This need can be distilled down to the misqualified and confused use of personal power. I consider owning one's personal power to be one of the most important keys to one's spiritual journey. However, if that power is running amuck and seeking to control others, most particularly your romantic partner, the power is inappropriately used. When one is operating out of this venue, one will most probably attract a mate with low self-esteem or one who is a people-pleaser. This then brings one into a parent-to-child relationship and/or a king or queen-to-subject relationship. This might seem to work for a brief period of time, as both parties involved have followed the path of least resistance, flowing along and letting the negative ego stay in control.

This will not work on a long-term basis, however, particularly for lightworkers involved in the ascension process or any sort of growth process. For those of us consciously evolving, the imbalance of such a situation will come quickly into our awareness and, hopefully, both partners can use this aspect of the relationship to continue to grow, evolve and heal. Yet even for those who are less conscious, something will be unsettling, with ensuing arguments and episodes in which there is acting out by one of the partners as jailer, king or queen in an attempt to maintain control. If this pattern reveals itself in your relationship, it is hoped that you use this opportunity as a vehicle for further growth, purification and cleansing.

In *Soul Psychology* I have given detailed exercises you can use. I suggest that you work with some of these tools as a couple, for you are given the opportunity to rub yourself clean upon the sandpaper of each other by virtue of being in a relationship. As a couple you might also consider counseling, for the objective perspective of a qualified professional can at times be extremely helpful. You might also suggest thanking one another for helping to bring these negative ego traits to light.

It then becomes essential that you work on yourself, in communion with yourself, God, the masters and the subconscious mind. If you need to be in control so desperately, it would be good to find out why. There is probably a good reason for it, a reason that at one time or another served you well. Perhaps you were left as head of the household when you were ten years old and had to assume control in order to survive. The main thing is to realize that what was appropriate at one point is not appropriate now. Ask for divine healing. Ask for God, the masters and your monad to shine their light on the situation. Know that the universe is supported and sustained by Source, by God Itself, and it is not your function or your place to control everything, nor is it possible.

Surrender to God and release your control attitude into the violet fire of transmutation given by the grace of St. Germain. Use the tools I spoke of to work with the subconscious mind. Remember, life is a lesson and relationships are some of the best teachers you can possibly find. No one has to stay stuck. The whole process of ascension is moving into light and love, and this process is both a service and a joy. Doing this work within the context of a relationship provides support and companionship as well as special challenges.

If you find yourself functioning as the "subject" or the child within the relationship, the same advice is offered to you, but from the opposite end of the spectrum. You too have assumed your role because of a need to survive at some crucial point in your life. Perhaps you had very domineering parents who withdrew their love if you asserted yourself, but showered you with affection if you were the good little boy or girl who didn't assert yourself.

What was once appropriate is no longer appropriate. You can work with the tools to reprogram your subconscious mind. You likewise can ask for help from God and the masters, calling upon the violet transmuting flame of St. Germain and also Archangel Michael for strength. It is time for you to claim, own and stand firm in your personal power. It is also good to realize that as a lightworker on the path, you have done well to allow your relationship to reveal the hidden aspects of yourself that need work and clearing. Then you act to claim your power and heal that lost child within yourself.

If you need to look to someone for support and guidance, look to the pure essence of Father/Mother God. There is no difficulty or rift so great and no problem so deep that it cannot be worked on by you and ultimately healed with the light and love of God. And if you are in a committed relationship, you can anchor and support each other in the process. This would lift your romantic relationship to the level of a *divinely* romantic relationship between you, your partner and God!

## The Artist and Caretaker Trap

Art is one of humanity's highest callings, as it is the expression of the beautiful upon the Earth. Artists working on a higher level often work, in varying degrees, with the angels of art, music and beauty. Even for one with such a high calling, there are many dangers to the artist, primarily the danger of removing oneself from the normal functioning of the world. In relationships, this may entail dumping the entire burden of the so-called mundane into a partner's lap.

What usually occurs in relationships of this sort is a profound infatuation between two people, with art serving as one of the most potent aphrodisiacs in the world. Either the nonartist is taken into wondrous poetic realms by the artist or, if both partners are artists, they fly off together into a romantic heaven. Of course, if the artistic person is balanced, there is no giant chasm between the beautiful world of the creator and the world of daily life. But more often, the nonartist or one of the artists in a two-artist relationship will be left holding the bag. There can be a healthy balance between the artist and the partner. But what often occurs is that the more creative of the two sees an opportunity to retreat into a world of creation, and the other feels a certain responsibility to take care of every other aspect of life, which cannot help but lead to resentment and frustration.

We are not all meant to play the same parts. In fact, we are each uniquely designed to play certain roles. However, we are all called upon to find the proper point of balance within ourselves, our romantic relationships and our relationship with the world, which calls for an integration and a balancing that we each must cultivate. It is just too easy for the eccentric artist to cop out and let the partner pick up the slack of daily living. This is just not fair, nor does it serve to integrate either the couple as a unit or the individualized soul/monad in incarnation. In relationships of this type, the honeymoon often ends abruptly, when the frustrated "doer of the mundane" realizes that he/she is in this arena alone and cries out for support.

If you find yourself in either role in this kind of relationship, what is called for above all else is communication. Actually, good communication is essential to the health and well-being of all relationships; but for the moment we will limit our discussion to problems inherent in the situation of the artist and mate. It is essential to talk things out, share your feelings and use the tools I have mentioned. More than likely, all that is needed is a little shift, a bit more awareness on the part of the artist as to what the other person is doing and certainly the willingness to contribute. No one should be left bearing all the responsibilities.

If you have hooked up with a pure artist, and provided you don't mind, it might be all right to do most of the daily stuff. But *no one* should do it all. It is important to have awareness, appreciation and a certain amount of participation on the part of the other person.

If you fell in love with your artistic partner and at first didn't mind carrying the responsibilities of daily life, but now find that this type of lopsided situation no longer seems fair or right, then lovingly sit down with your mate and tell him/her so. If *you* are the artist, I encourage you to listen and be open to changes. They might not have to be big changes. Little changes can often go a long way, and slight adjustments might align things in their proper order. However, in order to do this, the issue must be addressed and both people must be willing to look at why they have assumed the roles they play.

For the artist, art is probably your true and divine calling, but not to the absolute exclusion of all else. The partner of the artist is more than likely highly elevated, moved and opened by his/her mate's work in whatever medium he/she is working. It is vital that you acknowledge that, but it also is important that you look deeper. Perhaps your eagerness to play caretaker and supporter has an unhealthy aspect, and your rising discontent is now bringing it to light. It may be that you falsely believe that constant caretaking and support is the only way for you to get the love you need. I am here to tell you that this is not true. You are lovable and deserving of love by virtue of being, because it is your divine birthright, because you are a child of God. Recognize and explore this.

An artist with a more worldly partner, or two artists, one of which is somewhat more actualized in the world, can be a wonderful balance. It is the extreme that throws things off balance. The nonintegration of individuals who, while utilizing their strong points, have not found the proper balance within themselves, puts this type of relationship off kilter. What is really needed in this instance, as in life and romantic relationships, is the continual working on one's own relationship to self. The more work done on self, the clearer and the more functional your relationship will become.

The relationship between the artist and the caretaker has in actuality a wonderful potential. My guess would be that although there is the codependence factor in operation, you also have been attracted to each other because somewhere inside, each of you recognizes that you really would like to incorporate the missing parts of yourselves that the other is demonstrating. This is the perfect relationship to be in and the perfect opportunity to expand your own horizons. Therefore I encourage you to work together on this, even as you will also be working alone. Then a very balanced, mutually beneficial and deeply romantic relationship can blossom and grow.

You who are involved in this type of relationship have a great opportunity to grow and evolve both individually and as partners, if you are willing to confront your specific challenges and make the necessary adjustments. This will lead to a point of balance that has hitherto never been achieved, either alone or in relationship. Thank each other for this opportunity and get to work!

## The Occultist and the Mystic

One of the more interesting bonding patterns, and one that is ever on the rise with the mass wave of ascension and the elevation of humanity as a whole, is that of the occultist and the mystic. Herein lies a great potential for doing one's service work in conjunction with fulfilling the need for a romantic relationship. When the occultist and the mystic come together as romantic partners, they will often be mission mates as well. Thus what is found here is a threefold purpose being fulfilled in this unique blending.

This aptly could be called a marriage made in heaven. Yet this needs to be qualified with a big "if"—if the two partners can also come to terms with the lessons and growth patterns born of the Earth!

It is a wonderful thing indeed when two lightworkers come together wherein the spiritual psychologist, logician and cosmic scientist, functioning through a highly active brain center, join with a more intuitive, feeling-based, love-centered mystic who functions through a highly active heart center. The work they can do for the planet and for each other is virtually boundless. However, these people are in no way exempt from the problems inherent in the bonding experience, and they will inevitably be faced with problems unique to them as well as the more common problems that arise out of living as a couple upon planet Earth.

It is wise to remember that in this case, relationships are the great mirror of ourselves. Relationships are also great purifiers and revealers for those of us who are open to growth and willing to bring to light facets of ourselves that have been hidden. For example, a true occultist might become so absorbed in the mechanics and configurations of the universe that he loses touch with the simple mechanics of daily living. He might tend to forget certain things that are rather important to his heart-based partner. (Often it is the male who is more the occultist and the female more the mystic, although that is by no means always the case.)

The occultist might be so immersed in the cosmology of the universe that he forgets the time tables of daily life as well as birthdays, anniversaries and the like. An overlooked or glossed-over birthday is extremely painful to the heart-based mystic, and it is indeed a time of honoring. Again we are faced with finding the point of balance within ourselves that allows us to be who we are to the fullest and yet integrate the whole.

Many lightworkers would like to be exempt from the practicalities of life, but this part of life must be faced and dealt with from whatever level one is at. Integration of all the bodies is a must, and none is too elite to be exempt. It is hoped that the more enlightened you become, the more you bring all the bodies with you. But as acceleration is happening at so vast a speed, it is inevitable that there is work to be done in this department by all of us.

Let us consider the mystic in this light as well. Here we find a person with much heart-love who is often a channel of one kind or another. She may channel books, poetry, lectures, painting and so on, and in her own way be as connected with the abstract as the occultist. What can happen here is that she may get as lost in the lofty and visionary spheres as the eccentric artist spoken of earlier. She may fail to connect with the more earthly matters, experiencing them as too weighty or too much trouble. The mystic would be less likely to forget birthdays and anniversaries, as these would have great emotional impact for her.

However, there is a danger for the mystic in neglecting the healthy functioning of her own emotional sphere, except in the aforementioned matters. She may allow herself to experience only those who have a direct link to the loftier realms of feeling. As with everyone, all aspects of oneself must be worked with and brought into alignment. This will ultimately make the mystic a better channel and romantic partner, for integration of the whole is a matter for everyone.

The marriage between mystic and occultist has enormous potential. This would be a blending of two people who carry a great deal of light. They have much to offer each other and much to give to the world. The basic resonance between the two would be of a very high and refined nature, and the love that is shared would contain a great deal of divine love. However, the basic danger lies in forgetting their human qualities and the fact that they are faced with some of the same basic difficulties and challenges inherent in all relationships. Each must take personal responsibility for working on the healthy functioning of the four lower bodies. They must also work at integrating the energies coming in through the soul and/or monad, which are very powerful and transformational energies.

Another point to consider is that the occultist often tends to be more psychologically integrated and the mystic more psychically developed. This offers a wonderful opportunity to provide balance for each other and help stimulate the missing facet within each other. Thus the occultist would learn how to integrate the qualities of the mystic, and the mystic in turn would learn how to integrate the qualities of the occultist. This would lead to a greater balance within the individual and a greater cooperation within the relationship.

The higher you go, the more integrated you *must* become. Be grateful that you have each other and the energies of soul/monad as well as the grace and blessings of the masters you invoke. In your bonding there is an opportunity for great advancement and service work and a speeding-up of the initiatory process. However, this can only occur if you are willing to take a good, hard look at yourselves (not each other, but *yourselves*) and work with the same tools that have been suggested for everyone else. You must be willing to overhaul your entire four-body system and rid yourselves of any and all contaminants, blockages and negative ego patterns you find there. In romantic relationships, we have the opportunity to do this *if* both partners are willing to truly help each other in this process.

For those of us doing the work of ascension, whether in a partner situation or alone, this is of utmost importance, and I cannot stress this strongly enough. The temptation to ride the high horse and think yourself beyond this work because you have passed this or that initiation is rampant. Therefore I go through this process daily as well as ask for the cleansing, healing, clearing of my field and so forth. None of us are exempt or too elevated — after all, this is the program. What is vital is that you recognize that the more light and love quotient we have, the more we are asked to serve. It is therefore crucial that we do this from as clean, pure and integrated a place as possible.

The pairing of two lightworkers provides the opportunity for each to hold the point of clarity for the other when one falters a bit. One partner can gently and lovingly help the other to become aware, and then that one can set about the work of realignment. By no means must either the occultist or the mystic think that he/she is better or higher than the partner and assume the role of false guruship. All I am saying is that in this unique bonding pattern, the two lightworkers can help each other help themselves and be a wonderful support for each another. Just as each must come to the point of the yin/yang, Shiva/Shakti, masculine/feminine balance within oneself, so too is there a point wherein the occultist and the mystic merge within each being.

Just as a balanced man has his point of balance and a balanced woman has hers, so some are designed to be balanced more on the occult side and some more on the mystical. The point remains, however, to balance and to integrate all four lower bodies as well as the higher ones and remain loving and open supporters within the relationship. The work continues — it just gets more refined.

So, occultist/mystic partners, keep up the good work. Keep working on yourselves always, and in love and support do the work required of all relationships. Hold ever steady in the light and to your divine mission, and you will indeed be doing the very best you can do. Then go out and have some fun, relax and enjoy each other. We occultist and mystic types can forget this side of life, so I urge you to remember to do what it is said of God: "And on the seventh day He rested." Do the work, but relax and enjoy each other as well!

## The Businesswoman and the House Husband

I would like to address a situation that we are seeing more and more in our changing times. This is the age of the divine Mother, and among the many new energies and transformative patterns that are now occurring upon planet Earth is that of the anchoring of the divine feminine. As we have been living in what has been aptly called a man's world for a long time, this shift requires much adjustment on the parts of both men and women.

New structures and patterns are evolving today between men and women that are very different from what has been considered the norm in our society. Both men and women may find themselves a bit at sea amidst the constant restructuring going on today. It is not uncommon, for a variety of reasons and in many variations on a theme, to find the woman being the main breadwinner who goes out into the world and the man staying at home.

This can be caused by a variety of circumstances, such as the basic worldwide economic situation. The man might be burned out by a job he has had for twenty years, or he might simply enjoy working at home with the children. Or the woman might seek to actualize a certain career ambition. It might be that in our computer age the man continues to work, but by way of computer, fax and so forth, while the woman wants to be out in the arena of worldly affairs. The main point is not to prejudge the situation, particularly if you find yourselves operating from within one. Remain open and communicative with your partner to make sure that each of you is happy in the roles you have assumed.

Is the part you are playing in such a structure truly all right with you? Have you *chosen* to be out there or are you feeling forced, feeling that your partner is being lazy or copping out? If you are the one at home, is that all right with you, or are you feeling trapped? If indeed it is not all right with you to keep functioning in the manner in which you have been, it is your obligation to lovingly and gently, but honestly, communicate this at a time when your partner is receptive. However, if the role you are playing feels right for you, then make a mental/emotional note of it or even perhaps put it into the physical by way of writing. Then, out of courtesy, check to see if your partner is okay with his/her role. If the answer is no, you have some serious communicating and readjusting to do; but if the answer is yes, then play your parts with the utmost joy and devotion and do not allow other parties to interfere or try to lock you into old belief systems.

The important thing is that the relationship feels right within you. Then remember that this is what you need to honor. One suggestion, however, is that you do not lose sight of the feminine principle active within the woman or the masculine energies functioning within the man. A woman coming home after a hard day's work most probably would be delighted to be greeted with flowers. Words of appreciation for the man who has been working at home would give him the acknowledgment he needs in order to feel useful and purposeful. Changing *roles* does not necessarily mean changing *needs*. A woman still needs to feel like a woman, and a man needs to feel like a man.

The feminine principle is being reawakened upon the Earth, and this is one of the reasons why women increasingly find themselves in the workplace doing a wider and wider range of work. Women are serving to anchor the feminine energy in all areas of business, government, education, science, the humanities and the arts. Another reason that women increasingly are out in the workplace is purely economical. It is more and more the norm that both partners are making financial contributions to the unit. From a deeper esoteric level, this again reflects the balancing and integration of the masculine and feminine principles.

This balancing and integration is happening on many levels. Men are learning to soften and to honor the feminine within them and women are toughening up and bringing forth more of the masculine energies. All this, in effect, leads to more balanced, whole and integrated individuals, partnerships and, ultimately, the planet itself.

I simply ask you not to judge yourselves in any way if you find yourselves in a role reversal or a partial role reversal. The thing to remember is that it is perfect and right as long as it is right with both partners. But be aware that what might feel right at one point in your relationship might suddenly feel off base at another. Stay open and honest with yourself and your partner, keeping the lines of communication open and active at all times. Remember that there is no outer standard you need try to conform to. What you need to do is fulfill your own mission as it unfolds and be willing to do the necessary work each step of the way.

We are each unique and therefore each relationship will be unique. For ourselves and for each other let's remember to "judge not lest we be judged." We should then proceed to live as we see fit and be willing to change when and if it is appropriate.

## Relationships with the Same Sex

What has been said also applies to those who are in relationships with a member of the same sex. Everything that applies to a heterosexual relationship likewise applies to you. Many of the difficulties that arise out of a role-reversal relationship also apply to you, in that there are a great many who are prejudging your situation. The main thing to remember is that God and the masters are not judging, so don't take other people's judgments to heart. The other thing to remember is that you face the very same challenges of integrating and balancing the four-body system and ultimately the soul and monad, as does everyone else, in addition to balancing the masculine/feminine polarities. Even in relationships between members of the same sex, this balance will need addressing. The yin/yang energies are an aspect of the cosmos itself.

While it is true that you have the outer world to contend with, ultimately you have the same work to do on yourselves and your relationships as everyone else. The tools I suggest, the communication, the work on oneself, apply equally to you. Each one of us is dealing with the whole of ourselves and must do basically the same work.

## The Interracial Partnership

The interracial couple shares much of the same burden of judgment by society as does the same-sex couple. It is unfortunate that the bulk of humanity still functions from so limited a perspective as to place judgment on your relationship. Any relationship is hard enough to maintain without this added burden. A part of the divine plan is actually being fulfilled through interracial marriages, for they demonstrate the true unity of all humankind. This is the unity that we are creating upon Earth as the golden age manifests.

Beyond that, the same dynamics are at play, and couples in this situation would do well to explore all that preceded in this chapter and all that follows. The only thing I might add is, take a good look within to see if you are truly in love with your partner and are committed to him or her, or if you are in some sort of rebellion against either family or society in general. If the latter is the case, you need to be honest for the sake of yourself, your partner and the relationship. Face your true motivations rather than continue in a relationship that has no real heart. However, if the former is the case and you feel deep love and commitment to your partner, go the whole nine yards with your relationship and reap all the benefits of a committed partnership. Commit to doing all the necessary work on yourselves through the process of integration and self-balancing.

## Summary

I have addressed some of the more common ways in which couples bond. There are, of course, other ways as well as many permutations within those that have been discussed. You might want to look at the various archetypes and assess which roles you and your partner fit into; then explore the many possibilities via the archetypal lens. The main point I want you all to bear in mind is how relationships between two people manifest as the result of the relationship that each one has with self. It is here that the bulk of the work lies and where the alignment, integration and clearing must take place.

Because you are in a relationship, you can be of great value and support to one another in that process. You can reach the highest, most integrated potential not only as an individual, but as a couple. Remember also that being in a relationship has allowed much to surface, and what is brought into the light and revealed is more easily cleansed than that which is hidden. Therefore, thank your partner for this service, as it is a service indeed.

The other key point is that basically we are looking at relationship through the personality, the soul and ultimately the monad. Since you are most likely reading this book because the subjects of both relationship and ascension are of value to you, you will be accessing energies from the soul/monadic levels. Consequently, there will be more of you involved in the relationship and more energies to deal with. Thus there is a greater and deeper quality of love for you to experience and integrate, and there is more light within you. By virtue of the nature of light, it both lightens your aura and reveals the darker spots that need cleansing and balancing.

You are on a most wondrous journey, that of ascension and romantic relationship, with great potential to make rapid growth in both areas. The issue of bonding reveals much about us, but I remind you that as lightworkers on the path of ascension, *you have asked for this.* You have asked that all be brought into the light and that all negativity be transmuted and transcended. And you have asked that light, love, unity and joy remain unfettered.

Remember that God is within every relationship and that your relationship with God is one unto itself. No one is ever really alone, and all are being called to a deeper, fuller, more bountiful and beautiful experience of the unity of God. Work gently to express this unity in your relationship with yourself and with each another. Then you will expand in your relationship to God and in unity with all life.

# 3

## *Unconditional Love and Commitment*

B efore discussing the topic of love, it must first be stated that *unconditional love is love.* Anything less is an aspect of love that has become distorted. In the striving for unconditional love, initially we may embrace only a fraction of what we are seeking, but at least we are following the pathway toward living in the light of true unconditional love. The true nature of love is that it stands in the light of its own being, and it remains unconditional at all times. To borrow a quote from William Shakespeare (who was, in fact, St. Germain), "Love alters not when it alteration finds, nor bends with the remover to remove. Oh no, it [love] is an ever-fixed mark that looks on tempests and is not shaken."

This is not to imply that we do not love at all, for we most certainly do. But for most of us, and indeed for all of us at times, we love most incompletely. There is no judgment implied in this, for what we are about is growing in our capacity to love unconditionally just as we are growing in our capacity to contain light and embrace wisdom. Since this is a process, we would do well to allow our relationships to help us hold to ever greater standards in this matter and work diligently in learning how to truly exhibit unconditional love.

### Unconditional Love of Self

As with all that has been discussed thus far, the subject of unconditional love must first start with oneself. "As above, so below" in this instance is equivalent to "as within, so without." We can never demonstrate that which we have not yet attained, incorporated and activated within ourselves first. Therefore, I ask you first to look at the level and quality of the love you have for yourself. Many of us are not very good at self-love at all and are far better at giving love to others than to ourselves. However, if we do not truly cultivate self-love, then we will find that we are unable to keep giving whatever we have not allowed ourselves to receive.

It is imperative that we each learn how to love ourselves unconditionally. This might take a greater or lesser degree of work, depending on where we are. Some of us have a lot of negative programming to overcome from family, school, work environments and the world in general. The faulty programming is believing that we must prove ourselves worthy of love in order to receive the love that is already there for us simply by virtue of being. From our conditioning, we each had a different set of rules to follow and expectations to fulfill before we could receive love that is there. Unfortunately, we have taken this into our consciousness and have allowed it to become part of our subconscious programming and belief system. We are therefore unable to freely love ourselves, for no one can truly live up to these imposed standards. Ultimately, we all find ourselves incapable of unconditional self-love.

In the area of unconditional self-love, one must first be right with oneself before one can be right in a relationship. Ideally, in every relationship we should come from and hold an attitude of unconditional love, but this will not be possible until we can hold that attitude toward ourselves. I have given many tools for you to work with in *Soul Psychology*. Two additional tools I have found to be of great value are *A Course in Miracles* and a set of tapes called *How to Build High Self-Esteem* by Jack Canfield.

There is also the option of finding a well-qualified therapist who incorporates the spiritual with the psychological. Again I remind you that this is a process, and considering how most of us have been raised, it is a process that requires much attention and devotion. However, since God is love as well as light and power rightly used, this is a most important theme that runs through the whole of Creation and one that deserves all you can give it.

Love is one of the great divine qualities we are all developing and expanding as we tread the path of ascension. Therefore, all are encouraged to work on this most divine aspect of self, both in yourselves and in the arena of your relationships.

## Never Use Love as a Weapon

Of course, *true* love is unconditional and therefore could never be used as a weapon, but all too often people in romantic relationships will use the giving and withdrawing of expressions of affection as a tool of manipulation. This can run the gamut from mild manipulation to withdrawing love and replacing it with anger and, in the most extreme cases, violence.

Violence of any kind should *never* be tolerated, and this pertains to violence of a psychic and emotional nature as well as physical violence. When violence is used against the person we supposedly love, we are distorting love in the most vile way possible and making a weapon of it by either figuratively or literally thrusting a knife into the hearts of the ones who have opened their hearts to us. This example is obviously of such an extreme nature that I use it only as a wake-up call to any and all who see the slightest signs of violence in the behavior of their partner. This is *not* to be tolerated; either the behavior must abruptly end, with appropriate counseling to follow, or the relationship must end.

If you know that you are prone to anger and violent outbursts, I suggest that you immediately seek help via counseling, support groups, books, tapes or whatever other means you find most helpful. Never *ever* let this loose upon your partner or anyone else, but immediately start the process of eliminating it from your program banks, faulty thinking and gut-response system. Love is the opposite of fear, and anger is the acting-out of fear by lashing out at others. There is help. No one needs to stay stuck, and if you find yourself stuck in that violent place, please, for the sake of yourself and all concerned, do not wait another minute! Seek help *now!*

In the lesser extreme we return to the theme of using love as a tool of manipulation by the giving or withdrawing of one's affections. The classic place where this occurs is in the bedroom. One partner or the other finds that he/she can exercise a good deal of control over the other by being sexually available in order to get something or in order to illicit a desired behavior from the mate. This is unfair as well as destructive.

Two people coming together in sexual union is a highly spiritual and sacred act. That is not to infer that it is not a pleasurable and often playful time, for it is all these things and more. What it is not, however, is an act to be used to control your partner. Sex is so powerful and intimate that we are most vulnerable during this time, and it should never be used by anyone against another. Often we are equally vulnerable and open in its anticipation, and when it is withdrawn or denied as a means to an end, sex becomes a weapon we wield rather than an intimacy we share.

As lightworkers, hopefully we are using sexual intimacy to further bond, to raise the energies through tantric means or to simply enjoy ourselves with our mates. However, these issues relating to manipulation can also manifest in us. Since we are on the path of ascension, hopefully all are working diligently to get to the core of these problem areas.

This applies outside the bedroom as well. We must be watchful not to use withdrawal of affection as a weapon by tuning the other person out or becoming cold and detached because we are dissatisfied with something in our relationship. We must not assume that our partner will get the point from our lack of being there. First, even for those who are more psychically developed, our partner most probably will *not* get the point of this behavior, but will feel confused, hurt or angry. Second, this is not the appropriate mode of communication. Good communication must be clear, open and direct.

I have seen couples trying to punish each other by humiliating them in public or in other social settings, which invariably results in both partners becoming even more hurt and angry. Here is another classic example of what *should* be love turned into a weapon. Nothing good can ever come out of two people's negative egos locking horns and having a go at it. The negative ego can be a very tricky and subtle thing and can sneak up on you and take control if not closely kept in check.

It is obvious that issues will come up between two people, particularly when involved in a relationship of a romantic nature. This is to be expected, even welcomed, because growth, love and ascension are all made easier through being able to see the dormant and hidden arise from the subconscious — that is, of course, if properly handled. I suggest that you both remain honest and open with each other. When a tender issue comes up, wait until the initial surge of emotion is over before you attempt to talk about it. Then from a place of relative calm, hold hands for a moment and call upon both of your souls and monads to overlight you in your discussion. You might also ask for the help of God and the ascended masters with whom you feel closest. Then and only then, when you are aligned with your highest aspects (soul/monad), begin to share what is bothering you and enter into true communication regarding your issues. By practicing such a simple technique as this, by just waiting until after that first surge of anger or resentment and by linking with your divine I Am Presence, you can come from a place of clarity. The environment of a loving and committed relationship can serve to propel both you and your partner further into the very heart of love and light. It can bring you ever more deeply and fully into the essence of that unity we call God.

## Remaining Unconditionally Loving During Severe Testing

Sometimes our love is indeed pushed to the limit and we find ourselves confronted with a challenge such as being lied to or cheated on. We feel that this indicates the betrayal of the shared love and commitment, and we want to withdraw our own unconditional love and commitment. I pick this extreme example to emphasize that the highest level of love is unconditional, which means love under any conditions. So in *all* situations we need to strive to remain steady in unconditional love, which is staying steady in the love that is of God.

Ultimately, how you might deal with a given situation is for you to decide. In the case of an affair, perhaps it might be appropriate to end that commitment, for it could be that you and your partner are moving in different directions. But whatever you decide, if you are on the path of ascension, it will serve you well to remain ever steady in unconditional love, while you strive to hold your mind steady in the light. Then from that place you take the appropriate actions.

Another extreme example would be if confronted with verbal and/or physical abuse. It is imperative that you leave that situation if help is not immediately sought or if you feel that you are in any danger on any level while your partner is getting the needed help and doing the necessary work. However, remaining in unconditional love would apply here as well. I am not saying that it would be easy; it could be difficult in the extreme. I am saying that unconditional love is an aspect of God, and you who can hold that within yourselves *no matter what* are demonstrating God upon the Earth.

This equally applies to instances where divorce is the only sane choice or the mutual decision or just the natural unfolding of evolution wherein you and your partner are no longer functioning on the same wavelength. The latter would be quite understandable if you had come together while in early college years and one of you opened to spirit and just zipped through several levels of initiation and the other remained at the same level. There could be several reasons for divorce, which should not be the first choice, but is often appropriate. However, there is no reason not to remain unconditionally loving if you are aware that you have the capacity to do so.

My point is not to focus specifically on issues such as divorce. What I am focusing on is the divine opportunity that arises out of even the most severe situations *to remain unconditionally loving no matter what*. This does not mean that we should be unconditionally approving of the behavior of our partner. It means that even if we part with our partner, we part from a place of love and release them with an attitude of unconditional love to follow their path. This is not always the easiest thing to do, but it is the highest, and it is ultimately the most freeing. For then we are not kept bound to them in anger, but rather remain bound to God in love.

## Unconditional Daily Living

For those of us on the conscious path of ascension, it falls to us to set the example and tone of a Christ/Buddha rather than act out of the dictates of the negative ego. If both of you are on the conscious path of ascension, then the one who is more centered at a given time can serve as an anchoring point for the Christ energy to be demonstrated in the relationship. This is one of the benefits of a partnership between lightworkers. Hopefully at least one of you always will be able to hold to the light and to unconditional love.

All of us are vulnerable to the pressures and stresses of daily living. Some of us are more delicately constituted than others, as the energies of transformation are continually at work within the four-body system. Missing a good night's sleep, eating too much or too little, getting stuck in traffic and/or pollution can at times make us quite irritable, vulnerable and perhaps even a bit testy. It all depends on what one's personal issues or weak areas are.

Some of us are still prone to a certain amount of jealousy, fear and anger. This is not to say we should feel free to use these things as excuses and allow our negativity to dominate, for we are all about the transformation of these energies into the higher Christ/Buddha-like centeredness and functioning from the frequencies of our monads. What I am saying is, these issues and the transcendence of them is why we are here in the first place and what we are doing in the process of ascension. We can work to maintain the attitude of unconditional love as we go through our daily routines.

One thing we can do in the course of a committed romantic relationship is stay in the moment and take care not to let resentment build. This brings us once more to the importance of keeping the lines of communication open and feeling safe and secure enough with one another to communicate what's on our minds. What is definitely hazardous to a relationship is to hold things in for a long time and then blurt them out in a type of volcanic eruption of emotion. If we stay current with our feelings and with each other, then there will not be the opportunity for this negative-ego buildup.

If you find that during a period of communication you are getting trapped in relating from the negative ego's perspective, *stop!* Call time out and realign. Perhaps you need to go within yourself first. You would be better off meditating or journal-writing for a while. If this is the way you feel, let your partner know. More than likely you are both in need of some alone time, and it would be good for both of you to take time off, too. When you reconvene your discussion, make sure you ask to be overlighted by your monads, God and the masters. Be careful that you do not simply drop the discussion, but make sure that you are coming from as clear a place as possible. It might be a good idea to tell your partner that it is safe to speak his/her truth and that you want to be sure it is safe to speak your truth as well. Couples should always feel safe within the group body of their relationship and know that no matter what problem arises out of daily living, the love between them remains unconditional.

One thing that goes with the territory of being in relationship is that compromise in certain areas is inevitable. As harmonious as the two of you might be, undoubtedly there will arise a difference of opinion in some areas. In actuality, sometimes *because* of the compatibility factor, you might both find yourselves drawn to or pulled away from the same aspects of daily living. For example, both of you might dislike doing the laundry or vacuuming. What is important to you as a couple is that you learn to compromise, whether in the area of differing opinions or having the same distaste for specific chores. If neither of you can stand doing the laundry, take turns. Or if your partner is working harder in other areas, you might just consider doing this as service to help balance things out.

On the other hand, if one of you likes to fill up the house with furniture, paintings, collectibles or what-have-you and the other is a minimalist by nature, then it will take some serious compromising on both your parts. However, if you are serious about being in a committed, unconditionally loving relationship, then you should be more than willing to do this. The very word "relationship" contains within it the need to relate, and you are obviously in it to do just that. So keep the lines of communication open, remain unconditionally loving and work always to relate from the highest aspect of yourselves, and you should manifest an effective romantic relationship that will exceed your expectations.

## Commitment

It is also important to focus on the committed aspect of your relationship, which means to give 100 percent to the relationship, while still having 100 percent left over for your individual pursuits and independent needs. Perhaps the percentages don't tally, but they serve to express the point. Commitment means not running away the minute you encounter difficulty, but working problems through and finding the solution at the highest levels of your beings. It means considering your partner first before taking off with your friends or inviting people into the home as if you were still single. It also means knowing that you can trust your partner on all levels and that he or she can find that same level of trust in you. This will take a bit of thought, an awareness of the partner's needs and a willingness to be committed enough to work through issues.

If you are not doing this, why be in a relationship in the first place? What makes a romantic relationship so wonderful is the richness and support that you bring to each other. It should be founded on love and remain ever respectful of that love by honoring one another in the commitment you have made to each other. Therefore, unconditional love and commitment should always remain in the fore of your consciousness as you function day to day as a couple—that unique group body of two.

## Forgiveness through Acceptance

No discussion on unconditional love and commitment could be complete without including the element of forgiveness, which is, simply stated, to hold to your attitude that love is unconditional no matter what. While there are certain instances when an apology is the appropriate thing, forgiveness should be part and parcel of the expression of both love and commitment.

To love unconditionally means that you are accepting the other person for who he/she is and not asking your partner to justify his or her preferences or desires. Nor are you asking your partner to justify his/her choices about food or clothing. Hopefully, you have come together out of true love and have enough in common with which to keep building your relationship to each other, yourselves and to God. That there will be some restructuring and reconfiguration in this process is inevitable, but there must first be acceptance, and this acceptance must be given by each partner and felt by each.

Without this quality of forgiveness and nonjudgment, there will always be an underlying stress factor. This is completely unnecessary and inappropriate to any relationship, but especially to one based upon furthering the process of ascension for yourself and your partner. It would be like walking on eggshells all the time, which makes it inevitable that one will lose his or her balance. I have seen too many couples operating this way and have seen the terrible stress it puts on each of them on a daily basis. This is not the way for an enlightened person to behave! Each of you must realize that there will be certain fundamental differences between you. So never feel the need to apologize or seek forgiveness for simply being who you are.

I am not referring here to major areas of contention or to specific infringements wherein an apology and discussion is the appropriate course of action. I am referring to the basic tendencies and nature of each of you. Even when you have an abundance of things in common and are looking at life from primarily the same lens, there will be basic differences. For example, you might both be doing a lot of work on the physical body, trying to eat as healthily as possible, taking supplements and doing hatha yoga. One of you makes this a major point of focus, however, whereas the other one focuses more on other areas.

You might be the one who is tempted to reach into the cookie jar, and maybe you don't feel the need to show up at every scheduled yoga class. Perhaps you are even a bit over or under your ideal weight, but you *must* have the freedom to function as you do without feeling nervous about it. On the other hand, you might be the more committed to this health goal and your partner is sneaking cookies, skipping yoga classes and spending time on excuses for his or her behavior. Either way, please understand that this kind of behavior in itself can cause far more damage than eating a cookie or missing a yoga class!

In a romantic relationship built upon the ideal of ascension, unconditional love and commitment, forgiveness in matters such as the above should not even be an issue. In this case and the many permutations of cases like this, I am talking about a built-in forgiveness and an acceptance of who your partner is. Those of us on the path tend to be quite serious at times, and this can, and often does, serve us well. However, we must not be invasive with our seriousness to the point that our partners feel the need to apologize for following the path as they see fit. Another way of looking at it is to not get unduly attached to helping your partner learn his or her lessons, but rather to focus more on learning the lessons that God and the universe are giving you.

## When Forgiveness is Truly Necessary

There will be times, of course, when an apology is called for and when the one apologized to must decide whether or not they want to forgive the partner. I quote, "To err is human, to forgive divine." My advice is the same, because I believe holding to the Christ level of being is always of paramount importance. Take the high road whenever you can, for you are after all in the process of raising up and elevating every level of yourself. I do not mean to be in denial about the fact that your partner has exhibited a form of behavior that calls for an apology. Most likely you have felt wounded by his or her actions. I am saying, give your partner an opportunity to make that apology and provide an environment in which he/she feels safe in doing so.

If your partner is as committed to the personal path of ascension as you are and equally committed to the relationship and ideals of unconditional love and forgiveness, he/she probably feels quite badly about having hurt you. This would be especially true if he/she realized he had let his negative ego lead the way and run a bit rampant, perhaps by lashing out in anger or by being overly selfish and ignoring your needs in the process. It is hoped that your negative ego will not get in the way and that you will follow some of the guidelines of communication I have suggested, allowing your partner to make her apology and allowing your heart to be open enough to forgive her.

There may be extreme issues, however, that are brought to the fore and need a careful and in-depth discussion, such as the matter of adultery, which I have attempted to address in the Golden Key section of this book. Matters of such an extreme nature as abuse should lead to a qualified therapist's office and will take a great deal of communication, exploration and work. Issues of this sort might reveal that the relationship has indeed run its course and should be ended for the mutual benefit of all concerned. At the very least it will indicate a deeply rooted problem that deserves the utmost attention. If parting is the called-for solution, then that too should be done from a place of unconditional love and forgiveness.

The main thing to remember about the art of forgiveness is that in a committed relationship no one should ever feel the need to walk on eggshells lest he be called to judgment by his partner. We all have our little quirks, our preferences, our unique ways of functioning, and as long as the lines of communication are kept open, each must be allowed to follow her own personal path through her daily paces and through the path of ascension as well. There should never be the need to feel guilty or to apologize for simply being who you are.

On the other hand, since you are now functioning in the group body of relationship, you should keep in mind the areas where compromise and mutual decisions are appropriate and remain open and sensitive to your partner's needs. If you err in this regard, have the courage and compassion to make the needed apology. If you feel that you are the one who has been hurt, tap into the nature of compassion, acknowledging your partner's courage and honesty in his or her ability and willingness to ask for forgiveness, and by all means forgive him, even as you would want to be forgiven.

To err is human, and mistakes are bound to occur within every relationship, no matter how focused you are on the process of ascension or how committed to each other and to the light you are. People get caught in their own needs, and none of us is perfect or we would not be here in the first place. Yet to forgive is divine. I urge each of you to stay ever more open to that divine attribute within you and to actualize it to the best of your ability within the boundaries of your relationship.

There is one additional facet to be addressed when speaking of forgiveness, and that is the ability to forgive *oneself*. If we do not allow ourselves to make mistakes, learn the needed lesson and move on from there, we are creating a stagnant pool of guilt. We will become trapped in the murky waters of self-flagellation. This serves neither our partners nor ourselves, and it certainly does not honor the divine being we all are. To stay stuck in guilt is to stay stuck in false negative-ego programming. To make mistakes, then ask oneself just what the needed lesson was, learn the lesson and move on, is to be truly manifesting the process of ascension.

Unfortunately, most of us have been well trained in hanging onto guilt and not trained in the art of self-forgiveness. Therefore, please use the tools I have provided, along with any other techniques that work for you, and lift yourself above those murky waters of entrapment. What applies to romantic relationships likewise applies to the relationship we have with ourselves.

Remember that we are each here to grow, and mistakes are part of this process. So use the law of unconditional love and forgiveness when dealing with yourself. This is often harder to do in relation to oneself than to another, as the messages of blame and guilt have all too often been implanted within you from the time you were born. If this is an area that needs a lot of work, use the tools provided and do the work. We must clear ourselves of shame and guilt and live in an attitude of self-forgiveness in order to achieve this. We are children of God, meant to learn the lessons of our mistakes, but never to carry the guilt of them around. We are therefore guiltless, joyful and freely living in the light of divine forgiveness. We thus forgive ourselves and live in the peace of unconditional love, for it is meant that we live in freedom and joy.

# 4

# *Competition and the Path of Ascension*

## Doing Our Personal Best

The urge to move forward and better our conditions our relationships and ourselves in general is intrinsic to our nature as human and divine beings. Djwhal Khul states in the Alice Bailey books that "all moves onwards and upwards." This pertains to humanity, to the ascended masters and to the cosmos as a whole. This, then, is a basic impulse within all of us, and it is the very force that moves evolution forward. Therefore, doing one's personal best at all levels of one's being is natural and very important. Doing this in a noncompetitive way with one's partner often proves quite another matter. But it is important never to compete spiritually, financially, in the career arena or in any other area.

Your intent should be to keep growing, keep evolving and keep propelling yourself forward upon the pathway of ascension. This is between you and God alone. It is a matter of doing your personal soul/monadic best to move into a deeper unity with self and God, and this remains a private thing between you and God at a very deep level. Hopefully, this can also be shared and supported between you and your mate.

It is in the silent recess of our divine communion that God is seen and touched and known. It is in the quietude of meditation that we embrace the otherwise unembraceable, hear the voice of the silence, know the unknowable and dance within the stillness. All this is meant to be shared, for it is in these very places that the One is known as the many. Yet the journey is a very private one in the ultimate sense, and what we need concern ourselves with is making that journey in as pure and clear a manner as possible. The path to God is not a race or a competition. It is a journey that we must each make in solitude. Paradoxically, it is also a journey that we make with the entire human race wherein we are all advanced by the advancing of each of us, for indeed we are all inextricably bound together.

## Spiritual Support vs. Spiritual Competition

All too often the element of spiritual competition enters into a relationship between lightworkers. This does not serve to accelerate the ascension process or the quality of the relationship, and it is best to eliminate even the potential for this to occur. The easiest way to do this is to make sure to focus on the fact that by virtue of being in a committed romantic relationship, you have formed a unique group body. Your mutual ascension process is therefore deeply and uniquely connected. When one makes progress, the group body makes progress. When one taps into a greater light or love quotient, it becomes available to the whole. On a larger scale, this applies to the acceleration of humankind as a whole. Yet it applies most directly in the group body of the couple.

If one of you has had a particularly rewarding day at the workplace, there is a feeling of deep fulfillment that comes from doing your work successfully and reaching new levels. This might leave you with a feeling of overflowing joy and accomplishment, so much so that it cannot be contained. You then find yourself buying your partner flowers or showering him/her with extra affection or perhaps taking her out to dinner to celebrate. The point is that *joy and fulfillment want to be shared* and will almost always spill over into the relationship. What has uplifted one will ultimately bring upliftment to the two of you together.

This is also the case with your individual spiritual achievements. When one of you finds that you have entered into a higher, more love-filled place of spiritual beingness, that joy and love will express by outpouring to both of you. Your partner can be looked at in terms of the ascension buddy system I spoke about in *Beyond Ascension*. Why then should there ever be any competition in this sacred area in which all are indeed united? It is only due to faulty thinking, to hanging on to a belief system that has no basis in reality.

## Fame and Recognition in the Spiritual Arena

If one of you is more publicly recognized as a spiritual teacher because of the manner in which you are called to express your wisdom and love, I caution you both to pay attention, striving to keep any sense of competition from creeping into your relationship. One of you simply has a more public mission than the other, and so might be recognized as a well-known channeler, writer, speaker, painter, singer and so on. This is not better than the work that the other one is doing; it is simply a different kind of work. It is vitally important that both of you keep remembering this so that you can remain mutually supportive and not competitive.

Competition has no place whatsoever on the spiritual path and is in fact diametrically opposed to it. How can one part of the whole compete with any other part of the whole? It cannot, for how can God compete with God? However, the negative ego can and often does compete with another person's negative ego. If you are a couple on the ascension path, please connect daily with each other's monads as well as your own, to make sure you are functioning from that wondrous level of unity that is God.

Also realize that one of the reasons you are functioning as a couple is more than likely so that the more public one of you has the support and grounding of the other in order to do your work. From the monadic point of view, competition simply does not come into the picture. Therefore, it becomes even more imperative in such a situation to commune daily with each other's monads as well as with your own, so that you stay steady in the light and love and purpose of your divine I Am Presence.

From this point of view it will then become apparent that it is as important for the more publicly known lightworker to support his/her behind-the-scenes partner as it is the reverse. You are both a vital and integral part of the divine plan manifesting from within your relationship — perhaps even *because* of your relationship. Keep honoring each other in the unique roles you are playing, for it is the group body of two that has brought forth the functioning of the whole. Bear in mind that in saying this, I am not implying that each of you individually would not have brought to fruition the particular part that destiny would have you play. I am simply bringing to your attention that you have done this as a group unit and that you would do well to acknowledge that fact and give each other the proper honor and loving respect for the roles each of you plays.

There might have been a hundred different pathways you could have followed in becoming a famous lecturer, for example. But the fact is that you have done it with the help and support of your mate, and he or she should be honored for this. Conversely, it may have been your divine destiny, through silent meditation, to bring forth enough love and light to facilitate the outer manifestations of these qualities upon the Earth. But by virtue of being in relationship with your mate, he or she has drunk of the divine nectar you have brought through in silence, and your partner is out there sharing with the world what you have brought into the relationship. So your partner needs to be honored and supported for that role.

Fame and public recognition belong to the personality, not to the soul/monad. These higher aspects of you care only that the work gets done and that the divine plan is enacted to its fullest potential. To those lightworkers who find themselves with half of the group body gaining more recognition than the other half, remember that it is only the soul/monad fulfilling its highest calling and actualizing its mission. Keep ever centered in your I Am Presence and you will both see that what one of you is doing, *both* of you have succeeded in bringing about. For it is the will of your highest selves that this be so. Stay centered in the divine within, and it will follow that you will act in accordance with the energies of unconditional light and love, wholeness and support.

## Success in the Marketplace

In the third-dimensional world, money and power are often seen as two parts of the same whole. It is said that those who hold the purse strings are in control. Unfortunately, this is the case more often than not. "Money is power" is another common phrase, and this has unfortunately been the case in our world for quite some time.

In the system that we hopefully are moving out of, the major breadwinner was generally the person in control. We now live in a time when the cosmic energies are calling for change, and we are seeing more and more women holding prominent roles in the workplace. However, what is *not* meant to happen is that the same patterns continue with only the roles reversing. What is hoped for is a society of equality wherein each person fulfills his/her part of the plan and is honored for that.

As lightworkers, we are being called to bring forth the new energies of transformation into manifestation. But what happens when one of the partners of a relationship suddenly receives vast sums of money for fulfilling his/her mission? For example, say your spouse has been a loving, supportive homemaker while taking acting classes and getting an occasional bit part now and then, when suddenly she is cast in a TV series or a big-budget movie. Suddenly she is bringing in large sums of money, which now seem to dwarf the amount of money you have been bringing in over a period of many years. What most likely will happen is that patterns that were in effect before the shift will continue. So if you are presently equating money with the wielding of power and don't want that attitude to rend you asunder, give up that attitude *now*!

We are each valuable because we simply are. We are each truly in our power when we have connected with our *inner* power. You don't need to have large sums of money in order to own your personal power. You do need to connect with Source and clear the negative ego of all attributes that seemingly keep you separate from Source. Hold the mind steady in the light and merge your heart with the heart of the universe. Own your personal power and see all humanity through the lens of unity. This is the way to bring about the change that is so needed upon our world.

As things stand now, it is the wealthy who control our society, and thus we have a world misaligned and crying out for change. However, as the saying goes, "To travel far, we must begin near." What is nearer to us than where we currently are? And where is there a more perfect place to express the changing of values than from inside out, first with oneself and then within the unique group body that a relationship creates?

Let us take the opportunity that being in a relationship affords us and conduct ourselves as equals within that relationship regardless who has more earning capacity. If lightworkers all over the world were truly to implement this in their personal lives and relationships, the effect would ripple outward and little streams would join with other little streams until a vast ocean of values based on love would wash away the old values. We need to realize that earning money is just something we are a bit more adept at than our partner and recognize the areas in which our partner is more adept than we are. When we recognize that it is by the joint efforts and talents of each other that the partnership finds its very existence, we will be well on the way toward changing the world.

So what if our partner suddenly becomes a financial gold mine? So much the better for the whole! What if we suddenly find our own work in high demand in the marketplace, bringing in vast sums of money? All the better for the both of us, but we must be sure to stay aligned to spirit and keep our relationship to self and God in proper perspective. True power is inner power. It is the ability to stay focused and centered no matter which way the tides of fortune blow.

We must remember that; we must hold fast to our truths and keep very close guard that the negative ego does not reign supreme, falsely thinking and acting as if money is power. So let us stay aligned with our monads and remember to live from our I Am Presence and our spiritual value systems. For some of us this might mean making minor adjustments, and for others, major ones.

Learn to view your relationship as a mini world, which it is, and then structure your world from the highest possible vantage point. This means that whoever is the more successful in the marketplace is simply fulfilling part of the plan. There is no competition involved and no wielding of power over the other. Together you form one whole, each adding to that whole by the actualizing of your particular gifts to your fullest capacity.

Remember the equality that exists among all of humanity when viewed through the lens of the monad and the vantage point of God, and act in accordance with this vision. If each of us would look to see where we are with this issue and use every available tool to elevate ourselves to the place where we are demonstrating true inner power, unconditional love and equality, the world would eventually have no choice but to yield to these higher visions. Meanwhile our relationships will grow to a higher, purer, more equal and supportive level, and couples will know an ease that could not be known when buying into the negative ego's concept of money-equals-power. Remember the biblical adage, "What does it profit you if you gain the whole world but lose your own soul?" [Mark 8:36].

We must first and always look to our own relationships and ourselves and bring that into the light of God. In doing this, we will further our own personal and group ascension process. By living and demonstrating this high level of beingness and behavior, our relationships to ourselves, to God and to one another will be all the better.

## Competition between Couples in the Same Line of Work

Often people connect because they have a major point of common interest. This often happens in the area of careers. It is not uncommon to find a marriage between two doctors, two lawyers, two artists, two business people and so forth. This has the potential of bringing a deep and wonderful level of sharing into the relationship, as the partners are speaking a common language and dealing with shared interests, responsibilities and so forth. But this type of relationship also holds the danger of one or both partners feeling in competition with the other, which is most destructive and painful in a relationship.

Couples in such a situation must take extra care to realize that while fulfilling similar missions, they have their own unique and individual lessons to learn and contributions to make. This is true for all of us, and it is a basic fact that our life situations will provide us with the teachings and lessons that we most need. It doesn't matter how similar our work is to that of our partner, it is still *our* work with all its joys, lessons, tests and opportunities. It therefore becomes imperative, for example, that two actors or two doctors who are joined in a committed romantic relationship do not allow themselves to develop an attitude of competition. They must keep affirming the fact that they are souls/monads upon the path of evolution and ascension, following their own particular calling.

In the way they are set up in our society, some fields have a high level of competition. Professions in which this occupational hazard is most prevalent include acting, the performing arts and professional sports. It is interesting to note that some actor/actress couples can really go at it with their negative egos in a state of constant competition with their partners, when one of them is a petite blond woman and the other a tall strapping man! There is no way in the world that they can be up for the same role!

Nevertheless, the field itself has competition at its very foundation, and unless the couple takes great care to keep the relationship on a spiritual level and to function as two souls/monads, they will be susceptible to this trap.

Other fields can be breeding grounds of competition as well. Two doctors, two attorneys, two people functioning in the business world can easily fall into the trap of negative-ego competition, feeling superior if they are earning more money, acquiring more clients, achieving more fame, working for a larger company and so forth. The same point holds true for any and all of us in this situation.

We must take the time to put God first, to connect with our monads and to call into consciousness the fact that our path is uniquely ours. What we are meant to learn from participating in a certain line of work is not necessarily the same as what our partner is meant to learn. It might be your divine destiny to learn the attribute of humility and service, whereas your partner's divine calling is to step into the spotlight and catalyze great changes within the same profession.

If you are coming from the judgments of the negative ego, the effects of such a situation can be quite inharmonious and painful. But if you are coming from the perspective of the monad and are aligned with your work, you can be open to learning the necessary lessons and doing your work to your utmost potential. You will then find in your partner a unique support system, as he or she is involved in the same kind of work, speaks the same language, and is in a position to understand certain aspects of what you are going through that only an insider could possibly know. You proceed by honoring both the similarities and the differences that you share, and you know that each of you is fulfilling your own missions and doing the best you can in whatever situation presents itself to you.

Take a moment to still your mind, emotions and physical body. Know and invite your monad to anchor itself into all of your four lower bodies so that you become one integrated whole. Then if possible, do this jointly with your partner. Surrender and let go of all need to compete with your mate. State clearly your intention to function in cooperation with your monads. Take a unifying breath and let this henceforth be the way you live — mutually cooperative in noncompetitive support.

Always remember, you are working for God and not for the ego-self. By living this way, another person's success — your partner's or anyone else's — is *your* success, for your true identity is God, as is each person's. Competition is also closely related to comparing. *Never* compare yourself with others, but rather compare yourself only with yourself. In this way you will always be following the beat of your own drummer, and you will feel good about yourself and your continuing steady progress!

# 5

## *Our Sexual Selves*

Sexuality is a fact of nature, a basic core of the human structure. However, it is not one that functions simply through the physical vehicle. While sex is a physical act, it also involves the emotional, the mental and, ultimately, the spiritual aspects of one's being. When sexuality is fully expressed, a couple is sharing and communing deeply on several levels of intimacy at the same time. In its highest form, sexuality encompasses all four lower bodies as well as accesses energies from the highest level of self.

The physical level, being the most obvious, will be discussed first. However, I do ask the reader to bear in mind that in looking at the levels of sexuality, we are fragmenting that which in truth is not fragmented but part of a greater whole. Nevertheless, let us look at sexuality from the purely physical aspect. For each of us it operates as a physical release. In the male this is highly physicalized in the ejaculation of semen. The woman likewise releases some of her own fluids, but not to the extent that a man does.

Because of this physical release, many men want to roll over and fall asleep after the act. Women in general want to cuddle and hug. For the female of the species it is more difficult to experience sex on a purely physical level. Yet both men and women do this when they masturbate, it seems, whereby a basic physical need is given its due without a partner. This most assuredly is a physical act, but not entirely.

Almost always some sort of fantasy accompanies the act of masturbation, and we find that, depending on the needs of the individual and his or her level on the ladder of evolution or the particular need at the moment, the fantasy can be physical, emotional or mental in nature. However, on one level or another some thought and/or feeling process will be involved.

Different people have different sexual needs, but to look at this purely through a physical lens is incomplete. For example, you may come across the man who needs to "have it" at least once a day. While it is true that his body is producing more semen at a quicker rate than most, we must wonder why. There is always a reason, a cause behind every effect. Perhaps in his case it is because this allows him to release emotions that he would otherwise keep buried but which he feels safe to release in a physical manner through sex. Perhaps it is because this enables him to find a willing partner, a girl in every port, so to speak, and this feeds his otherwise low opinion of himself.

A woman, on the other hand, might feel herself sexually over-charged and find herself in the lower world of pornography or prostitution. This, however, can come out of various other needs. Perhaps she feels that the only way to get affection is by providing sex. Perhaps it gives her a sense of power over men, which her personality seems to need because she has previously been put down, controlled and manipulated by men. Perhaps it is simply a way to earn money, which would keep it in the realm of physical survival but not necessarily in the realm of sex.

Although sexuality is one of the most physical expressions between two people, it is limiting to look at it purely from a physical standpoint. Yet there is that phenomenon of chemistry so often spoken of where two people find themselves utterly attracted to and desirous of each other. There are indeed certain subtle physical energies at play in these cases. However, there is a mystery to this chemistry, because while certain people find an immediate physical attraction, another person cannot fathom what the attraction is. And therein lies the rub!

It is not so much in the seeing, although physical attraction and preferences certainly have this appeal, but something that is felt between the two. That is why we often can see a gorgeous being and, even while mentally acknowledging their extreme good looks, we do not feel that special attraction. The saying, "Beauty is in the eye of the beholder," is nowhere truer than in the sexual arena. However, it is not solely through the physical eye that beauty is beheld.

Sometimes it is a slow-burning fire that creates the greatest heat, as is evidenced in those cases where friends find themselves acknowledging sexual desire for one another that might end in marriage. It is not that the physical potential was not there from the outset, but simply that they came together first as friends. In actuality, true friendship is the best of all foundations upon which to build an enduring romantic relationship. Then you know that you are not acting out of some impulsive feeling that offers immediate gratification. You have experienced each other on the deeper levels of your being first and have the trust and grounding from which your sexuality is free to come to the fore.

For the reader's edification, the Hierarchy's view on masturbation is that it is perfectly natural. It takes preference over coupling with an inappropriate partner, either for a one-night stand or longer periods of time. In such an instance, the sharing of fluids between the two of you would then build an etheric bridge to the other that you do not want. So we must all be very careful about having so-called casual sex.

Even when you are in a harmonious relationship, masturbation is perfectly fine. This is an issue that has fallen prey to taboos and false beliefs, primarily out of a need for control on the part of traditional religious orders, parents and others. Do not be afraid of your own body or of being intimate with it. There is nothing wrong with masturbation. The only thing I would guide against is doing this to excess. I would guide against excess in all areas of sexuality, specifically if you are on the path of ascension. You do not want to deplete your energies by constant sexual release. However, masturbation has its place in the scheme of things, as does sexual intimacy with your partner.

## The Emotional Level

Emotions are tied to the physical expression of sexuality. As we have seen, it is almost impossible to look at the physical level of sex without taking the emotional level into consideration. Many people, mostly women (though this can be true of both sexes), will often choose to have sex in order to bond and receive the stroking and loving they crave. Sometimes it is not sex that is desired at a particular time, but rather warm touching and affection. If you are in a committed relationship, it is hoped that you feel safe and secure enough to ask for cuddling or a hug and an affectionate attitude from your partner.

However, if it is both sex and affection you are in need of, be honest enough to say so. More often than not your partner will be more than willing to comply. He or she simply needs to know. If you are the partner, however, and find yourself focused in other areas, it is hoped that you will have the sensitivity to communicate this to your mate. Take the time to help your partner feel loved. Tell him or her that as soon as you shift from the space you are in, you can plan a time when you both feel relaxed enough for a wonderful sexual encounter and that they and their needs are by no means being ignored. It was likely connecting with you that was their primary need, and you have given them that. Sex should not be ignored in the above example, nor should it be forced. As long as your partner feels wanted by you and feels your loving, caring affection, your partner will be happy to wait until both of you can fully enjoy the experience.

## The Mental Level

The mental level also plays a key part in the expression of sexuality. Sex is a deep and intimate bonding between two people and, more often than not, you want to be at a mental level similar to that of your partner, particularly in a committed relationship. This is not to suggest that you see things exactly the same, but true bonding and a lasting relationship generally occur between people who are resonating on a similar mental level.

This might not be quite so applicable when talking about a fling or a one-night stand. In these cases, it is more the physical (attractive looks, body chemistry) and the emotional needs that come into play. But I have seen, time and again, marriages and lasting relationships occurring between people of similar mental development. When coupling is attempted between people who have a great chasm between their levels of mental development, the relationship will often self-terminate due to lack of communication and bonding on this most important level of one's being.

Another aspect of sexuality on the mental level is the use of sexual fantasy. At times fantasy can be an extremely helpful tool to keep one's sexual energies flowing. Lovers often fantasize about one another while masturbating, and this further connects them in the mental realm. It also keeps the focus remaining on the relationship. It is equally all right to allow other sexual images into your mental field during sex, for to do so often acts as an aid to one's release. But there is some caution that must be used in this area. For example, if you are using a particular fantasy figure over and over again, this can form an imprint on your mental field that is inappropriate for that person as well as yourself. By the same process, if you are a public figure whom others find extremely attractive and are thus used over and over again in their personal fantasies, a mental bridge will be built between you and them. Then you will find yourself constantly bombarded by sexual thoughts coming at you from all directions.

I would not advise anyone on the path of ascension to pose nude or partly nude, thereby deliberately attracting this kind of attention. If you have done this at one point or another in your life, I would strongly advise you to put up shields (with the help of the masters) to protect you from such bombardments. It is a good idea for anyone with public exposure to do this as a safeguard from unwanted fantasy pictures coming into their auric field through the thought forms of those who find them especially attractive.

If you are the fantasizer, again I say, walk the middle path. Fantasizing can be a helpful tool, but not to the point of obsession or to the detriment of the one fantasized about. Regarding the use of public figures, you may even state before you begin your fantasy that this *is* a fantasy, and you want to keep it contained within your own auric and mental field. Make sure that you also request that your sexual fantasy will never hurt or impinge upon anyone in any fashion. These precautions would solve many difficulties encountered through the use of fantasy.

Ideally, your fantasy would be of a more general nature, with you or your partner at the center, and it would not involve the constant invocation of a specific person who is vulnerable to your thought form. It is best to limit your sexual thoughts and fantasies to your partner, with whom a bond already has been formed by joint agreement. This would be the ideal. But it is important to have the ideal set before you so that you are clear in which direction to move if you so choose. There are no hard and fast rules regarding this, save that of harmlessness.

When discussing thought forms and the mental realm, one must look at some of the ways this can and does manifest on the Earth. One of the oldest and most negative forms can be seen in the use of pornography, child pornography heading the list. Just about everyone, except for those responsible, would agree that child pornography is just about as low as one can go, being a form of child abuse. However, pornography itself, including video tapes, X-rated films and magazines that function in that capacity, do naught to elevate the sexual nature of humanity, but only debase it.

Immediately apparent is that rather than integrating the person as a whole, pornography serves to separate individual sexual parts, objectifying the person, whether male or female, and in the process it totally dehumanizes them. We have all indulged in this activity and there is no judgment in this, but in the process of initiation and ascension, there is the movement from what might be called lower-self sexuality to higher-self sexuality, and it is *that* we are speaking of here.

This is not to be confused with the tasteful portrayals in art or photography that seek to show the beauty of the human form. I am addressing pornography itself. Realize that this is a process and does not necessarily happen all in one day. Sexuality is an enormously powerful force, and God and the inner-plane masters are fully aware of this. Strive for the ideal, but do not be hard on yourself in the process. All of life, and indeed the path of ascension, is a process. Looked at through that lens, your sexuality is simply another facet of yourself in the process of transformation.

Couples will often play out consensual bondage fantasies in an atmosphere of complete safety and harmlessness. This type of sexual play, from the masters' perspective, is all right as long as both partners feel safe at all times and it is done in utter harmlessness and playfulness. On the other hand, one must be aware of the harm that can occur through such practices as sado-masochism, serious nonconsensual bondage and indeed any form of sexuality that causes pain to another person. If this is something that attracts you, please realize that you have some reprogramming work to do in this area.

These practices are, in essence, giving the negative-ego free rein to act out issues that are in dire need of addressing and correcting. Many people are still so entrapped by the functioning of their negative egos that sometimes what is entirely off base from the higher, more integrated viewpoint becomes common practice, and because it is common we somehow accept it as all right. This simply is not so when confronting issues such as those mentioned above.

If you notice any of these tendencies within yourself, understand that this is a part of you letting yourself know that it is in need of deep and intensive healing. Tell yourself that you forgive yourself for acting out your pain in such an inappropriate manner, then seek the aid of a qualified therapist in order to work through the underlying issues that caused this behavior in the first place. Most of all, do not judge yourself, but do what is needed to make the appropriate attitudinal and emotional corrections.

Please know that there is no judgment in presenting these matters as I have done. There is, however, a clear and direct call to use your discernment and know that these extreme behaviors are indicative of parts of yourself that are in great need of help and adjustment and healing. Therefore, I ask only that you are open to looking at these issues from the viewpoint of the higher self, and then doing all within your power to heal the wounds that have created these behavior patterns within yourself.

## The Spiritual Level

For those upon the path of ascension, the depth and level of intimacy during sex can be brought to the most sublime heights. You are more fully integrated within your four lower bodies as well as the higher bodies, so you are more complete within yourself and have more to bring to the sexual union. You are also most likely to use discretion in regard to who you relate to sexually, for you are aware of the bonding factor and the sacredness of the sharing of fluids. Last, you are bringing in the level of soul and/or monad and, therefore, God.

You might even be using certain sexual encounters with your mate as a means to raising your energies in the practice of tantra yoga. For you, sex is an integrated act between integrated people with full and complete awareness that you are bringing the emotional, mental and spiritual bodies into the act as well as the physical. The union between two people at this level offers much, and it is recognized to be the very special and sacred coming together that it truly is. Sex then involves the total being and traverses the realms from the pleasurable physical orgasm to that of a joint melding with monad and God. Count yourself lucky indeed when both you and your partner are coming from this vantage point, for then sex has the potential to be one of the most sacred, beautiful and enjoyable experiences that a couple can share.

## Pleasing Your Partner

There are two people involved in whatever level of sexuality you are expressing, except in the case of masturbation. Whether sex is of a more physical/emotional nature or brings in the levels of the monad between two ascension-oriented people, there is always the factor of physical pleasure to consider, and that means both giving and receiving.

Everyone's body rhythms are different. Certainly there is a clear differentiation between the rhythms of a man and a woman. The woman is usually slower to climax. Each woman responds to touch differently, as does each man. Partners in sex have the same responsibility to communicate in this area as in other areas. Don't be afraid to tell your partner what works for you and to ask for what you want.

The bedroom is one of the key places where the selfish/selfless balance needs to come into expression. Since everyone's body works differently, two people in a romantic relationship must become familiar with the way their partner's body works. If this is not done, you will have a buildup of frustration that will inevitably find its outlet in inappropriate outbursts rather than the flow of pleasure meant to occur when each partner knows the needs and desires of the other and is willing to meet them. I am not speaking here about sexual abnormalities, but about true and honest sexual communication so that both partners are equally satisfied. Those who are drawn to the more off-beat expressions of sex will ultimately find each other and work it out themselves.

Those of us who function under the more normal sexual modes, however, which definitely includes experimentation, are usually more reticent about expressing what works for us. This should be worked through by the couple so that each is fully satisfied and neither is doing anything that goes against the grain. Because it so often takes a woman longer to reach the point of climax than it does the man, if she feels he is impatient or has "checked out," she will never climax. If, however, he remains fully present, she can help bring herself to climax in the loving and supportive presence of her partner, and that is okay.

What is not okay is to feel emotionally abandoned by your partner. There may be cases where the man takes longer to achieve orgasm than the woman. It then is left to the woman to remain sensitive to her partner's needs so that both are satisfied. It is important that both of you are fully present and willing to communicate your needs and to have your partner's needs be communicated to you in return. In this way sex can be a most wonderfully satisfying and bonding experience.

## Sex and Fun

I feel the need to inject here a few words about the fun element of sexual union. Taking into consideration all that has been said in regard to pleasing your partner and the many levels of sex, it must be understood that sexual union can also be a time of lightness and play. One need not approach it with seriousness. Sometimes both partners need to release through both sex and laughter. So let some of your sexual encounters be playful ones. Playfulness is as much a part of sex as is affection and bonding. Just remember to respect your partner's needs at all times. As long as you both do this, you will both be satisfied and sexual bonding will be a wonderful experience for you both.

## Soul Passion and the Lightworker

During various stages of the ascension process it might be appropriate to cut back on sexual expression or even to live the life of the celibate. Thus sex might take a back seat to the activation and utilization of energy for purposes other than sex. This is by no means a hard and fast rule, although almost all initiates will pass through this phase during a certain period of their growth. It might be that the needed adjustments were made in a previous life as a disciple, so this might not be applicable to the current life of the initiate. Or it might be that one feels pulled to the path of celibacy for a variety of reasons and so chooses to follow that path. This by no means infers that this path is right for everyone. Nor does it mean that those following celibacy during a particular phase on the path must stay with that choice throughout the incarnation.

The question then arises for many lightworkers as to what the appropriate behavior in the sexual area is. Quite often we have put our own taboos upon ourselves by thinking of the physical vehicle as separate from the whole or from God, and we have become quite confused in the area of our own sexuality. Add to this the conditioning factor of our particular upbringing, our religious backgrounds and our desire to merge with God, and we often become quite inhibited in the area of our own sexuality. If this is the case, work must be done to release limiting programming and beliefs. Certainly, promiscuity and all forms of pornography should be avoided, but where it comes to love in our romantic relationship with our partner, we should allow ourselves to be totally free and uninhibited. There are very few rules regarding sex, save these: harmlessness, keeping your partner's needs in the fore, mutual respect and mutual communication.

Passion is a natural and normal part of the expression of both love and sexuality, and there is nothing antispiritual in this. Our goal is to integrate the bodies so that they can function as a unified whole. It is not our goal to deny any of our four bodies. There is a raw sexual passion that is often equated with animal passion, and sometimes lightworkers fear these feelings rising from within. However, as long as these feelings are not cut off from the feelings of love, mutual respect, consideration and tenderness, there is really nothing at all to fear in the expression of this depth of passion between you and your mate.

I use the words "raw animal passion" to express the deeper and more intense passions of the human being. I am not here referring to degrading, lust-filled and debasing passion. I am stating that two people in a loving, committed relationship need not fear exploring the depths of their love through a passionate sexual union. Sexual intimacy, in fact, serves as one of the great bonding factors between couples, and lightworkers are no exception. Follow the path that seems most appropriate at a given time, but do not fear the special intimacy of romantic passion, whether physical, emotional, mental or spiritual.

In this area, as in all others, the ideal is that of integration and completion. There are times when we are more emotionally focused in the sharing of tender words and poetry or listening to beautiful music. There are times when we are more mentally focused, as when, for example, we put our heads together to find a solution to a financial situation. There are other times when we are more spiritually focused, such as during prayer or meditation. There are likewise times when we are more physically focused such as during the time of lovemaking.

Let the disciple, initiate or, for that matter, the incarnate ascended being have the freedom to express the full range of their love in this manner, with all of the passion and excitement that goes into sexual union. To explore the full range of passions, feelings and physicality is most appropriate; why else would you be in a romantic relationship in the first place?

Yet I must address the fact again that at a certain stage during certain phases, you might feel that sex is not for you and that living the life of a celibate is. This can and often does occur between committed couples, as well as single people, at various points on their path. The main thing to keep in mind is that what you do should come from within your own being, *not* from someone saying this or that, or that a given behavior is correct and appropriate. For instance, such blanket statements as "Sexuality must be transcended by all upon the path of ascension" are simply not true. If you remain open and honest with yourself and stay in communication with your partner, the answers to your many questions will most assuredly come from within.

I would, however, urge you to reach a mutually satisfying agreement with your partner before suddenly embarking upon the path of the celibate or going from the sexually elusive or nonphysically expressive mode to that of the passionate lover. Whenever you feel the need for a major shift, it is only fair and right that you communicate with your partner and get his or her feedback. It is important to reach some sort of consensus before making any major changes in the expression of your sexuality and in other areas of your lives together.

We all need to honor where we are at a given point on our paths and to openly and honestly communicate that with our partners. Sex is made sacred or profane by what is in our hearts. As long as we keep our hearts aligned and open to the heart of love itself, there is no reason to deny ourselves the pleasures and wonders of a fulfilling and complete romantic relationship, including passion and intense lovemaking (unless we so choose). There is no right or wrong in this regard, only the honoring of where we are at a given point in our journey.

As long as we know we are truly honoring ourselves, our partners and God, our actions will take the shape and form of that honoring, be it in an intensely passionate bonding in lovemaking, through the life of the celibate or indeed anything that falls in between. In sex, as in all else, we want to hold to our truth and stay centered in light and love.

Always remember that the spiritual path is the path of integration and balance. One of the wondrous aspects of the spiritual path is that you can have the best of both worlds. Being spiritual or ascended does not mean the rejection of Earth life. Ascension is descension of the soul and monad fully into the physical vehicle and into all three lower bodies to bring heaven to Earth. Ascension is fully embracing earthly living from the perspective of the soul and monad. The divine Plan is to manifest God consciousness fully into physically incarnated masters. In conclusion, enjoy romance and sexuality as one God being to another. Share love, passion, joy and pleasure for the greatest good of all concerned.

# 6

## *The Differing Elevator Syndrome:*

### Being on the Path of Ascension When Your Partner Is Not

All of humanity is on the path of ascension. As the forces of evolution carry us onward and upward, all are a part of this divine truth. However, there is a vast difference between those who are consciously on the path of ascension and those who are not. We who are consciously traversing the realms of spirit are actually carrying different energies within our four lower bodies and bringing through the sublime energies of the soul/monadic realms. Thus we are functioning at quite a different frequency than those who are not engaged in this process. So it follows that our needs and desires change. God-realization becomes our very reason for being.

We are living at a time when the energies of enlightenment and the opportunity for ascension are accelerated in a way that has never been experienced on Earth before. The thrust and force of change is so much upon us that the very forces of the heavens are seeking out any and all who feel the seeds of spirituality sprouting and taking root at this time. These seeds are growing and ripening at lightning speed. The ascended masters on the inner plane are drawing ever nearer to humanity, and all of us who find resonance with the song of spirit find ourselves drawing closer to the masters, God and our own souls and monads.

Thus a relationship that would have plodded along at a more comfortable pace before is now stirred up by the fact that one of the partners is responding with the full force of his or her being to the spiritual stimulation now occurring in the world. The other partner might not be quite so ripe for change and might not understand what is going on. If you find yourself seeking a spiritual path alone within a relationship, you are most likely the one who has sought out this book. I want to assure you that you are not alone, for this is a situation that many lightworkers face at this time.

What the eventual outcome of such a relationship will be varies with the couple and the adjustments that each person is willing to make within the relationship. It is important to hold a great deal of compassion for both yourself and your partner as you explore the issues involved. If you have held an attitude of judgment toward your partner who seems less interested in matters of the spirit, it is crucial that you release that judgment now. The path of ascension is not one of judgment but of discernment, so it is with a discriminating eye that we shall proceed.

Being on the path of ascension when your partner is not is difficult, and at times it can be very frustrating and unfulfilling. It can leave you with a feeling of being alone in a crowd of two. If you have suddenly awakened to vast levels of being within yourself and in the blink of an eye, have seemingly fallen out of step with your given group of friends, you may be feeling quite lonely and confused. This is obviously a difficult place to be, but it can be quite difficult for your partner as well. If you have suddenly acquired a whole new group of like-minded friends, your partner might be feeling very lonely and confused.

Understand that although you are being called to follow a difficult path, it is one well worth any inconvenience that life throws your way. Every challenge is a lesson to be learned to help further your path of ascension into the light, and your relationship has become another means by which you are to grow. The question of whether you ultimately will stay in such a relationship is not the issue at this point. What is at issue is that you come into the full honoring of who you are, stand firm within the realms of love and light that have been made known to you, and proceed to explore your relationship and life in general through the lens of your soul and monad.

## "Judge Not, Lest Ye Be Judged"

First make sure that you are not in a place of judging your partner. If not held in check, this can lead to falling into a mode of constant criticism and putting down your partner's belief systems. Such an attitude will do nothing to open his or her eyes to the truths that you have encountered. Rather, it will do much to engender disapproval and criticism. You will also have fallen into the dictates of your negative ego rather than follow the road to ascension that you seek. Judgment and criticism will create a situation of two personalities at war rather than two divine beings communicating their various viewpoints.

It is imperative that you, who hold the more inclusive perspective of the nature of things, do all in your power to remain faithful to that vision and communicate from that perspective. If there is any judging or criticizing going on, make sure it is not coming from you. If it does indeed come *at* you, I suggest calling to your higher self and the masters to help shield you from any and all forms of this negative attack. But by no means let attack come *from you*, and do not attempt to force-feed your truth to your partner.

There will be some cases in which you will find that a partner is hungry for the higher perspective and hidden truths of life. Then all it will take on your part is a sharing of these in order to help awaken what was waiting to be awakened. However, if your partner is not ready to open in this way, no amount of cajoling or lecturing is going to do it. So why create bad energy between you? Simply do your best to communicate your awakening. Share about ascension, but do not try to force your point of view onto your partner. Each of you must have the freedom to follow your own paths to your highest and fullest potential. This might be hard to hear, but God cannot be force-fed to anyone. If you hope to enlighten your partner, do it by living the truth and being an example of love in action. How we walk our talk is ultimately our greatest teaching method, so let us all be as loving, caring and compassionate as we can be at all times.

As we make changes in our lives, it is important that we be tactful about how our partner chooses to live. For example, if we are in the process of purifying our diet and see our partner continually eating junk food, to point that out at every meal would only serve to hurt, anger and alienate him/her. Share your understanding of diet once, maybe twice, then wait to see if he/she asks you any more about it. If he is overweight, he probably feels bad enough about it. We do not need to keep at a partner about this.

If you have spent time with your partner enjoying horror movies and now find them repugnant, simply don't watch them with your partner anymore. You don't need to badger him about it or keep telling her the damage it is doing to her aura. I am not saying for you not to be who you are. What I am saying is, allow your partner to be who *he* is, even while working at some kind of resolution and harmony you both can live with.

## When Your Elevators Are at Opposite Ends of the Spectrum

You might ultimately find that the two of you have grown in such different directions that it seems your relationship cannot function as a unit any longer. I would definitely not advise either of you to reach a quick decision about this matter out of anger or in an abrupt fashion. If you find that you are in that position, I suggest you deal with it in as loving and supportive a manner as possible. It is often quite helpful to seek out a therapist while you are in the process of making a decision. This gives you the opportunity to check out whether either of you is coming from an emotionally reactive space rather than deeply considering the situation together.

Sometimes it might be that your differing ends of the spectrum form a unique point of balance for both of you. The more grounded partner who is not consciously on a spiritual path might be happy in his role as primary provider. This would give you the time and money to take various spiritual courses, buy the books you wish to read and so forth. Perhaps your partner enjoys the time you spend in spiritual pursuits. Perhaps he enjoys the way you harmoniously decorate the home or the way you prepare healthy meals.

You just might have something quite workable, and I would caution against any form of hasty decision even if you seem to function at opposite ends of the same spectrum. That might be the very backbone of why you both have been able to flourish as you have. Give yourselves time to look at all the various possibilities before rushing into a major decision.

On the other hand, a separation might not only be appropriate, but necessary in order for each of you to live your lives to the fullest possible potential. If this is the case, I suggest that you part the same way you came together, and that is in love. I am not referring to the romantic type of love that drew you together, but to the principle of unconditional love. It is important to bring forgiveness for each other to the process of parting. There should also be an honoring of what each of you has gained by being together. Then from that place move forward.

Separation is a difficult matter even for the most enlightened, so the help of a qualified therapist or spiritual counselor is advised here. It then becomes the responsibility of you who are on the path of ascension to use the many available tools mentioned throughout my books to continue the process of cleansing and clearing your own negative ego and to keep building your light and love quotient to ever higher frequencies.

Throughout this process, it is important to steer clear of all guilt and self-blame over the fact that your relationship did not work out. Please bear in mind that it worked for as long as it was meant to and that neither of you need hold any guilt because of what I have aptly termed "the differing elevator syndrome." There is no such thing as failure. Yet sometimes two people do grow apart, and in these spiritually charged times this happens quite often. If separation and/or divorce have become your choice, let go of guilt and self-blame. In actuality, there is no blame, so nothing needs to be forgiven. As much as possible, cultivate a sense of gratitude, because all that has gone before has led you to the level of spirituality you now embrace. Then follow your heart's calling and "be about your Father's business."

## Choosing to Stay Together

Of course there will be those who find that a workable and healthy balance has been achieved from the two of you operating at different ends of the spectrum. Others might find that although it is challenging for you to be at different levels of spiritual unfoldment, the love and essential values you share far outweigh the challenges. Those of you who find yourselves in this category will more than likely choose to remain together. If this is the case, keep in your minds and hearts that this was your choice, and do everything in your power to make it work for you.

As in all situations, keep love as the focal point of your relationship and play up the positive things you share. It is a matter of whether you see the glass as half empty or half full, and it is hoped that you will view the glass of your relationship as full as possible. Keep the lines of communication open and always try to communicate from as clear, integrated and spiritual a place as possible.

In your case, there will probably be more areas in which you differ than there will be with couples who are more aligned in their spiritual work. This does not imply that they are better off than you are, for they will be dealing with specific difficulties that confront two lightworkers who come together. But when two people view spirituality through a similar lens, they will probably get excited over the same or similar spiritual events, books and so forth. In your case, what is of great interest to you might be of little or no interest to your partner. That is why it is so important to focus on the love you share and on the areas of mutual interest you have. It is so crucial to allow one another the freedom to explore and participate in the interests unique to each of you. For example, if you do not like a certain type of movie and your partner does, then give him/her the freedom and the blessing to see what is most appealing. Perhaps he can have his night when he goes to see a slam-bam action film and you stay home and meditate. Then you might set aside a date night when you share an activity that is of equal interest to both of you.

However, if spiritual events are not of interest to your partner, be prepared to attend these alone. This might not always be the case, as you might be the couple who shares a certain degree of joint spiritual interests. Sharing spiritual activities that are of mutual interest would be a wonderful way in which to expand and deepen the relationship between you. But if you find that a specific event is calling to you and it is not of interest to your partner, pursue what interests you. In fact, this should be an issue that is discussed in general. Neither of you should feel as if you must be the other one's shadow. Nor should either of you feel stifled and unable to express yourself to the utmost and pursue your visions. The best way to deal with this is through open communication before the fact. Then freely and without guilt, go where your hearts and spirits call you.

No relationship is easy, no matter how many shared interests and values there are. Keep reminding yourself and each other that being together and staying together through the process of transformation and the knowledge that you are looking at the world through different lenses was a joint decision. Keep honoring yourself and always hold yourself to the integrity of your divine calling. Likewise honor your partner for being who he or she is and for playing the part he is playing in your relationship. Always keep the channels of communication open. Then follow the joint pathway of your loving, committed relationship while following your heart and staying in communion with your soul and I Am Presence.

# 7

## *In Search of Your Soulmate: The Deeper Meaning*

In order to put the vast topic of the search for one's soulmate into proper perspective, we must look at it from the highest and most inclusive vantage point. We are all part of one great whole, extensions of ever greater and fuller levels of beingness and unity. What we are ultimately seeking is to merge back with Source. This occurs in varying and graded succession, but must ultimately lead back through all 352 levels of the Godhead, which is our journey through the Mahatma, Avatar of Synthesis.

Although we indeed merge and blend with the next level above us, we retain our individuality. It came through Melchizedek, and through Djwhal Khul in the Alice Bailey material, that the body one manifests on the higher planes is usually the same body in which one takes one's ascension. Some ascended masters choose to take the youthful form of that body. Others will maintain the appearance of the age they were when they took their ascension. In part, this is so their disciples can recognize them. This can be seen in the cases of Djwhal Khul and Sri Yukteswar of the Self-Realization Fellowship and lineage, to name just two.

A major point of significance is that one retains one's specific gender. That is, the masters retain a feminine or masculine appearance through all the cosmic dimensions, all the way back to their cosmic ascension. This is a vital point when discussing the matter of soulmates and, from a much broader aspect, the divine feminine/masculine principles intrinsic to the cosmic structure itself. This includes how various ascended planetary and cosmic masters function through the yin/yang forces of nature as well as the pairing of the archangels and the elohim who likewise function through male/female counterparts. (Please refer to *The Complete Ascension Manual* for a specific chart on the pairing of these incredible cosmic beings.)

It might be wise then, to review a topic I have endeavored to explain in detail in the above-mentioned book. This is the fact that we are each a soul, an extension of an oversoul. The individualized soul functions as one of twelve that belong to a soul family (oversoul), and the experiences gained through each soul's unique incarnations hopefully contribute to the development of the oversoul itself. But there comes a point when one of the more dedicated and spiritually motivated members of that particular soul grouping is given the task of doing the work for its entire oversoul.

Each oversoul is also one of twelve oversouls that belong to a specific monad. The oversouls merge with the greater monadic family, and the monads group themselves into ever-expanding wholes as the ascension process continues. What can be clearly seen is that we are dealing with successive mergings into greater and greater group wholes, or spiritual families. This is a very important point to understand if we are to have any true perspective when approaching the subject of finding one's soulmate.

## Soulmates and Twin Flames

The process of finding your soulmate is not what one generally thinks. Oftentimes another soul is part of your soul family, but that person's development is along quite different lines than yours and is *not* by any means the mate you think you are seeking. This can apply to the monadic realms as well: Two individuals may be a part of the same monad, but their work and means of evolution might not be in harmony. In such instances, if you encounter one another, you may find that you do not especially bond, as your specific contributions to the whole are not aligned. This is usually, but not always, the case.

On the other hand, you might encounter someone from a different monad who functions much more as a complement to the way you function. When the two of you meet, you might be certain you have met your soulmate when in fact you have met someone from a different oversoul and probably from a different monad altogether. But because you are each holding similar positions in relation to your monads, you immediately recognize that there is joint work *to do.* You will probably have compatible natures, which will make it feel as if you are part of the same oversoul.

The fact is, most of humanity, lightworkers included, have a definition of soulmate that is simply not applicable from the soul level. The understanding of soul extensions is only now coming to light, and therefore there is still a general misunderstanding of what a soulmate is. This also applies to the term "twin flame," which is often talked about with very little thought or understanding.

Your twin flame is indeed someone special and unique to you. However, it first must be understood that this person, like a soulmate, is not usually, if ever, from the same oversoul or even the same monad. Your twin flame is a being with whom you have bonded through eons in both your outer-plane and inner-plane work. It is this *past shared work* that makes it seem as if you are connected through the oversoul or monad. More often than not, your twin flame will manifest in the sex opposite your own, and you will feel as if you are indeed two parts of the same whole. There may be specific lifetimes in which you have come in as the same sex in order to do a particular type of work. However, on the inner planes you will more than likely each hold either the masculine or the feminine principle in order to function in as complementary a fashion as possible.

The oneness and unity you feel when encountering your alleged soulmate or twin flame is likely due to the fact that you are meeting a being with whom you are closely and intimately connected in your spiritual mission. That being is not necessarily your other half. The truth is that we are each complete because we are the incarnated divine, made in the image of Father/Mother God. We are each Shiva/Shakti, and at our highest levels of integration we will manifest that within our own beings. However, we each hold more of either the male (Shiva) or female (Shakti) energy within us. This accounts for the fact that the ascended masters themselves embody more of either the male or female energies and consistently function with the energies thus embodied, taking a form also consistent with these specific energies.

We can also look at this from the point of view that oneness is All That Is. Therefore, when we reach the level of what we call ascension or enlightenment, we view ourselves as one with all beings and all forms of life. It is interesting to note that although we remain ourselves, we merge with all, and that while playing our parts within the whole, we feel ourselves to *be* the whole. This is the divine and blessed paradox of God and of life itself. "While pervading the universe with His entire Being, yet He remains."

In this light, let us explore the unique parts that we each have to play, remembering always that even as we expand within greater and greater wholes, still we remain. Also remember that in our embracing the oneness, we each have our specific roles to play, as do those with whom we are to interact. Thus during a lifetime we may encounter more than one soulmate — those special and rare beings with whom our purpose is aligned, beings we recognize as dear and special parts of ourselves. The tie is deep and the joy they provide is a joy that should be expressed.

Sometimes we find ourselves partnered with a person who does not feel like one of these soul-mate connections, and they may not be. Perhaps they are fulfilling a different function for us, as we may be for them (discussed at length in the preceding chapter). These two people might find a balance, not out of a particular spiritual alignment but one that provides a grounding factor. They might share a deep love, but not the same spiritual values, and in these situations the spiritual partner will often find companionship among other kindred souls. What most often occurs in these situations is that soulmates or soul companions are found among their group of spiritual friends. The fulfillment that was sought but not found through their mates is fulfilled through these soul-mate friends. If a person is so constituted that he or she cannot be in relationship with anyone who is not of a soul-mate nature, he might wait until he can blend the two facets of his life into one before settling down. Or a person might even choose to leave an existing relationship in order to be alone or to wait until the right soul companion comes along. We all have different needs, and what is of primary importance is that we stay faithful to what our own heartlight is guiding us to do.

I realize that the understanding I am presenting here about soulmates and twin flames is not very glamorous. My job in writing this book is not to present glamour, but truth. The fact is that it is very rare to meet a soul extension from your own oversoul. It is a little more likely that you will meet someone from your monad, but even this is rare. Every spiritual couple wants to think the partner is the other half of their soul, but this is highly unlikely. (I know I may get some flack from couples who believe differently, but I am sharing with you only what the ascended masters have shared with me on this subject. I was not very pleased to hear their guidance about this myself, but I am sure that you are seeking truth, not glamour or illusion.) This does not discount the profound bonding that takes place in the relationships that have been defined thus far.

## Mission Mates

Mission mates present us with a unique and interesting form of partnership. It occurs when two people who are probably not from the same oversoul or even monad come together and form a deep bond out of a sense of having a particular spiritual mission that they are to accomplish together. When this bond also takes the form of a romantic relationship, they do indeed have the best of both worlds. It offers the support of love and commitment as well as that of a partner who shares basically the same mission and spiritual destiny. This does not mean you play exactly the same roles, but you will work together to fulfill the same purpose and be parts of the same whole.

Perhaps one of you will be more the mystic writer and the other more of the occultist and lecturer. Or perhaps one will be the writer/composer of beautiful spiritual songs and the other the performer of those songs. There is an infinite number of ways this can manifest, but the point is, you will be doing it together in a shared and mutually supportive union.

If you are both rather advanced on the path of ascension, the work that can be done is tremendous and of extreme value to humanity. If you are both centered in your monads and make God the center of your work and life together, you will have a relationship of the highest order.

## Monadic Mates

This leads us into the realm of monadic mates. If you are a monadically centered mission-mate couple, the work you do has the potential of elevating humanity in ways not available to those who are not in such an elevated inner-plane position. The pairing of monadic mates occurs when both beings are monadically centered. This could be between two individuals from the same monad or from different monads. This is much more common than individual souls coming together from the same oversoul.

This pairing of two monadically centered individuals allows the purpose of the monad to be fulfilled, which is the overshadowing by God of all they do. To live then means to serve, for service is one of the attributes of monadic existence and why you have been called together in the first place. Monadic mission mates therefore have God and service work at the fore of their relationship, for it could not be otherwise when so overlighted by the monad. But if one loses his or her focus on the mission, most likely a relationship of this high calling will come to an end, as service and God are the primary reasons it came into existence in the first place.

This is equally true for those who share a mission but who are not mated in a romantic or sexual union. Sometimes two people come together who share a great vision and the monad of each stands beside them and within them in order to manifest that mission. If the mission is no longer the primary objective for their being together, they will frequently drift apart and another avenue for the monadic intent will be sought by one or both.

Whenever you are operating from the monadic realms, you are both watched and supported by the planetary and cosmic masters as well as your monad. The purpose is to see light and love and power, rightly used, manifest on the Earth. If a given vehicle for that expression is not taking hold, a new one will be sought, for neither the monad of the individual nor God will accept less than the highest level of expression by those of us who are capable of expressing it.

All of us, whether in a service-oriented mission-mate relationship or a romantic mission-mate relationship, must discern if it is coming from the realm of the monad. If it is, we should indeed rejoice and keep a close watch so that this high level is maintained at all times and the monadic mission is brought forth on the plane of matter. If we are not yet so connected with our monads as to have found our monadic mate, let us work daily upon our path of ascension so that we too shall know the glory of the monad — the mighty I Am Presence — as well as have the opportunity to serve it and the greater whole.

## Group Monadic Mates

Group monadic mates do not fall into the category of romantic relationships, for here we are dealing with a larger group body. However, it might be the destiny of two people within that group to form a romantic bond. The work structure of group monadic mates occurs when there is a coming together of various ascended beings or near-ascended beings. These beings are merged within the group body of their particular monad. They come together from their various monads to form a particular monadic grouping in order to work together on both the outer and inner planes on a joint venture of service. They form a unique group consciousness and bond for the sole purpose of being agents of the divine Plan. This type of relationship offers them the opportunity to advance along the lines of cosmic evolution. They can and do anchor into their fields the higher dimensions, chakras and bodies as well as heightened light and love quotients, which will enable them to move quickly through the higher levels of initiation when their tenure on Earth is over.

They also work as a balancing system for one another in several different ways. One way is simply by coming from different monads. Although serving a similar purpose, each one carries a slightly different energy. Thus each person's energy complements and supports the others. Working closely with one another, they form a kind of check against negative-ego manipulations. This is not to imply that there will not be slip-ups, but as long as each person stays open to the mirroring effect of the others, this can work wonders to keep the negative ego at bay. All of us, no matter how evolved we feel, must be ever watchful over that sneaky negative ego! This applies even to the inner-plane masters, although on a completely different scale and at a much subtler level.

All things considered, functioning within a specific monadic grouping can be one of the greatest service vehicles available to us on Earth. The good news is that all of us will eventually find ourselves merged back with our monad, without a loss of individuality but with a greatly heightened sense of love, wisdom and being. From that high place we will all have the opportunity to serve humanity, continuing onward and upward into ever higher and more inclusive realms of being.

## Sex on the Inner Planes

I must admit that addressing the matter of sex on the inner planes seems both humorous and quite serious. It has been the brunt of many jokes, but it is serious because it involves the attribute of love, and love is indeed synonymous with God.

When two people who are deeply in love on the Earth plane are separated by what is commonly termed death, but which more appropriately should be called transition, does the love between them stop? I venture to say it does not. It may seem to fade, and if one makes an early departure, adjustments are most certainly made. But love is love, and by its very nature it is carried forward into the realms beyond. When one is in the process of passing, he or she is met by loved ones — a fact which is now common knowledge — and are most assuredly greeted by a beloved mate from their most recent incarnation who has already passed over.

The only time this does not occur is when you have two people who are at very different levels of spiritual development. In these cases, they are still met by loved ones, but they will more likely encounter a husband or wife from an *earlier* incarnation, one whose frequencies are more aligned with their own and who will be recognized as a beloved. The more evolved individual will have a similar experience, although in that case, contact with the soul/monad and the masters will be just as important as connecting with a former husband or wife. The more evolved being will have a more expanded view of being one with the whole.

This brings us to the understanding that on the inner planes we cannot hide from the truth as we can here on Earth. Therefore, the true nature of another being will stand revealed, and one cannot help being drawn to the most suitable mate. On the inner planes, each being knows the other by their inner light. Therefore, though there are hundreds of husbands or wives from former lifetimes, we will be drawn to the one with whom we truly belong. At the same time, a soul might have some unfinished business and therefore a strong desire to be with the mate it was with last, even if only briefly.

## The Astral Realm

Sex on the lower astral levels is quite similar to sex on the physical plane, except for the absence of either a physical vehicle or its etheric counterpart. If the people involved were acting out of the lower frequencies while still on Earth, they will continue to play that out on the lower astral until they tire of it. They will then find themselves, either individually or as a couple, elevated to the higher levels of the astral realm, where a deeper comprehension of love and a purer expression of it will take place in their sexual union.

In order to understand this, you must first understand that the astral realm itself is quite like the physical. The major difference is that on Earth you have those of varying frequencies lumped together in crowded cities or functioning in the same work environment. But in the astral realm things are much more clearly delineated, which allows those of similar natures to play out their parts and learn the needed lessons. Those who are more highly evolved can pursue the higher nature of God within themselves. They can also explore the vaster mysteries of cosmic truths unencumbered by those who on Earth would have vibrationally dragged them down.

So we can see that in the astral realm, things function much as they do on Earth. Yet unlike Earth, things are not so hidden from astral sight as they are from physical sight. Also, the regions of the astral run the gamut from the lowest expressions of the basest human savagery (almost all of our current humanity has evolved far beyond this point) all the way to the most resplendent regions. To behold someone from these higher realms would seem to the average Earth person like beholding a god!

## The Mental Realm

Upon the mental realm one finds beings of various degrees of development. Those who find themselves in the lower mental worlds are but relative children in their capacity to think and understand compared to those who find themselves in the higher mental worlds. Although the mental realm can be regarded as the next plane above the astral, it can also be considered to coexist with the astral, for although the mental realm is higher, it interpenetrates the astral realm.

Let us consider an average couple in order to demonstrate this point. Joe and Jane, for example, have rejoined each other after both have passed through the great transition that humans call death. They are expressing their love and making a life together for a time on certain levels of the astral realm. In addition, both of them are expressing in the mental realm. They are practicing the expansion of their mental capacities, yet having an anchor and "home" on the astral. This is not unlike Joe and Jane on Earth, who conducted their physical-plane lives through their emotional and mental vehicles while still on the plane of dense matter.

On the other hand, there are beings who have dropped their astral vehicles just as we here on Earth drop our physical vehicles at the time of death. These beings are free to function through their thought or mental bodies of light, freed from the encumbrance of both the astral and the physical vehicles. They might be called back into incarnation at some point, but they will be graced with a period of unfolding purely through the higher mental worlds during their inner-plane stay, and this is a most delightful, enlightening and wonderfully freeing experience.

We are then left to wonder whether, or how, these beings enact sexual union. Some do not, as they choose to use this time to develop their mental faculties and further their understanding of the divine Plan. Yet some most certainly do engage in a type of sexual union. I use this term in a broad sense. It certainly involves a specific coupling, and it certainly is expressive of a unique intimacy between them, but it is of quite a different nature than what we on Earth think when we use the term "sex."

What occurs is more of a melding of minds, a total blending of beings. This union is not altogether without form, as there is still a form in the higher mental worlds, but it is refined beyond that which can be expressed in words. The merging of the forms occurs in a way that is hard to explain. Form follows thought, rather than thought following the form of the physical. It is the merging of these mental forms that we can most readily equate with the act of sex. It is far more appropriate to consider this merging of light/mind than an act of sex, for the very word "sex" cannot help but conjure up images that are simply not appropriate on the higher regions of mind.

Yet it is equally inappropriate to say that these realms are devoid of sex altogether. We remain in a dilemma as to how best to express what does occur. The terms "intimate bonding" and "union between couples" more closely approximate what actually occurs than simply saying they are having sex on the higher mental regions. If one were put on the spot to say whether or not sexuality is expressed on these higher mental worlds, one would do well to say there is, but it is of quite a different nature than you are apt to imagine.

To summarize, I would state that yes, there is sex in the higher mental worlds, and it is preceded by thought. The saying "thoughts are things" is a profound statement of fact on these higher mental regions. There is a coming together of two individuals who function and unite through the bodies provided by the level of their beingness in the realm of mind. Love indeed enters into this union, as love itself is an attribute of God.

Therefore, for those of you who are concerned about whether or not you will be able to be with your mate as you enter the higher mental worlds, I answer with a resounding *yes!* However, as above, so below — and even more so in the case of the higher mental regions. As there are those who, during certain lifetimes or portions of a lifetime on Earth, choose to be celibate, so there are those on the higher mental worlds who choose to use this time in the pursuit of cosmic wisdom and the various functions of mind. Yet that path is only for those who choose it. For you who wish to continue your love relationship through your higher mental bodies, it is quite a common practice, as the levels of unity that are possible within these mental worlds far supersede any levels hitherto experienced.

## The Causal (Buddhic) Realm

It is in the buddhic realm that one functions as the soul. It is upon the causal realm that all the good, the beautiful and the true that a being has stored up through many cycles of evolution on the lower realms eventually finds its place. Nothing but that which is of a divine nature goes into building the causal vehicle, which is the vehicle for soul itself. What occurs with mates is quite interesting in the causal or buddhic realm. A type of specific couple bonding occurs, but from a place totally reflective of unity. We are now dealing with souls and the group bodies and families of souls that exist in a world that reflects only unity.

At this level there is again a coupling of souls as mission mates for the purpose of doing specific work together. Sex on the causal realm takes the form of a bonding of essences rather than the joining of specific bodies. The coupling of soul bodies might exist for a certain span of time, but this will ultimately give way to a higher form of bonding that does not involve the coupling of soul bodies at all. One of the major reasons for this is that all continues to evolve, and it is on the causal realm that even the body of the soul is relinquished. One is left with an individualized monadic expression that is an extension of the monad itself.

A master, of course, can form a soul body through an act of will, just as the master can form the four lower bodies with which to express self. But in essence, after a longer or shorter stay on the causal realm, one relinquishes that body and moves up within the ever-expanding whole into the atmic, monadic and logoic realms and eventually into the cosmic realms beyond.

During the process of incarnation, one gets to experience the causal realm before becoming a permanent resident. During these stays one can and often does have more of the "normal" (if such a term is applicable) type of sexual union. That is to say, one can continue to bond with one's mate through the buddhic vehicle. This could be called a type of intercourse, but it is the intercourse of two souls that is so deep and all-embracing that to call it sex would be somewhat misleading. There is a merging between the two that approximates certain aspects of sex, but this more appropriately could be called intercourse of souls. This is vastly different from the sexual intercourse between two people on Earth.

## The Atmic and Monadic Realms

There is such a unity between the atmic and monadic realms that to try and differentiate between them would be a disservice to both. On the atmic realm or plane, one is totally connected with the monadic vehicle. On the monadic realm, one *is* the monad. Yet to be as connected with monadic source as one is on the atmic plane is to be the monad as well. The difference is that what is utterly pure and unfettered becomes even more pure and unfettered. It is truly hard to separate them, as those on the atmic plane serve only the monad, being a direct expression of it. And those on the monadic plane serve only the monad by *being* it.

The difference is slight, but when full monadic merging occurs, one is then totally and completely free from any separation from Source. On that plane one is totally unified with the monad and has become Source Itself. This is speaking from a planetary point of view, not a full cosmic ascension point of view.

Sex on these planes fades away, though coupling does not. However, let none fear for the loss, for it is a place of such unity that whatever has been gained through the act of sex — the love and bonding — *is the very nature of these planes*. Therefore, nothing is ever lost — not intimacy, individual identity or the particular mate one might choose to have and work with on these planes. What does occur is the fading of particular needs, for these planes contain within their very nature the fulfillment of all needs.

## The Logoic Realm

It is appropriate that we continue our discussion by bringing the logoic realm into it, as we have now entered realms that uniquely merge and blend one into the other. When a monad reenters the logoic realm, it brings with it all that its many cycles in the various worlds have given it of the nature of goodness, beauty and truth. What happens upon entering the logoic plane is that there is a direct and correct knowledge of logoic intent, and it is that which the individual now serves. Yet one has by then entered into such a vast group body and consciousness that calling one an individual expresses but part of the truth. One does indeed remain an individual, unique unto itself, yet one fully functions as part of a greater group body and whole. Each is both the one and the many. Because this is the case, one can, and often does, have a particular being with whom one works and serves. This is one's divine complement or counterpart, which all the elohim and archangels have. Many masters of both planetary and cosmic standing also function by way of this divine coupling. This is not something that *must* be, because by the time such heights are reached, one has bonded with one's ultimate mate, which is the individual merging with its mighty I Am Presence or monad. On a planetary level this is uniting with God, fulfilling the ultimate union.

However, even as one has achieved this ultimate union, blending with that higher aspect of self and balancing the masculine and feminine within oneself, there is still a tendency to be a bit more yin or yang even within this perfect balance. This is because the basic form of the cosmos itself works on the divine Father/Mother principle. And because of this, it is not at all uncommon that great masters and cosmic beings alike choose to work with their divine complement.

Each of the seven planes mentioned in this chapter will eventually become integrated when you take one of the seven levels of initiation. If you know your initiation level, you can easily trace the plane you are working on and the plane you are now striving to integrate.

## Merging with the Master

There are various ways in which the disciple or initiate merges with a higher master. One of the most profound examples of this is invoking a penetration by such cosmic masters as the Mahatma (who embraces all 352 levels of the cosmos), Melchizedek or Metatron. You invoke their divine presence to permeate your being, thus making those extremely high energies available to you as well as to all of humanity and the Earth herself. This enables the master to express and function more fully and freely through you.

To use the Mahatma as a wonderful example, the person who asks for a penetration of his energies then functions as a type of walk-in, allowing the Mahatma to function within him/her. This is not the type of walk-in situation in which one leaves the body to allow another to walk in and live through it. It is a profound example of merging with a cosmic master by allowing that being to penetrate you with his/her divine essence. This is actually quite a common practice, as the master will seek to merge and blend his or her energies with any number of initiates for the purpose of protection and to further facilitate the spiritual development of the initiate. In this way the masters are able to express themselves more freely on Earth.

It is interesting to note that some disciples or initiates feel themselves to be in a type of marriage relationship with a particular master due to the bonding and unifying factor. This is the case with nuns who put on a wedding band to signify that marriage between themselves and Jesus Christ or God has taken place. They consider themselves brides of Christ. In truth, this can occur with any planetary or cosmic master.

The master also merges in group formation with those he is guiding. They (the initiate, disciple or younger master) learn by being enfolded within the auric presence of those masters with whom they are aligned. This has to do with the formation of a group body, which occurs through the unified work of advanced lightworkers. To quote from scripture, "Where two or three are gathered together in my name, there am I in the midst of them" [Matthew 18:20]. This is a wonderful concept that all disciples, initiates and masters at every level should be aware of. When two or more of you join in divine intent, a third entity is created, comprised of yourselves, your I Am Presence and the master who is working with you. A group body then arises out of your joint intent.

This can be a wonderful way to approach a marriage as well. Join hands, invite your I Am Presence to overlight you both and ask for the master or masters with whom you feel most aligned to join you. Through this joining, recognize that a third entity, a group body, has been created. Then make every effort to function as that group body as well as individuals. This will give you the benefit of continuing your individual work as well as working within the love, support and purpose of your greater group whole for the upliftment of humanity.

This group body becomes even more powerful when it is created in conjunction with the ascension buddy system. Ascension buddies can be marriage partners, two friends or a group of friends. It can serve to uplift a marriage or romantic relationship. The ascension buddy system will elevate any relationship. It is also a wonderful tool for mutual support and spiritual acceleration.

## Bodies of the Masters

Although it must be obvious to those who have had personal contact with any of the masters that they do indeed have form, it seems important to state this: A master is one who has achieved liberation from the Earth and who functions from at least the monadic plane. For the purpose of contacting their disciples, and in order to fulfill specific missions, the masters create vehicles on the etheric, astral, mental, causal, atmic, monadic and logoic plane, and sometimes on the physical plane as well. Thus they are able to make direct and personal contact with their disciples in ashrams and schools of learning.

Having the ability to take a form enables them to visit the disciple and the disciple to visit them. Some specific manifestations of this are Djwhal Khul's Synthesis Ashram on the inner planes, where many disciples come; the beautiful manifestations of the etherialized form of Mother Mary so that she may impart specific blessings and teachings; the appearance of Sananda and Lord Maitreya to the inner eye of disciples; the appearance of the Christ (Lord Maitreya) on Earth; and the advent of Sai Baba and his incarnation in a physical body. The masters are drawing ever closer to humanity, as are the angelic beings and higher extraterrestrial intelligences during these heightened times of spiritual acceleration.

## The Unique Accounts of Saint Germain

Saint Germain has been known to visit many disciples in an etherialized form, a form that functions much like the physical, although superseding it. In such a manner was Guy Ballard, now known as Godfré Ray King, contacted and taught. These contacts ultimately brought about the *I Am Discourses* that served, and still serve, to motivate many disciples on the path of ascension. Many women disciples also tell of being visited by Saint Germain and, in etheric form, being made love to. This is somewhat reminiscent of the stories of Zeus appearing to various women in many guises and becoming their lover.

One might wonder if these stories are indeed true and, if so, why a being of such divine stature would manifest in this way. We discussed earlier the great power involved in sexual union, as well as the fact that the masters are functioning through self-created bodies (the mayavarupa body) on various planes in order to serve specific functions. There is also the fact that the Mahatma merges with his disciples through an act of penetration. It follows then that a master who carries specific energies might use an act of seeming sexual union to thus penetrate a disciple and further merge his energies with that disciple. He would do this if he deemed it the most effective way to unite and commune with a particular disciple.

Granted, this is not commonplace, nor should it be, for almost all disciples are struggling to rid themselves of the dictates of their sexual nature and assume mastery over that powerful aspect of their beings. However, if a master has the ability to elevate the disciple through this type of union, then should this be seen as wrong? I think not!

However, caution must be exercised here lest teachers in incarnation who are not ascended to such divine levels use this as an excuse to sleep with whomever they choose. This practice is *never* to be considered by any earthly teacher, no matter how advanced they think they are. If anyone has such a teacher, my advice is to remove yourself from his teaching and seek the light of truth within yourself. This type of situation is utterly and completely unacceptable, and we are not speaking of such matters here. We are, in fact, speaking of a deeper penetration by a divine and cosmic being who is using a form for precise and specific reasons, and only when it is appropriate.

One must also keep watch that the rumors of such occurrences do not exaggerate their frequency, which they often do. This is a delicate and unique situation, one that is hard to convey clearly. I would caution all disciples *not* to make this their intent with any master. Instead, set your intent on merging with your own I Am Presence. If such a vision does come to you, challenge it thrice in the name of Christ. If it is not of a high and pure frequency, such a challenge will stop it full force. If it is of a divine nature, you will know that you are protected and that the master appearing to you is an ascended being. This is a sensitive issue where extreme caution must be exercised on all planes.

## Splitting of Souls and Oversouls

There are some unique cases where an individualized soul or oversoul will indeed split to form true soul twins. In the case of the splitting of an individual soul, the purpose would be to better express and serve, utilizing the various aspects of that soul in the form of two rather than one. This would be the case when there is a split within the oversoul.

In rare cases, this joint decision is made by certain cosmic and planetary masters, the soul and monad and the presiding Planetary Logos. This is done to fulfill a greater part of the plan through this unique formation and to facilitate the growth of the soul involved. This is the only time when the use of the word "twin" is truly applicable, as the two indeed have come from the same higher self. This type of split is rare indeed. I want to make it clear that this is so rare that the masters almost guided me not even to mention it. Because it has occasionally occurred, however, I have included it for your edification.

## Your Pet Mate

The important role that pets play in the realm of relationship cannot be understated. Directly below the human kingdom is the animal kingdom, even as the angelic kingdom is directly above the human. The human kingdom is a bridge for the animal kingdom to evolve into its next level, but this will not happen for every species now encountered on Earth. Some species will die off, but the group soul to which that species belongs will not. It will eventually manifest in a more appropriate form and continue its group evolution, for all life is evolving. Therefore, though the forms of animals might change with time, the group soul continues.

When we talk about our pets, we are discussing beings of an already developed nature who sometimes have quite developed emotional bodies and a form of mind principle in activation. This includes dogs, cats, elephants and horses. It also includes birds, who are actually part of the devic kingdom. These animals are awaiting the opening of the door to individuation, which will occur by the activation of *manas* (mind) and their separation from the group body. At that point they become individualized souls and begin treading the path of human evolution.

The relationship between an individual and his/her pet is a mutually beneficial one for both their evolutions and emotional well-being. A particular animal is ready for individuation when it begins to break away from the generic group body that is usually the pool for the cumulative experiences of a given species. It begins to retain a separate identity through a succession of incarnations and grows through its interaction with humanity. This is why it was designed that an animal take the role of pet or "animal baby," as they are often referred to. They are indeed our animal children, and the emotional bonding between us is truly mutual.

We often feel so bonded with our pets that we consider them family members. This is not to be taken lightly, for they *should* be thought of this way. Even the more elusive ones such as the cat, who is not as outwardly expressive as the dog, is quite involved in the activities of the household and all the emotions of its members. This is equally true of the elephant and the horse, although not nearly so outwardly apparent.

We are not being sentimental when we imagine our "animal babies" to have certain feelings, for indeed they do. We will likely encounter the same animal again and again throughout its incarnation process, for the bond continues to grow. At this period in history we have our share of animal psychologists and psychics, and although all are not truly tuned in, most are. The emotional needs and feelings of our pets can easily be discerned by anyone who is willing to take the time to become sensitive to them.

If you therefore find yourself the proud parent of a Persian, alley cat, mutt or Maltese and feel a deep and loving bond, know that you are not off on a tangent with your love, but are helping to facilitate the plan of God. Animals can occupy a special place in our lives. Certain people have a destiny with the animal kingdom in general or with a particular species. Others have a destiny with a particular pet they are assisting in their journey toward individuation. The pure, unconditional love that loyal pets afford us is one of the best examples of the nature of unconditional love that humanity can find.

Animals also serve as companions to the elderly, guides for the blind and deaf, herders and crucial team members in various kinds of rescue work. Since animals can be calming, they are sometimes employed to sit quietly on the lap of a fearful dental patient, giving them a dose of drug-free calm.

As a beautiful example of man's harmonious relationship with the animal kingdom, one can look to the tradition of the Native Americans for whom the animal kingdom, has served as guides through many centuries. We can thus see how closely tied we are to the animal kingdom, both inwardly and outwardly, and how much animals have to offer us as teachers, servers and friends.

Let us therefore not exclude those most wondrous creatures when considering our soulmates. Your puppy today was most likely your dog in a previous incarnation. The bond runs deep and long, and many have experienced manifestations of their pets from the other side of the veil. So please try not to have undue concern when you lose them. They will be there awaiting your arrival — and indeed are probably watching over you even now, if they have passed on. The tie between humanity and those animals on the path to individuation spans the ages, as does any close relationship. In some ways it is perhaps the tenderest one of all.

# 8

## *Spiritual Parenting*

### Choosing Your Parents

It is quite common among lightworkers to hear people discussing why they chose their particular parents. We wonder how this is possible, given so much conflict between parents and their offspring. However, from the viewpoint of the soul, oversoul and monad, the parents one has chosen are indeed the perfect parents. This does not seem to be the case when we find ourselves incarnated into a disharmonious situation, and to be sure, there are extreme examples of this in every walk of life. But if one looks at it through the lens of the higher self, one would see that all is as it should be for the needed lessons to be learned by both parents and offspring.

To become detached in this matter is often very difficult, particularly if you find yourself in an extreme situation, such as an abusive alcoholic or drug-using child or parent. To help you understand this process, let us look at it from as high a vantage point as possible.

There are many factors at play in the process of a soul being born into this world, and many cosmic factors must be taken into consideration. From the vaster cosmic lens, the timing of your birth is of utmost importance, as you incarnate to follow specific cycles of the zodiac in order to complete the assimilation and relative perfection that being born under the influence of specific zodiacal energies brings into play. The rays must be mastered and incorporated into our being and the various archetypes played out throughout our evolutionary process. So too will each of us cycle through the various signs of the zodiac, experiencing the major influence of each of the sun signs.

Therefore, the coordination between parents, conception and birth is watched closely and involves the participation of the lords of karma. This becomes quite a technical matter, particularly with the increasing number of induced births, and must be watched over and guided most specifically, as it is always the free choice of parents to avail themselves of this option. In almost all instances it is not advisable, as the timing of the birth should be under the direction of the soul and the oversoul. Therefore, when this option is chosen, the birth is carefully watched over and guided by beings of a very high nature. They want to ensure that the soul has the specific zodiacal influences that will provide it with the opportunities it needs to fulfill its karma and destiny.

We are all here to grow and evolve through every available means, and if we learn to keep that in the forefront of our consciousness, we will not waste precious moments grumbling, but will try to use all events as opportunities for growth. We are most likely to be born to those with whom we have had previous blood ties. This particular grouping of individuals provides the opportunity in which the type of karma intrinsic to a family unit will be allowed to work itself out. So it is often the case that the parent in one life will have been the child in a previous one. Patterns of behavior will arise again and again until they are ultimately brought to light and worked through. This, of course, applies to soul groupings involving other types of relationships, many of which already have been discussed in this book. However, there is something unique at work when this takes shape in the genetic family unit.

We can see that we do not randomly pick our parents. Rather, it is a mutual agreement made between three souls — two parents and the child — the oversouls and monads of each and the lords of karma. We are each drawn to such an agreement, although it is one that is definitely made consciously from the soul level and agreed on by all concerned. There are always other possible choices that can be made; however, the areas that need to be addressed will always come into play so that they can be resolved.

One further factor must be taken into consideration in choosing our parents. We each have a specific mission on the Earth, which will involve such things as particular talents and abilities, physical bodies, mental and emotional factors and the parents who can best provide us with these qualities. You can see that this is quite an involved process and that much is taken into consideration by all concerned. The main point to focus on is that once having made this choice, it is best for us to accept it and get on with the process of learning the lessons at hand and advancing our ascension process.

## The Power of Parental Programming

Our parents' power is great indeed. Until very recently, humanity has acted out of the processes of the negative ego, and still does to a large extent. This has been considered the norm, albeit an extremely dangerous and harmful norm indeed! This type of thinking is then imparted to the child without any conscious awareness on the part of the parents.

The only way the dangers of negative-ego parental programming can be brought to light and overcome is through proper education — education for child and parents alike. Without proper understanding of how the negative ego functions and how it can be cleared, cleansed and purified, parents will continue to unconsciously program their children with faulty belief systems. Likewise, without proper education as to how this negative programming is affecting us, as the children of such parenting, we will be stuck in the cesspool of the negative ego's faulty thinking and continue to be contaminated by it. Luckily, the power of the subconscious mind is being brought to light. Through various tools such as affirmations, positive thinking, self-esteem workshops and the like, people are at last beginning to reparent themselves.

The destructive power of negative-ego thinking is so enormous that I cannot stress the point enough. In *Soul Psychology,* this issue is discussed at length. No matter how much we build our light and love quotients, we must ultimately take the responsibility to heal, cleanse and purify ourselves of negative-ego-based thinking. It becomes our responsibility to reparent ourselves in this regard, as almost all of us have been programmed and parented with faulty belief systems.

It is not only our parents who have done this, nor are they to blame. In fact, I ask you to please release any and all blame you might be holding onto in relation to your parents. They are human beings who, in most cases, simply did the best they knew how. The majority of parents do not set about willfully to program us with faulty thinking and negative-ego beliefs. This is simply the way they functioned and the only way they knew *how* to function. This, in fact, is *still* the way society functions as a whole, which can be seen at every level.

Our teachers then continued this process by working through a school system built on a foundation of competitiveness and comparison. Our friends picked up on this and threw it back in our faces. We likely did the same to them in turn. Then most of us found ourselves functioning in a work arena that continued to perpetuate these same patterns of negative-ego programming: competition, separation and ego strokes and strikes. No wonder we find the subconscious in such a state and are having such a hard time learning how to think positively and bring through the levels of divine love and light! The negative ego keeps getting in the way and doing its thing unless we work extensively with it.

## The Importance of Self-Parenting

So we are called upon to take a fearless look at our own subconscious selves and see where the blotches and boils are. Then we can set about the task of self-parenting and reprogramming our subconscious thinking structure and the inner-parent/inner-child relationship. We must do this with full and total awareness that we are dealing with our inner child, which has its own specific set of needs and has grown attached to certain modalities of believing and behaving. We must be loving but firm parents to our inner child and assure this part of ourselves that we do not mean to destroy it, but simply reeducate it so that we may function at a healthier and higher level for the benefit of the whole.

Once we are awakened to the power the negative ego and negative subconscious thinking have on us, the task of reeducation then falls to us. This is not a bad thing. In fact, it is one of the best insights we could possibly have into the subtler ways in which we function. What has hitherto controlled and overpowered us by virtue of our unawareness now reveals itself to be an aspect of ourselves that we can take charge of and master. We can use positive affirmations and decrees, victory logs, dream logs, listening to affirmation tapes and so forth.

Since I have given many tools and discussed their specific usage at length in my previous books, I will not repeat them here. But I will repeat how essential it is that we let go of these false belief systems by reprogramming and reparenting our subconscious minds in the most positive ways possible. This should be done in every aspect of our lives. Negative-ego thinking impacts all areas of our lives, because our conscious and subconscious minds set the tone regarding how we feel about ourselves.

Consequently, if we have low self-esteem, we generally have it in all areas, but if we change these feelings by reparenting ourselves to have confident and positive feelings about ourselves, these will also permeate every area of our lives. The words and images we hold in the silent recesses of our subconscious minds are reflected in the world of our daily lives, creating loud echoes. Let us then reach into these seemingly silent corners of ourselves and change all negative ego-based programming into self-love and joy. Let us never forget that we create every aspect of our reality by how we think consciously and subconsciously.

If we fall into the category of the awakened lightworker or the self-aware individual who is in the process of reparenting our inner child and subconscious, the question then comes to mind how to transfer this new understanding to our children. Perhaps we have children who are no longer infants, but who are old enough to feel the sting of the negative ego both in the outer world and in the way it impinges on the child's own inner world. If that is the case, I urge you to share your process of new understanding and reprogramming in whatever ways best suit the particular situation and your child's level of comprehension.

## Parenting Our Children

If your children are old enough to comprehend, tell them that you understand the nature of what they are going through. Share with them that you are also going through similar trials and difficulties, but that you have found that you can change this by working on changing your subconscious negative beliefs. There is no need for them to think there is something wrong with them because they are following a path laid out for them by the world at large. It is a good thing that they are uncomfortable with the limiting structures of society. You can support them in building the inner resources in order to have the strength to be who they are.

Bear in mind, however, that this is a child *you* have parented, and although you are not to blame for being who you are or were at any given point in their growth process, sometimes outside help is advisable. With a spiritual counselor or a transpersonal psychologist, your child can discuss things that he or she might find difficult to discuss with you. Frequently children can freely express just so much with their parents. The stigma of seeing a counselor should be transcended, and this can be looked at as working with a spiritual teacher.

It is also a good idea to work with your children yourselves. Perhaps you can do joint positive affirmations, both from books you work with and from those they come up with on their own. It is good to be aware of how much peer pressure impacts your children. If they have a sensitive nature and are not fitting in with their peers, this can have a devastating effect. Encourage them to talk with you about their day and how they are feeling about it. Ask what is going on in school. Ask them how they feel about their grades, if perhaps they feel inadequate because they are not as high as they think they should be. Are they active in sports, and/or do they want to be? Perhaps they are competing in a sport and not getting the results they think they should. This can cause a great deal of pain. It will be wonderful if you can talk with them about it and perhaps help them reframe the way they are looking at things. You can work on success affirmations together, but more importantly, you can work on self-esteem affirmations that have nothing to do with outer success.

Take a good look at the schools they are attending. Schools that might be good academically might not provide the best support for self-esteem and creative expression. If you find this to be the case, you might want to consider an alternative school that better meets the emotional and creative needs of your children.

There have been some wonderful advances made in child psychology, some of which are quite effective in getting to the core subconscious feelings. Art therapy is one technique that comes to mind, in which much of the child's inner world is drawn forth through the medium of crayon or paint. No one is either too young or too old to work with the various tools of reprogramming and reparenting the subconscious mind.

## Parenting the Infant

If you are a new mother or father and are aware of the power of subconscious programming, you are in a unique position to begin at a very early age to fill your children's subconscious mind and feeling world with the most positive images you can think of. During their time of sleep, which is the bulk of their existence in infancy, you can play soft, healing music. There is wonderful music available for little ones, and many of your own spiritual and new-age music tapes would be suitable as well. You can talk to your children and tell them how wonderful they are and how loved and safe they are. Decorate their rooms with beautiful colors, angel pictures and soft, sweet things. It is a good idea to place a picture of one or more of the masters you work with by their crib. Archangel Michael is a wonderful protective influence for little ones.

As the infant grows in awareness, be careful to always remain unconditionally loving. *Never* withdraw love if they misbehave, no matter what the situation. As was discussed earlier in this book, true love is unconditional love. Any other expression of love is a distortion of true love.

Unfortunately, many of us were brought up with the threat of love being withdrawn or with the feeling that we had to prove ourselves worthy of love. Well, the buck stops with us. The damage this can do often takes a lifetime to correct. Since we are all aware of it, let us *never* do this with our own children. While we are at it, let us start this very moment to give our own inner child only total unconditional love. We have the power to do this, so let us claim that power *now* and begin to demonstrate, both to our children and to ourselves, the nature of unconditional love. The best way to ensure that your children grow up psychologically and spiritually healthy is for you, as their parent, to be right with yourself and right with God. Most programming of children is actually done energetically and subconsciously through the vibrational frequencies we radiate.

## Parenting Your Unborn Child

Closely aligned with the subject of parenting an infant is the importance of parenting an infant who is still in the womb. This brings us to certain matters that must be addressed before continuing.

The soul preparing for incarnation spends most of its time building the four lower bodies. This is a process that begins at conception and continues at greater and greater levels of involvement as the fetus grows. Therefore, what actually occurs is paradoxical. On the one hand there is the soul that remains free in its own realm but still functions to a greater or lesser degree, depending on the level of its evolution, on building the four lower bodies. On the other hand, because that soul is already intimate with the vehicle it is building, it is connected with the thoughts, emotions and physical world of its parents, especially the mother.

Both the mother and the father, as well as close friends and relatives, affect the growth of the soul, and they all play a part in programming its inner subconscious nature before actual incarnation. Of course the two who play the biggest role in forming the soul's four lower bodies are the parents, with the mother foremost. The fetus is physically anchored within the mother, and therefore every thought, feeling and emotion is directly transferred to the fetus through this intimate connection.

## Abortion

This leads us to one of the most controversial issues of our time—that of abortion. There is a great deal of confusion about whether one is committing murder in the process of aborting a child. The ultimate answer is an unequivocal no. However, in having an abortion, you are, in fact, aborting a process in which the soul is deeply involved. It is not an issue to be taken lightly, for an abortion does indeed have an impact on the soul. This soul is tied to the mother and is indeed impacted by the thought forms and feeling world of the mother. If one is considering an abortion, one must be sensitive to this fact. Although we do not have the power to kill the soul, we do have the power to disrupt the functions of that soul while it is engaged in the process of building the vehicles of expression on Earth.

If one chooses to have an abortion, it is vital to send messages to the soul, telling it that it is not that it is unwanted or unloved, but that you are making the best decision you can for all concerned. Ask it to detach itself from the building process, then let it go with love and blessings. Talk to that soul and tell it that you will meet again at a more appropriate time and that you are releasing it to seek another vehicle with which to continue its rounds of birth. Be sure to communicate that you are letting go with love and to ask that soul to do the same. Having made that decision, proceed to act with love, then let go and truly get on with the next phase of your life.

This is not a choice to make lightly, but having done so, do not carry any form of guilt around with you. As you have released the soul, likewise release yourself from feelings of blame. You simply do not have the power to kill the soul. Ultimately, it is at the moment of birth that true joining between soul and its vehicles occurs, and even that proceeds in stages. Nevertheless, it is at birth that the soul enters incarnation. Therefore, if you have had to make this choice, please know in your heart that the soul is free, and that you should likewise be free to pursue your life.

There is one other important point you should be aware of. Sometimes a soul will choose consciously to participate in the building of the vehicles with full and complete knowledge that this process will be aborted. That is because this soul has chosen to work off a certain portion of its karma in this way. This would likely be the case when that soul is consciously on the path of ascension, aware of karma and choosing to work through all of it as quickly as possible. This type of ultra short incarnation would also include many crib deaths and spontaneous abortions.

## Late-Term Abortion

I specifically asked the Hierarchy for their view on the controversial issue of late-term abortions. They told me they do not recommend this, as the bonds between fetus, soul and mother are very strong at this point. However, neither do they judge it or considerate it sinful. They again bring up the point that we are not yet dealing with the child, since the soul of that child will not fully enter the body it has prepared until the time of birth. Therefore, they say, this should not be thought of as murder, even though many people think of it as such. However, they acknowledge the fact that the appearance of the fetus during these later stages is like that of the newborn. It is quite understandable that viewing a developed fetus would cause some to think that they are looking at an infant.

However, the Hierarchy would like us to look at the fetus through the eyes of our own higher selves and monads. This would put us in touch with the dual nature of the effect that a late-term abortion has on the soul. In late-term abortions, the process of building has gone on for an extended period. A lot of work and connections have been made between the soul preparing the bodies, the bodies themselves and the parents, especially the mother. This causes a wrenching that early abortions do not, so they are not encouraged. But if one finds oneself in the predicament of having to make such a decision, or if one has made this decision in the past, remember to talk to that soul even if some years have passed, because the bond remains. Tell the soul that you are releasing it in pure love and that you wish it to go forward in the light. Then release it in love.

It is important that lightworkers do not allow themselves to see only through the limited lens of the personality on such a delicate and sensitive issue. We are all souls and monads, and we shall continue our path of evolution and ascension no matter what. The issue of abortion is not one to be taken lightly, nor is it appropriate to view it from the perspective of the negative ego, personality or lower self. In this, as in all aspects of your life, remain in integrity with yourself and with God. Keep your motivations pure and loving, and trust that all will unfold in divine order.

You can see how complex this matter is. View this and the upcoming topics through the greater lens of soul, monadic and cosmic perception. We must keep in mind that we are not simply dealing with children, but with souls who have come into incarnation through us. We are also dealing with the unseen inner child who lives within each of us. The ideal is to use the best means available to parent both our inner child and the children whose care has been entrusted to us.

## Prebirth Environment and Communication

We now have scientific proof that certain physical substances affect the growing fetus, including cigarettes, alcohol and drugs. Food impacts the fetus positively or negatively depending on the type and quality of the food. We are also becoming increasingly aware that what we intake spiritually, mentally and emotionally impacts the growing fetus. The soul who is building the four lower bodies within the womb of the mother can be considered in much the same way we would an infant, in terms of the type of environment we provide.

The impact of vibration is very important to the growing fetus, so noise pollution should be avoided whenever possible. In its place one can listen to soft, beautiful music, perhaps even placing the speakers of the stereo player near the belly of the mother. In this manner both parent and child can experience the energy of such music. The fetus will pick up the harmonious vibrational frequencies, which aids the soul in building its vehicle of expression. In addition, the mother will be transmitting vibrationally her own peaceful feelings to the fetus in her womb.

Prebirth communication between parents and child has a far-reaching effect. We are dealing with the idea of a soul being linked to the fetus rather than the fetus being one's child. Nevertheless, the bonding between the lower bodies, the soul itself and the parents is so deep that one should act as if it is the *whole* child with whom they are communicating. This is a good example of how two truths can be integrated when, in speaking of the unborn infant, we include both the soul participating in the building process and the manifestation of that building process. So as you read this subsection, bear in mind that the term "unborn infant" applies to *both* the soul and the fetus.

The inner subconscious and conscious nature of the mother is in moment-to-moment communion with the unborn infant. Every fluctuation of mood, every modality of thinking, every surge of emotion, is transferred vibrationally to the infant growing within her. We briefly mentioned sound in the context of beautiful music, referring to specific works played to the unborn on a short-term basis. If this has such a profound effect, just think what an exposure to beautiful classical music on a longer-term basis would do to create an atmosphere of harmony.

But the personal taste of the mother also needs to be considered. If she does not find this type of music to her personal liking yet feels that she should play it for her unborn infant, the infant will be getting vibrational impacts of negativity from the mother. In this case, that type of music would not be recommended. This would only cause a battle of energies between the healing quality of the music and the energies of distaste from the parent. That is why we seldom like to give hard and fast rules, because each individual person must be honored. We advise the parents to find music that is not only harmonious to them but also beneficial to the infant. There would then be only one harmonious vibration transmitted by the parents and the music, thus achieving the desired effect.

People often wonder what the effect of reading to an unborn infant is. The answer is twofold. On one hand, the soothing sounds of a parent's voice gently enfold the infant in a feeling of restful calm. It is not the words themselves that matter as much as the tone in which they are read. Of course, whatever one chooses to read should be positive and harmonious. One might consider reading from sacred scriptures or poetry or from "new thought" writings, all of which generate a spiritual tone and feeling. This will reach your unborn infant, who will be uplifted by it. A second benefit of reading to an infant in the womb is that the parent aids the soul in building its mental vehicle. This will add to what the soul brings to the mental vehicle, thus accelerating the mental processes.

Through exposing the infant in utero to uplifting music and literature, it will be stimulated in mental, emotional and spiritual areas. This aids the soul in developing all the bodies and enables the higher self and monad to more readily find a point of access on the earthly realms. Most of this will be affected by the evolution of the soul coming into incarnation, but that soul can be aided greatly by the energies transmitted to the unborn infant through the efforts of the parents.

The reader must be made aware that because the human condition is as it is, there is of necessity a vibrational wall of protection that surrounds the unborn infant. This does not limit the benefits of communicating with the infant, but it does act as a cushion against constant onslaughts of a negative-ego-based parent and environment. Although it does not make them immune to outbursts of anger and violence, a certain shielding does take place, or else many fetuses would never reach full term.

Remember also that this soul is linked with its appropriate parents so that the vibrations imparted to it through those parents are not alien to it. Fortunately, the fetus has some shielding from the chaotic energies of such parents and other harsh stimuli so that it can grow and develop. And the womb itself creates a fluid environment in which the physical form can safely come to term.

To parents who are bringing the new-age child into incarnation, it is suggested that they ask God and the masters to place a special protective grid around the unborn infant. This is often done even without the request of the parents, as the frequencies of the incarnating soul are such that some of the harsher elements in the Earth's vibrational sphere could throw its work off balance and cause a great disturbance and discomfort to that soul. But this grid activation is more quickly and completely anchored around the unborn infant if the parents request it. I also suggest that each parent make this request again after the birth of the child for extra protection.

Throughout the pregnancy, harmony between the parents should be maintained whenever possible. No anger, shouting or abusive language should be exchanged. Of course, this is an ideal, but at all times we should strive for it, especially during this stage of the parenting process. As much as possible, this type of attitude should be maintained during the birthing process and carried forward into infancy, throughout childhood and into adulthood. This is an ideal, again, but what better motivation is there to move toward this ideal than at the time of bringing forth a soul in its new journey on Earth!

## Birthing in Water and Welcoming with Love

The Hierarchy tells me that water birth is a wonderful way in which to welcome the newborn into the world of matter. Water's fluidity is reminiscent of the subtler realms from which the soul has come. And of course the fetus has spent nine months surrounded by fluid. So the child born through the process of water-birthing will find itself in a familiar and embracing environment in which it can acclimate to the Earth plane. The four lower bodies as well as the soul entering the plane of dense matter will appreciate this method of coming into the world. With water-birthing, there is far less shock to the newborn than is encountered by birthing in most other ways. The gentle touch of water is familiar and comforting. One must remember how long the fetus has been immersed in water and how accustomed to fluid the soul is, not to mention the fact that the human body itself is composed mostly of water.

Of course, this might not be the appropriate choice for every couple. What *is* appropriate and essential for every birthing process is that the child be welcomed into the world with the utmost love and joy. Whenever possible, the child should be placed on the mother's abdomen to continue the bonding process that has begun on inner realms and cement it on the earthly realm. Then the mother should hold the infant to her breast and envelop it with love. The father should also immediately hold the infant against his heart in order to bond further and to envelop the newborn with love. Whether through water birth or other methods, both the mother and the father need the time immediately after the birth to hold the infant to their hearts and welcome it with love.

## An Esoteric View of the Birth Process

Let us now look at the birthing process from an esoteric standpoint. Again, we are not really dealing with babies, although the physical form is indeed that of a tiny newborn infant. What we are encountering are *souls* — and ultimately monads — using the process of incarnation to further themselves upon the path of ascension. However, the process of birth, just like the process of so-called death, puts that soul in touch with certain aspects of itself in a unique way.

In actuality, the process we call death is a simple matter compared to what we call birth. In the former, there is a liberation from the dense forms of matter, whereas in the latter there is a confinement within dense matter. *From the esoteric point of view, the processes of birth and death are completely reversed in the perception of those who dwell in the worlds of form.* Yet both are indeed divine processes, parts of the same whole. And both contribute equally to building the divine qualities into the individualized soul and monad. Upon its return to the greater monadic groupings and to God, the soul brings with it all that it has incorporated during its many sojourns in the worlds of matter. Thus it enriches both itself and the whole, which we call God.

## Birth Bardo

There is a birth bardo that each soul goes through that is similar to that of the death bardo. This actually begins when the soul first connects with the newly formed fetus at the time of conception. At this time the soul is shown the various karmic connections it has with its new family. It is also shown the opportunities it will be given, certain astrological trends, world trends and its purpose for this lifetime. The reason it is coming into the world through the two parents it has chosen will become increasingly clear. The arena of friends, work and physical environment will flash before its inner eye.

During the birth process, the soul looks on all this in one last attempt to hold to its vision and reason for coming into form. The soul will desire to hold to this vision, but it will not be able to do so, for it must be free to experience the world anew in each incarnation. This will change as the Earth and the souls evolving here gain ever greater light and love and as the vibrational frequency of the planet as a whole is raised. But for the time being, the soul must forget, at least consciously, most of its past and future visions.

This causes the soul a great deal of pain, as it seeks to keep its ever-shrinking vistas of illumination open. This causes less pain for less developed souls, because many of their aspirations are tied to physical existence, as they are more comfortable within the confines of the four lower bodies. There is always a degree of discomfort in coming from the more bountiful into the more limited, however, and fitting oneself into the infant form always takes some adjustment.

So a certain degree of trauma is always associated with the process of being born. Some of this is inherent in the birthing process itself, but much can be averted if the birth occurs in as loving and supportive an environment as possible. Nevertheless, a certain degree of trauma is experienced when coming into the limitations of the four-body system and feeling the physical shock of entering into this vibrational sphere.

## Past-Life Effect on Infant and Parents

The past lives of the incarnating soul have an impact on the infant. Past lives have not only contributed to where and to whom the infant is born, but they have a direct bearing on the lives of both infant and parents. For example, in some cases, all the souls involved will have agreed that the most rapid way to work through certain karma is by having the unborn infant spontaneously abort, be stillborn or depart through a crib death. I realize how traumatic this is from an earthly point of view, and I am not attempting to suggest that anyone who has had this type of experience even remotely try to deny it, let alone suppress the powerful and painful impact of such an experience.

However, I present these situations from the viewpoint that the Hierarchy presented them to me, which will give you the freedom to incorporate this understanding into your experience. Because of the pain of such an event, both the parents and the soul who was or would have been the infant of these parents rapidly work through much karma. The Hierarchy seeks to impart this expanded vision to you. They also wish to make you aware that despite the fact that we are ultimately dealing with souls and monads, some will choose to remain in baby or child form when they pass into the inner planes at a young age. This can occur if both that soul and its parents have the need for a parent/child love connection to be worked out on the inner planes.

If such is the case, rest assured that the infant or child on the inner realms will be taken to an appropriate place where it is cared for and watched over until the parents make their transition. Once that occurs, they are reunited and have the chance to enact on inner spheres what was abruptly cut short on Earth. Please know that if you are one who has suffered the earthly loss of a child, you will find that child again in the inner realms. That one will be there waiting for you, just as it is never far from you while you remain on Earth. This can be a most difficult trial indeed, but the Hierarchy requests your trust that all will be healed and made whole.

Others will choose to return to the adult soul consciousness when the transition happens in infancy or before birth. Remember that they are souls just as you are, and nothing in heaven or Earth can, or wants to, keep you apart. You will be together, for such is the law of love.

## The Permanent Atoms

This topic relates to building the four lower vehicles, which will ultimately come to expression when the baby is born. During each of our incarnations, we as souls are constantly rebuilding and restructuring our bodies by the work we do on them from a spiritual point of view. Much of what we call karma we have built into the permanent atoms of the physical, etheric, emotional and mental bodies. These are our own individualized and encoded inner-plane karmic recording devices for each of our bodies. These wait to be called forth into incarnation when we again take form as individualized souls.

In a sense, we build ourselves out of ourselves. Put another way, we build our bodies out of the substance of our bodies and the semipermanent vibrational frequencies and imprints on our permanent atoms. The reason I say semipermanent is that in the case of a liberated or fully ascended soul and monad, what is brought forth comes exclusively from the causal and monadic realms. Such a one is veritably freed from the lower worlds and all the karma thereof. Such a one functions out of the mayavarupa body.

It is vital to bear in mind, however, the place of these permanent atoms, as they hold our imprints and structure our bodies based on what we have built into them. This is true, although on a higher level and turn of the spiral, we build our bodies on what we have contributed to the causal and monadic vehicle. Although the permanent atoms will not be brought into play in an incarnating ascended being, because so much of what one has done is stored within those atoms, this information is transferred into the higher components of the ascended being. These permanent atoms thus have a lasting effect on all our sojourns into the world of form. They do not have the same effect on a liberated ascended master that they do on one traversing the path toward liberation. But since what has been built in the past transfers to the higher self and eventually to the monad, these permanent atoms always function, though they function quite indirectly in the later stages of our unfoldment. The saying that nothing is ever lost has a profound meaning when looked at in relation to the permanent atoms.

I find it quite amusing to note just how complex are the processes of birth, death and parenting. Yet how ultimately simple it really is once we understand that all of it is a cosmic play in which we, as souls and monads, get to play the role of parent and child again and again until we fully and finally ascend. Then we realize the wonder of the illusion of it all, and we honor the great wisdom that has been garnered in our play through these realms of illusion. The paradox is quite awesome, and I cannot help but call to mind that glorious phrase from the *Bhagavad-Gita*, "While pervading the universe with my being, yet I remain." What is true for God is true for the children of God, and thus we move through the various roles each lifetime assigns to us, yet always we remain monads. From a cosmic perspective, one might say that in truth there is no such thing as children, but rather souls incarnating into babies' bodies.

## The Blank-Slate Theory

Some earlier schools of psychology and philosophy declared that children were born as blank slates. Of course this is complete nonsense. Every child has likely had over 200 adult past lives and is therefore born with unique personalities, gifts and tendencies. The job of the ideal parent is to guide and direct, but also to allow the unique wisdom of the soul of the child to unfold according to its inner direction.

Taking into account all that has been said in regard to karma, picking one's parents, permanent atoms and the entire range of subject matter covered in this chapter, the idea of a child being a blank slate is so far from truth that it would not be worth mentioning were it not a belief still held by many. God is all, and all those who incarnate are aspects of God unfolding, evolving into greater and greater aspects of what they ultimately are. Therefore, if you are a parent, enjoy your role to the fullest, but never forget that you are dealing with a soul on a long journey who has taken form through you. This soul will grow and evolve back from whence it came—God. You are sharing coparenting responsibilities not only with your spouse, but also with the child's oversoul and mighty I Am Presence!

## It Takes a Village

Hillary Clinton wrote a wonderful little book called *It Takes a Village*. She is right in one sense, for the village or community serves as a support system for the child and the parents. This includes grandparents, extended family members, teachers, ministers and rabbis, baby-sitters and neighbors. From an ascended-master perspective, Hillary Clinton is totally right, for we are speaking here of group consciousness.

Paramahansa Yogananda said that the single most important factor in the spiritual path until total mastery is obtained is one's environment. If a child is constantly corrupted by the "village," it makes the parents' job exceedingly difficult. We are always dealing with groups and group bodies. This is a cosmic fact to which we become increasingly more attuned as we evolve. However, nowhere is it more evident on Earth than in the care and nurturing of our children.

## The Hierarchy's View on Spanking

From a hierarchical point of view, spanking is not recommended. There are, of course, times when a light slap on the bottom is appropriate, but this should always be as a call to attention rather than to inflict pain. It should never be done when the parent is angry or out of control. The masters tell me that it appears quite ludicrous when they observe an out-of-control parent whose negative ego is running amuck, slapping a child in an attempt to control the child who is out of control and running amuck!

The ideal would be to refrain from this type of punishment totally, as it cannot help but give the child the message that physical pain is a way to get what one person (the stronger one) wants from another (the weaker one). A child must be guided and disciplined by way of example, communication, tone of voice and natural consequences.

In our interactions with our children, we make lasting impressions, as they are quite vulnerable to the adult world. By no means should anyone other than the parents slap a child, the more obvious examples being teachers, baby-sitters, ministers, nuns or rabbis. This surely conveys to the child that the outer world operates through physical violence. The infliction of pain is something that has no place in the Aquarian age.

The Hierarchy requests that parents take a good look at this issue in light of all that has been said so that they can reevaluate, without guilt, past behavioral patterns. Then they can seek to align themselves with the most effective ways to guide the souls entrusted to them, then align themselves with the higher frequencies and the thrust toward wholeness and harmony that are being brought forth on Earth at this time.

## Letting Go of Parenting Roles

One of the more difficult things for a parent to do, yet one that ultimately *must* be done to one degree or another, is letting go of the role of parent. That does not mean that all parental expressions and instincts should cease. It merely means that there comes an appropriate time for the parent to fully recognize the child as an adult and give him or her the respect and freedom they give to any other adult. Put simply, there comes a time when continuing to play mom or dad is quite inappropriate.

It is the tendency of parents to want to overparent and continue a level of parenting that becomes unhealthy to child and parent alike. While doing the utmost to be the best possible parent to your children, you should always remember that those you call *your* children are, in truth, God's children. They are souls incarnate, and you must allow them to grow up as children of God. Obviously I am not referring to the young child, but rather to the young adults and adults who have their own unique destiny to fulfill within the plan of God. These adult offspring will benefit greatly from your support, but they must be free to follow the calling of their souls and try out their own wings.

This should be fairly easy to grasp, as most of us are both parent and child, and all of us are children to our parents. As children of all ages, we know how uncomfortable it felt if we were overparented by our own parents and how we ached to grow up and function as adults. Some of us, no matter how old we are, are still engaged in the battle of separation from overprotective or meddling parents. For this reason, we should be able to see clearly enough how important it is to release our children at the appropriate time and allow them to pursue their divine destiny without interference and with our total support.

Granted, this is not always the easiest thing to do, but it is one of the most important things we can do for both our children and ourselves. As parents, if we get too tied to our children, we will not follow our own divine calling or feel the freedom to take the needed steps on our own path of ascension. As children, if we remain too tied to our parents, we will not exercise our freedom to follow our hearts and claim our own divinity. Our task lies in finding that point of balance between being both child and parent and in owning our own divine birthrights as sons and daughters of the Most High. All parenting is coparenting with God. And don't forget that your child has had hundreds of other sets of parents from previous incarnations.

The best way to facilitate a healthy relationship with your maturing children is through open and honest communication. Take the high road and endeavor to truly listen to one another, communicating from the level of your soul and your I Am Presence. Great strides can be made when communication occurs from spirit to spirit. All parents and children are children of God, and all deserve the respect of the divine beings that we are.

The child constantly serves as teacher to the parent. There is really no clear delineation as to who is child and who is parent in the larger sense. Just as we are at once both student and teacher, so are we likewise both parent and child. Toward the end of our lives the roles often become reversed on the physical plane, as those we term the elderly begin a process of drawing inward and in many cases become as little children. Their care then falls to us.

With certain nutritional and health discoveries, however, as well as the process of ascension, the physical aging process will become increasingly obsolete. Nevertheless, we have done this reverse parenting for ages, so it does bear noting. The higher we ascend, the more light and love will be able to find expression in these relationships as in all aspects of our lives.

## The Mother/Son or Father/Daughter Relationship in Couples

There are romantic relationships in which the mother/son or father/daughter theme is the basis of the relationship. This does not refer to those relationships where one of you is better at finances and earning the daily bread while the other holds a more home-based focus. I am addressing here the unhealthy playing-out of unresolved parent/child scenarios within a romantic relationship. This type of theme is usually not very successful, even if it appears to be for a while. Sometimes these relationships go on for years, but ultimately one or the other awakens to what has been occurring and usually with a great deal of resentment.

If you find yourself in this type of relationship, it is important to understand that you are *both* participating in it, as it is apparently fulfilling a mutual need. There is no one person at fault here. In fact, neither is at fault. What must be looked at are unhealthy patterns that are within your power to correct and uplift by bringing them into the light and working them through. Most of us engage in this type of relationship at one time or another. However, the sooner we realize that there are core issues within our programming that need addressing, the more quickly we can deal with them.

If you are a couple involved in this scenario, counseling would serve you well, provided you find a therapist or counselor who works from a spiritual as well as a psychological base. You can then set about exploring your need to function in whatever role you have assumed and get to the root of the issue that prevents you from being, and functioning as, an integrated whole. This again boils down to being right with self and with God. Romantic relationships are wonderful areas in which to see whether we are right with ourselves so that we can make the needed adjustments. Trying to make our partner either our parent or our child is a signal that we are *not* right with ourselves.

True integration can occur only when you are willing to look at what is keeping you from expansion and integration. As well, there must be a willingness to work with the tools that allow you to heal limiting patterns and move into being whole within yourself. The goal, then, is to find the healthiest integration of self in all four lower bodies as well as the soul and monad.

## God, the Ultimate Parent

If we are to see ourselves as children of God, then it is God indeed who is the ultimate parent. Father/Mother God does the ultimate parenting, and that parenting manifests from within our very own souls and monads. However, it is a tricky business to allow God or our monads to function as the ultimate parent.

First and foremost, we must be careful not to make God into our pre-conceived notion of what we *think* a parent is or should be. For instance, those of us raised by strict father figures whose lack of self-esteem made them behave as a tyrant, might tend to make God into a strict judgmental figurehead. Conversely, we may try to make God into the parent that enforces no discipline at all, who lets us think that we could get away with murder. This parent would allow us to act out whatever we pleased, due to perhaps very low self-esteem on their part. We therefore grew up thinking we could do whatever we wanted with no consequences whatsoever.

We must bear in mind that we are not here to limit the limitless and fit God into our childhood programming. We are here to explore our God-selves from the highest possible vantage point and allow our I Am Presence to communicate directly to us the nature and intent of God in as inclusive a way as possible. Then we must be willing to expand our vision and widen our lens in order to experience ever deeper and vaster aspects of the One.

The second area where seeing God as parent becomes tricky is with our tendency to view God through the lens of the religion in which we were raised. We may try to squeeze God into the limiting mold of that viewpoint. We must be mindful of this so that our experience of God and truth can be as limitless and pure as possible. Therefore, in order to evolve within Father/Mother God as souls and monads, we must allow ourselves the freedom to clear out our faulty belief systems. We can call upon God and the masters to help us with this process.

There is no limit to the limitlessness that is God, nor is there a ceiling covering the heights at which we may know Him. We are children of God and there is naught that Father/Mother God will not reveal or give to us, the children of the One. We must free ourselves from our preconceptions, know ourselves to be the monads, the sparks of God that we are, and seek communion with the One who is the very essence of ourselves. The *Bhagavad-Gita* says, "God is Brahman and that thou art." Christ/Lord Maitreya has said, "I and the Father are one." The scriptures say, "Ye are sons and daughters of the Most High." The Huna teachings of Hawaii refer to the higher self as the Aumakua, which means the utterly trustworthy parental self. Ideally, we are meant to parent our physical children and ourselves in the way that our higher self parents us.

Let us therefore know ourselves as one with the One. Through the ascension process, through study, meditation and clearing, and with the help of God and the masters, we ever expand in uniting our consciousness with the consciousness of the One. We will then know ourselves as we truly are, and we will merge with the light, love, power, glory, peace, joy and wisdom that God is and that we are. This is both our birthright and our destiny!

# 9

## *The True Meaning of Marriage*

### Making a Commitment

Marriage is an inner commitment made between two people. It is a commitment to be life partners, to love and support one another unconditionally, for better or worse. This is not to say that divorce does not have its place, but it will be discussed later in this chapter. The focus in marriage at its highest level is love and commitment.

Whether or not the marriage takes the traditional legal form is up to the couple. However, that "piece of paper," as it has been referred to in recent times, has its meaning and place. In a like manner, so does the wedding band, symbol of the complete circle of the bond between two people. So too does the marriage ceremony, whether traditional or not. I am not saying that these traditions are right for every couple, but that there is significance in these traditional forms. These are outer symbols of an inner commitment and something most sacred indeed.

Depending on the two people involved, the sacredness of their union might be much deeper than that of those who choose the more traditional path of marriage, as the true nature and degree of sacredness lies within the hearts and spirits of the couple. The marriage ceremony has a wonderful place, however, and it need not be thrown out when two people seek a deeper understanding of commitment. That would be akin to throwing the baby out with the bath water, and that is not the divine intent.

The divine intent that is the cornerstone of all marriages, whether traditional or nontraditional, is that a high level of unconditional love and commitment be upheld and that the couple entering into such a sacred union does so with purity of heart, mind and spirit.

### Gay Marriages

Humanity's opinions concerning homosexuality in general range from seeing it as the deepest sin to being avid supporters of gay marriages. Of course, humanity has its opinions about everything, so I asked the masters their viewpoint on this controversial issue. Their answers might surprise many. Certainly, they will delight the gay couple, and I sincerely hope they

will shed some light on this issue for humankind in general, and more particularly, for the families and friends of gay couples.

The masters have said that, from a hierarchical point of view, they are
in total support of gay marriages. Perhaps this sounds shocking to some, but
take a moment to consider. The Hierarchy views us as souls (and ultimately
as monads) in incarnation. They view each incarnation as an opportunity
for growth, wherein the soul extensions and their monads come into a
greater balance and unity with their own divine nature.

This is done more commonly through the mating of soul extensions of
opposite gender in order to balance the male/female polarities within each
person and within the group body of the couple. However, this is not always
the case, as sometimes two souls (I shall hereafter refer to soul extensions
as souls) come into incarnation with a more fully balanced male/female polarity already operative within them. This does not mean that they are more
advanced than the rest of us, but simply that this is their mission for a particular incarnation. These pairs of opposites have taken a unique blending
pattern within these individuals. This is not to be judged one way or another, but is simply a fact.

There are many subtle facets to the homosexual personality, and most
gay individuals have suffered unduly at the hands of judgmental humanity.
This is not divine intent, nor should heterosexuals be judgmental. We all
tend to judge because we have been *taught* to judge and because whatever
seems to function outside the norm is somehow upsetting and unsettling to
humanity in general. This should not and need not continue. We, as
lightworkers, have a greater responsibility to accept what is outside the
norm, for if we were to take a good, honest look at ourselves, we would be
astonished at just how outside the norm most of humanity considers *us!*

As for homosexual marriages, the Hierarchy is very much in favor of
our forming group bodies that are committed in love to one another. They do
not say that all gay couples should enter into an official marriage relationship, but that they should have the right to do so if they choose, the same as
any other couple. It is always the intent that they look for, and the level of
love and commitment between the partners is their primary concern. The
Hierarchy finds that official ceremonies can be of enormous value because
they anchor on the physical realm what has been created between the two
upon the etheric, astral and mental realms. They encourage all couples to at
least consider this. They feel that all couples, gay or straight, should have
the freedom to decide their own paths. Remember, "Judge not lest ye be
judged" applies in this and all matters.

## "For Better or for Worse"

Let us now consider one of the more traditional wedding vows, which includes the phrase "for better or for worse." Does this include abusive re-lationships? The answer is no, as no one should ever be subjected to the abuse of another. Does this mean that divorce is not an option? No, because there are indeed occasions where divorce is the best available option. What about psychic attack or disharmony? No, because no one should live with constant psychic attack. So we might ask, just what does the phrase "for better or for worse" refer to?

The underlying meaning of the phrase is that we do not simply bail out the minute our egos are offended or called to task. Only a short time ago people were not able to get out of a marriage situation as quickly as we do now. There is indeed a time when it might become totally appropriate to end the marriage or relationship for a variety of reasons, but the head-butting of the negative ego is not one of them.

Marriage, or any committed relationship, is not to be taken lightly. One does not vow to remain wed "as long as you shall remain in total agreement with me and support the indulging of my negative ego." Yet this is the sce-nario that humanity as a whole currently supports, and it is truly antitheti-cal to the very purpose of relationship, which is to bond in love for the sup-port of each other on every level of our being. Ultimately, the purpose is also to help each other overcome the trappings of the negative ego by bring-ing those issues to light and working through them. Through the lens of those on the path of ascension, this becomes an even more critical issue.

If we are lucky enough to find a life mate or marriage partner, we can be an invaluable aid to each other on our pathway of ascension into the light. We form a unique group body of two and are a spiritual team, being ascen-sion buddies in the fullest sense. We each benefit from the advancements of the other. The more light and love quotient our partner brings forth, the more that is brought into the group body as a whole. The more clearly one of us can see, the clearer the vision of the whole. We are there to help sand smooth the rough spots within our auras and caress and embrace one an-other in love and support.

On one level this is infinitely easier than trying to do it all by yourself. In today's world there are so many bases that need covering, it is a blessing to have a partner to share in the basic work of daily living. It is also a bless-ing to have the added spiritual support, as traversing these realms is by no means a simple matter. Bringing in ever higher, more intense quotients of love, light and power puts the four lower bodies into a constant state of re-adjustment to these new energies. This frequently leads to a greater sensi-tivity in the physical body as it struggles to anchor these divine and rarefied energies into the dense form of matter. Thus a partnership can be of great value in a multitude of ways to those of us who tread the path of spirit on Earth.

## When a Relationship Ends

There might come a time when what once worked to uplift no longer works to either uplift or support, and a separation might become inevitable. However, before discussing this, let me reiterate that this is not a matter to be taken lightly. Everything should be done to try and work through issues, as issues in general go hand and hand with being in a romantic relationship in the first place. Bringing into the light the darkness that lies hidden within our depths is one of the major benefits of a relationship.

It is important that this not be the result of a negative-ego battle if you *do* decide to separate. Rather, it needs to be because you have deemed it appropriate in a calm, rational, loving manner. If all marriages and partnerships were to end because two negative egos were in disagreement with one another, all marriages and partnerships would end this instant. Unfortunately, all too often a relationship ultimately ends over negative-ego conflicts. As lightworkers and beings on the path of ascension, I ask that this not be the case with you.

If you are meant to end a relationship, or if you choose to do so for the good of all concerned, do so with integrity of spirit and work to keep the voices of the negative ego to a minimum. Knowing ourselves as souls and monads, let us work to come together and stay together. If we are guided to part, let us do so as souls and monads and not as negative egos running amuck. We owe it to ourselves and to each other to always function from the highest possible place regardless where that place eventually brings us. If we stay true to our soul and monad, we will stay true to God and ourselves. Then all our actions will remain true to the all-pervasive love and light which, in essence, we are.

## When Divorce is the Best Option

There are, of course, times when to divorce is the best possible option. Following are some examples of when this may be the case: (a) The differing elevator syndrome has reached such great proportions that the couple can no longer see eye to eye, much less soul to soul. (b) There is either physical or psychic abuse. (c) The karma between two individuals has run its course, and there remains nothing left to bond them together. (d) The apparent destiny of the couple seems to lie in completely opposite directions. (e) The particular work the two came together to do is at an end, and both the ties of work and the feelings of being in love seem complete.

Sometimes couples will divorce because of sexual betrayal, which the injured partner cannot, or will not, see beyond. In such a case the couple might feel that the entire bond of trust between them has been violated beyond repair. We can see that there are a great many reasons why people choose to separate and/or divorce.

I would like to offer some ideas on how best to handle these situations. First and foremost, you should part as you came together — with love in your heart. This is often not easy, and in some cases it might seem quite impossible. But in the long run, if that place of loving can be found, it will serve as the healthiest pathway for both you and your partner to continue with your lives.

There is no greater bond than love, save anger. If anger and resentment are held onto, the two of you will remain bound in a psychic war that I can assure you neither of you wants or needs. If this is not resolved, it can bind you together to the wheel of reincarnation, but if you can find that place of unconditional love and forgiveness within yourselves, both of you will fare far better for it. If the two people can release each other in love, there will be a clarity and a cleanness between you that will be of great benefit not only in this lifetime, but in many lifetimes to come.

If just one of you can do this, you are, in effect, doing this on behalf of the whole. Then if your former mate holds onto anger and resentment, it will be more or less the sound of one hand clapping. It will find no resonance within you and will ultimately cease to be. But it is a good idea to ask for protection from your higher self and the masters if you know that there is one who holds deep anger toward you. This will act as further protection against the person's negative emotional and mental thought forms, until he or she gets tired of holding them against you who refuse to hold such thought forms.

By clinging fast to unconditional love no matter what, you will be clinging to truth itself, and to God. You will be remaining in integrity with yourself and with God, therefore, and your path shall not falter. It is easier for some to get through separation and/or divorce than for others. This depends on many factors, including what prompted the separation in the first place. No matter how hard it is for you to bear, however, the call to hold your mind steady in the light remains valid and of utmost importance, as does the call to remain in unconditional love. If you can do these two things, the better able you will be to weather any storm and enjoy all the sunrises of your life!

## Recommitting to the Commitment

Often one issue or another brings a couple to the brink of divorce, but rather than taking that option, they choose to take inventory of the relationship — to reevaluate, elevate and recommit. This can be done informally, or it can be done formally through participating in the ceremony of marriage again. For those who have lived many years as an unmarried couple, this may well be the time to commit to one another formally. The option to recommit to a relationship is certainly worth considering. In some cases it can serve as a tool to elevate a marriage on the brink of divorce.

Sometimes just by virtue of being together over a long period of time, a romantic relationship will seem to have dried up. This not only happens with sex, but also in such areas as taking an interest in what your partner is doing, making real attempts at communication and, in fact, just knowing what the other person is all about. There might be no great crisis, yet the need to recommit in these areas is as strong as it is for the couple that is experiencing major upheaval.

In my experience as a marriage counselor, nothing has quite the impact of getting remarried or stating vows of recommitment in one way or another. This gives the couple a chance to really look at things and see them as they are as well as how they would like them to be. If there are any overt issues, such as in the case of adultery, this is the time for a fresh beginning with a new, deeper and hopefully lasting commitment of trust being made between the two partners. This will take some work, to say the least, but it offers the opportunity to make that new commitment of trust and for that new commitment to be accepted and implemented between the partners.

This type of remarriage, or restating of vows, also allows any hidden or suppressed issues of a more subtle nature to be brought into the light. For instance, if one partner feels that the other is totally uninterested in his/her work, this inner feeling can lead to outbursts of anger that seem to come from nowhere. Taking inventory of their marriage gives the more aloof partner a chance to see how his lack of interest is affecting his mate. He can then take steps to correct this by taking a more active interest in his partner's life. That partner would then be able to let go of the built-up anger and hostility toward her mate and so would be less prone to inappropriate outbursts of anger.

If you are in a committed relationship, you might want to give serious thought to restating your vows of commitment. You are far clearer at this point about your needs and desires than when you first fell in love and began your romantic bonding. Much can be stated now by virtue of the increased awareness you gained through your years of being together and by your increased maturity and understanding.

Another very important area is the sexual aspect of your relationship. During the honeymoon phase this aspect usually takes care of itself. However, through the passage of time, raising children, tending to your spiritual life and your careers, parenting of your own inner child and maintaining your household and cars, sex is often relegated to an almost nonexistent status. I am not now referring to couples who have made the choice to be celibate for a time in order to better concentrate on raising their energies into the monad. However, these couples are not excluded entirely from this discussion.

## The Sexual Bond

Sexual contact is vital to maintaining the bond of intimacy in a relationship. Even for those treading very lightly and conservatively in the sexual area, there must be some sort of contact. Human beings, by our very nature, crave some kind of affection at all times. If we are in relationship and have drifted far afield from this aspect of ourselves, the renewal of vows might set the perfect atmosphere for a renewal in the area of romance. Whether or not you choose to have this as a prime focus depends entirely on the joint needs and desires of the two people who form that relationship.

But all couples need a little spark put back into the embers of a long-term relationship, no matter how they choose to manifest that spark. Even for very spiritually centered people, it is not recommended that they go longer than three months without sexual intimacy. This bonding is important. In certain instances when one or both partners choose to live the life of the monk, they might agree on refraining from sexual intimacy for as long as six months. After that it would be best to keep sexual contact to no longer than three-month intervals.

For two highly sexual people who have let that aspect of their relationship fall by the wayside of daily duties and/or spiritual aspirations, a recommittal and a second honeymoon might be just what the doctor ordered. If, in the rewriting of your vows, there arise underlying issues that contribute to your drifting apart in the sexual area, with that baggage out of the way, you can now reembrace one another as new lovers. Taking a vacation or second honeymoon might be ideal, as changing your physical setting can work magic in putting a spark back in your sexual life and leaving behind the daily chores and concerns. However, if you are unable to do this, take off a couple of days from the usual routine and devote it to dinner, candlelight, flowers and each other. You will be pleasantly surprised just how quickly that tiny spark surges once more into the flame of passion!

For those who are more or less on the celibate path, I would suggest using this time to make some sort of sexual connection. You can do this through tantric means while in connection with your monads and focusing mostly on love itself. However you choose to do it, make some sort of connection. Sexuality is a wonderful way to rebond. If you are absolutely certain that you are in a phase of no sexual contact, you can still take this time to express your genuine affection for one another through touching, cuddling, holding hands and massage. I am not saying that everyone must be sexually involved with their partners, but I do encourage even celibate couples to engage in some type of sexual bonding, because it creates a certain type of intimacy between the partners that is otherwise not expressed.

When the honeymoon is over, it is not recommended that sexual intimacy exceed three times a week. It can occasionally, but if this becomes the norm it will keep the couple far too centered in the energy of the second chakra. Having intercourse on a daily basis will do this to the extreme, and it is therefore not recommended for those on the path of ascension. Each couple deserves a honeymoon, but once it is over, sexuality should be integrated into the lives of the couple in a balanced way and not become the all-consuming passion that it often is.

In summary, I recommend that couples who have been in a long-standing relationship consider recommitting to each other by participating in a marriage renewal or rebirth. This can work wonders in helping you get to the core of issues you may not even be aware of. You then can work together to release them by making the necessary adjustments as you look deeply at yourselves, both individually and within your group body of two. This might be a good time to let go of the old and re-create the new.

A renewal will also serve to reconnect you in a deeper way and propel your relationship into new heights and new depths. Just as no one needs to stay stuck in faulty thinking, no relationship needs to remain stale and stagnant. Retaking your vows, recommitting to your commitment or perhaps even stating your vows for the very first time, is the magic that can add new life and luster to what feels a bit stale and brittle. I highly recommend this to all. Each couple is unique and will do this in their own way according to their needs and inner guidance.

# 10

## *God, the Consummate Union*

### Ecstasy

Hilda Charlton, a wonderful spiritual teacher, once said that the ecstasy of God union far surpasses any type of sexual union between man and woman. I was in my early twenties at the time, and I was convinced that she was speaking purely metaphorically. I indeed had been blessed with love unions between myself, God and certain masters, including Jesus/Sananda, Lord Maitreya, Krishna and Kuthumi. This most accurately could be described as a great and beatific heart expansion filled with overtones of falling in love again and again.

At that point I had not experienced any type of physical sensation, much less one that could be likened to sexual orgasm. When Hilda talked about union with God, she said, "The ecstatic energies of God run up your spine and fill every cell of your body." But I could in no way conceive of this being anything but a metaphor of expanding into the heart of God—until these energies began to flow within my own body!

I must admit, I was not at all prepared for what I experienced. The first time it happened, and for many years following, the point where I experienced these energies was in my heart chakra along my spine, directly behind the physical heart. What I am describing to you is *not* of a metaphorical nature. It was an experience of orgasm in the back of the heart chakra, but far more powerful than anything I had experienced before. It was indeed everything that a second chakra sexual orgasm feels like, except that it occurred in the fourth chakra.

This is not to say that expanding into the heart of God does not equally bring one into a state of complete bliss. This will be discussed later in this chapter. But Hilda was quite right in telling us that union with God far surpasses earthly sex. Ultimately, orgasm is experienced along the entire spine, the head being the final point of climax!

What actually occurs is closely related to the kundalini rising from the base of the spine to the top of the head. High frequencies are poured forth from the monad or from certain planetary or cosmic masters. These energies activate the chakra system in the four lower bodies to bring about this ecstatic experience. For centuries, Eastern traditions have taught that each of us contains the blending of the Shiva/Shakti, yin/yang, masculine/feminine principles within ourselves. Ecstatic experiences are one way that the union within us manifests.

Not everyone will experience this in the same way. Each of us is constituted differently, so each person's spiritual journey will be unique. This also applies to how the kundalini will move through your own four-body system. If it does not happen in quite the way I have described, it does not mean that you have not achieved this or that level. You might very well have surpassed the level of one having these experiences, for your four-body system already might have acclimated to this type of vibrational frequency, or this type of experience might manifest in a unique way with you.

For those of you who are experiencing this type of phenomenon, however, I feel that it is quite helpful to read about it, for often it is quite unexpected. Each time I had this type of ecstatic experience, it took some getting used to. One evening I put on a tape of angelic music, lit some incense, put on a small night light and intended to drift to sleep enveloped by the soft tones of angel songs. However, this was not to be the case.

When the music began, I immediately felt it go straight to my head area. I then began to experience what I can describe most accurately as wave after wave of orgasm generated within my head. Even after my many and diverse experiences of this type, I admit to being a bit overcome. The music played on, and for fifteen to twenty minutes these waves of energy continued to flow. I sensed that the frequencies of the music were tapping into areas in my brain, uplifting me to the realms of bliss. This type of sensation often occurs when I am in deep meditation and/or listening within to the masters.

Please do not interpret this to be sexual in the usual sense. These experiences occur along the spinal column when certain frequencies of energies are released from the base of the spine or when they are being incorporated into the physical/etheric body from either the monad, the masters or that indefinable essence we call God. Again, each body will assimilate these energies in its own unique way, so do not think that this is something that must be experienced by everyone. But if you do experience these sensations, it is always helpful to have some point of reference.

The universe is filled with a great many surprises, as it should be, since we are all on the path of cosmic discovery. However, it is of equal value to share our experiences so that we might be better prepared for them and have the ease of knowing that much of what we experience is common to many lightworkers, especially those rapidly advancing on the path of ascension.

## Lost in Love, Found in Love

One of the more common experiences is the feeling of being in love with God or a particular master or group of masters. Bhakti, or devotion, is quite a common practice in India, where the objective is for the disciple to merge in love and devotion with his/her particular master. Thus the lover and the beloved eventually become as one. In the case of Krishna (Lord Maitreya) or of Sai Baba, it becomes immediately evident that to merge with them is indeed to merge with God. Again, this is not unlike the experience of the Christian who, in love and devotion, seeks to merge with the Christ and therefore with God.

Obviously, this type of union is one of the heart, wherein the gender of that divine being who is upholding the sacred energy can be in either male or female form. There are many who take this path to its heights and depths with Lord Sai Baba, who holds the highest light and love quotient ever manifested on our planet. There are many who follow this bhakti path of devotion and merge with Mother Mary and many who follow this path by way of the Christ. Some choose to focus on either the divine Mother or the divine Father aspect of God. The point is that if you find yourself in such a relationship with any of the planetary or cosmic masters, you will ultimately merge with the God you are. Your own divinity is what they are representing to you, and the embracing of that divinity in yourself is where they are leading you.

People who are devout followers of such a path, whether with an individual master or with God, are often referred to as being God-intoxicated because the feeling accompanying such utter love and devotion so fills the individual with the energies of love divine that the person appears to be drunk on love. If you seek that experience of drunkenness, I would recommend this path most highly. Actually, this path usually comes to one because there is a great bonding that exists and has existed over many ages between master and disciple. It is actually a path that chooses you.

However, even as we are broadening our spectrum and seeking ever more and more the divine within ourselves, we too can experience a bit of the divine nectar of such holy love. Take a moment to focus on a being who represents to us this divine quality, such as Sai Baba, Mother Mary or Lord Maitreya. We do not need to shift our focus away from the true path in order to merge at more and more expansive levels within ourselves, but we can broaden our vistas to incorporate the intimate connection with one or more masters in such divine union. It is a wonderful way to expand and further open the heart space. The highest evolution of this path, however, will lead one back to one's own inner and direct connection with God. Thus it will lead one to experience oneself as God.

## The Marriage of Minds

With our ascension process as accelerated as it has become in recent times, many people are experiencing a mental overshadowing, telepathic linkage or merging between their own minds and the mind of a master or group of masters. Wisdom that has hitherto been unavailable to us is now being poured into our minds at lightning speed. This is one of the reasons there is such an abundance of channelers on Earth today. Many individuals are being put into telepathic rapport with planetary and cosmic masters who had not previously been available to us. This is true of the angelic kingdom as well, including the archangels themselves, and it also applies to certain groups of positive extraterrestrials, such as the Arcturians and the Ashtar Command.

Individuals are coming into ever deeper levels of direct contact with their own souls and monads. Thus they are finding that the clouds of unknowable things are suddenly clearing up. Looked at through the lens of relationship, there is a blending of minds between higher beings and higher aspects of ourselves that creates its own unique bond, union or marriage. So it is not only the heart, but also the mind that is involved in the consummate union between individualized soul, monad, master and God. There is a divine merging or marriage between advancing and ascending humanity and God, the likes of which our small planet has never before known!

One very interesting aspect is the anchoring of the Avatar of Synthesis, or the 352 levels of the Mahatma, within those who call it forth. This being is of such a vast and cosmic nature as to extend through all levels of our existence up to the level of the Godhead Itself. But of course the cosmos is structured in the "ask and ye shall receive" mode. So even a being of the magnitude of the Mahatma waits to be invited before attempting to communicate with or use that individual as a focus of his divine energies.

This appears paradoxical, as that which pervades the whole is itself already within it; on one level, this is accurate. Yet in order to work with this divine being consciously, you must invoke it yourself. I highly recommend asking for the Mahatma to be anchored and activated within you so that you might advance more quickly through the levels of existence and therefore be of greater service to the whole in the process. I call the Mahatma to your attention to show how far-reaching and vast are the various aspects of God seeking expression through us at this time.

This is a time wherein the wisdom and love aspects of the universe truly seek to come to light within the minds and hearts of humankind. People are filling the data banks of their minds with more and more knowledge so that the masters can more easily access and transmit ever higher and greater truths. The more familiar we are with any given subject, the more available and accessible we are to the masters in their attempts to further enlighten us on the deeper meaning and hidden nature of those subjects.

We can also ask the masters to place within our auric fields and etheric and mental bodies packets of divine wisdom. These packets, having been anchored on the higher levels of mind, can then be brought through us, with their help, into the denser aspects of mind, also known as the plane of concrete mind. By now you can discern the give-and-take relationship we have with the cosmos and those great beings who exist to serve us.

Sai Baba has said, "The mind can create bondage or the mind can create liberation." It is suggested that we all open our minds to the great downpour of wisdom now taking place. Ultimate wisdom comes from within because when the masters speak to us, they speak in our language and use metaphors and symbols that we best understand. However, if we want to hear the masters and aspire to hear the voice of our own higher selves and monads, we must create the space, time and openness to facilitate our listening.

True listening means stilling the concrete mind in order to hear the voice of the higher mind, the monad or the masters. It involves letting go of preconceived ideas about the nature of things and allowing the truth to be revealed. It involves inviting in the cosmic masters, such as Melchizedek, Lord Metatron and the Mahatma. There is no ceiling to stop our growth except that which our minds create. Therefore, let us make sure not to create limits for ourselves, as the vast wisdom of the cosmos is waiting, wanting to be revealed.

## Taking Time Alone

As with all relationships, as much fun as a couple might have with their close friends or community, there are times when they need to be alone with one another. This same type of aloneness in one's relationship to God is equally essential. Getting together with groups of people who are attuned spiritually is not only recommended, but also vital to world service work and the advancing of one's own ascension process. One is propelled by leaps and bounds by group energy, but it is a must to spend time alone afterward in order to process what has occurred.

Time spent alone on a daily basis is also crucial. One can do a lot of service work and even be blessed with a spiritual mate, but at some point during the day or at the end of the day, it is important to sit alone with the stillness to hear what the voice of the silence has to reveal. Meditation is of enormous value in that its focus is to still the concrete mind and simply be. Beingness itself is one of the main attributes of God. While it is true that God or the cosmos acts, it is equally true that God or the cosmos acts from a state of pure beingness.

It is imperative, therefore, for each of us to learn to tap into that place where we simply *are*, where we can experience our own beingness. The true objective of meditation is to do just that, to allow ourselves simply to be. The silence often has more to reveal about the true nature of things than any amount of words. In actuality, words and silence are the divine complement of each other. They form their own polarity balance much like that of the yin and the yang. As I am by nature both a lecturer and a writer, I obviously know the importance that words have in the communication of truth. However, the majority of the words I communicate issue from the depths of the silence within myself.

It is crucial for your spiritual evolution and ability to stay centered in God to be able to delve into that center of quiet calm, so I want to make you aware of the perfect polarity balance between silence and the word. Our society is much too focused on doing, thinking and achieving, without the balance of inner communion. Those in traditional religions, even lightworkers, are often much better at praying than they are at listening. They might be surprised how open God and the masters are to speaking back.

Having said that, I also want to reemphasize that other things can be incorporated into your alone time with self and God. This is a good time to journal-write and check in with your subconscious mind and inner child to see how they are doing. If you ask, the inner child will be more than willing to share with you what its needs are. Although not an aspect of ourselves to be indulged unwisely, neither is the inner child to be ignored. It is a part of each of us, and we need to take the time to check in with it before it has the chance to act out its needs in an inappropriate fashion. Invite the inner child to do a bit of journal work so that it might share with you if it is doing okay or feels totally neglected. Perhaps it needs a day of lightness, a trip to the mall or to the movies. Perhaps it needs this because you have become somewhat imbalanced. The process of journaling will allow these various parts of ourselves to have their say which, when appropriately handled, will keep us integrated and whole.

There are a variety of techniques and functions that journal writing embraces. As with the inner child, you can listen to the various aspects of yourself speak, such as the various archetypes or subpersonalities. You can also set down your intent of action in any number of areas in your life. The point is, this time is for you to be alone with yourself and God. It is a period of time away from the input of other people, where you can both process what is going on with you and rest in the silence of your essential being.

Sometimes this stillness is the perfect time to communicate with your higher self, monad and the masters. You might very well find that your journal writing takes the form of channeling these higher aspects of self. If you are one to rely solely on books, you might suddenly find yourself channeling wisdom that you would otherwise seek from an outside source. It is a good idea to allot some of your alone time to asking God, your monad and the masters to talk to you through the vehicle of your own higher mind. Sit in meditation, set the intent and see what comes through.

Perhaps it will be a poem or a clarification of something you have read but not fully understood. In other cases you might be surprised to find that you are an open channel to higher inspiration. I am not saying that you should strive to be that kind of channel or telepath, because that might or might not be part of your work. What I am saying is that there are levels and layers within all of us that can only be explored and brought forth in the solitude of our own beings. I greatly encourage you to use this most precious time for yourself.

## Your Alone Time Together

If you are involved in a romantic relationship, it is of great value to take alone time together. Take specific time to join together as monads, and from that higher group body meditate, seek guidance, inspiration and just *be*. This is different from the communicating process that has been referred to throughout this book. Since this chapter is "God, the Consummate Union," what I am referring to is joining the group body of two with the energies of the One.

Allow yourselves the time to experience your monads in the solitude of a meditative environment that the two of you create together. You might want to play some soothing spiritual music as well as light some incense and perhaps a candle. However you choose to manifest it, this can be a time when your souls and/or monads can be the center of attention, and from that center you can meditate on the greater whole of God Itself.

This is a wonderful way to bond as ascension buddies and take time out from all other aspects of your relationship. Whatever you create within that most sublime stillness and silence ultimately resonates as two souls and monads in unison with God. This is a wonderful gift you can give to yourselves and your relationship. I highly recommend that you take advantage of this precious gift and give it to yourselves and each other.

## Experiences That Accompany Your Changing Frequencies

In the beginning of this chapter some of the more divine and sensually delightful experiences were described. As the brain cells expand in order to bring forth more wisdom and as the heart chakra is activated because the love quotient is increasing, one might very well find oneself experiencing the wonderful sensation of orgasm in these various chakra areas, as well as along the entire spine.

As we go deeper and deeper within the realms of God, as we bring through more and more wisdom, love and energies, and as we become increasingly integrated with our monads and the masters, our frequencies shift and change. As a result, we can experience a wide range of changes and symptoms in our four-body system.

As the energy continues to shift as rapidly as it is now doing, however, one might find that (either in conjunction with these sensual experiences or quite apart from them) other less pleasurable energy fluctuations occur within the body. They occur because of the path you are on and because of the rapid shift of energies. If you are aware that these symptoms go with the territory, you will be less likely to get bogged down by them through fear and confusion.

The rapid transformation of humanity as a whole means that each of us will go through the needed transformations that our bodies require in order to hold these higher frequencies. I have seen too many people waste precious time in bewilderment and self-judgment due to these varying manifestations. There is nothing to fear in them, and they should be welcomed as symbolic of the rising kundalini and the preparation of the four lower bodies to hold increasing amounts of light.

Some of the more bewildering symptoms of the kundalini rising or of the raising of our frequencies are: a feeling of lightheadedness, a floating feeling, a feeling of being off balance or dizziness and a change in vision (such as seeing the auras of people and objects perhaps more clearly than the physical form itself). There might be a trembling feeling or a sense of impending doom that can leave the person wondering whether he is suffering from an anxiety or panic disorder. The person might feel agoraphobic and want to stay close to home. In some cases this is due to a buildup of stress, which plays itself out by manifesting this type of symptom. Even if this is happening to you, you have all the tools I have so far discussed that can help you use these symptoms as a springboard for growth. If they are consuming your life, I would also recommend working with a therapist/spiritual counselor qualified in this area.

However, do not rush to judgment. Let us take a look at these symptoms from the standpoint of the monad. Remember that we are in a unique relationship with God because we are consciously on the path of ascension. If what was mentioned earlier about the change of frequencies that results in spinal-system orgasms and orgasms of the heart and head are true, would it not follow that this profound shifting and stimulation within one's being might also produce other symptoms?

If the expanding of the brains cells produces an individual climax in the head chakra, then the symptoms of lightheadedness, dizziness and feeling off balance are minor in comparison and should not surprise you. It is all a matter of the lens through which we view these manifestations. It is much easier to accept and enjoy the pleasant ones than the unpleasant ones, but all of these physical reactions have their roots in the same cause. Therefore, it is important that we view all these reactions from an attitude of love.

This leads us to ask about the fear that can arise. Why do we often feel such an acute sense of panic with the second group of symptoms? The answer to that lies in humanity's innate fear of death. It is one of the worst feelings, and many who experience these symptoms report a feeling of impending doom or death. The truth is that during such an accelerated process we *are* dying to the old within ourselves while we are birthing to the new. Sometimes it is difficult to let the old go so that the new might be brought forth, as the ego might be screaming *no!* What I ask you to remember at these times is that the higher self and monad are rejoicing with a resounding *yes!* So it will smooth the process and bring reassurance if you learn to listen to *that* voice. It is resistance that brings pain, so the more gracefully you can allow the old to leave, the easier your transformation will be.

The shaking and trembling occur because we are 100-watt light bulbs suddenly receiving 1000 volts from the cosmos. This is quite an adjustment for all of us, particularly for those with more sensitive electrical systems. As to not wanting to leave the safety of one's home and enter into the marketplace, many on the path of ascension are prone to steering clear of the noise and clamor of the marketplace and remaining within the walls of the sanctuaries they have made of their homes. Although there are those who travel around the globe anchoring the light into either troubled areas or power points, many desire to remain cloistered within their home-based ashrams.

So do not judge yourself by the standards that the world puts forth. Know that these symptoms are a call to, and a manifestation of, further growth. I choose to look at these through the more inclusive lens of transformation as we proceed on our paths of ascension. Whether it is the voice of our subconscious minds begging for our attention, higher energies seeking to anchor in our bodies or the spontaneous rising of kundalini from these energies, it is the voice and movement of growth we are hearing and feeling.

## Other Symptoms of Spiritual Acceleration

One further area of transformation that the lightworker will almost always notice in achieving ever greater union with the divine is the effect of detoxification. This is relegated almost exclusively to the physical/etheric realm, although some very definite changes will also occur in the emotional and mental bodies.

Most of us doing ascension work will invariably make some dietary adjustments. The foods we eat will be more nutritious, we might want to take various food supplements and we might desire to receive bodywork. We might also begin doing bodywork on ourselves, as in practicing hatha yoga and/or various breathing exercises. I am sure that the more creative among us will think up and explore much that is not mentioned here. Of course the changes we make on the physical will move into the other bodies. For instance, if one is in the process of cutting back or giving up sugar or caffeine, the emotions will feel somewhat deprived for a while, and this area will need some attention.

It is important to realize that when the body is detoxifying, in cleansing out the toxins the body will go through necessary adjustments. This is a positive thing, so it is important to understand that healing is taking place. This understanding applies to all forms of dis-ease and/or physical imbalance. As one integrates higher and higher levels of ascension frequencies, the physical body and nervous system must readjust.

At one of the Wesak celebrations, I touched a woman on her third eye with the divine nectar of Sai Baba and she lost vision in her left eye. Her body was not accustomed to the higher-level frequency of shaktipat that was transmitted. This symptom shortly passed, but it is an example of what can happen in the process of spiritual acceleration. The ways symptoms can manifest are infinite. Things are not always what they seem. So don't judge yourself or others about these manifestations, for they might be a sign that the person is accelerating spiritually far beyond the rate of the average lightworker. The focus of all our spiritual work, whether detoxification of the body or meditation, is the integration of the four-body system. We can see how each aspect of our being plays its part and how that part interrelates with the whole as we journey on our path.

## Safe in God's Love and Light

The subject of God as the ultimate union is vast indeed. As the relationship between couples stretches us to the limit and puts us to the test, how much more does our relationship with God! The love, light and safety that the union with the divine brings forth, however, cannot be equaled by any earthly relationship no matter how deeply we love. Therefore, as we proceed along this journey we should be ever aware of the vast energies of love, light and protection that are provided by God.

Those who walk this path in lieu of having an earthly partner should take comfort and joy in the fact that no matter how alone we feel we are, we can never be *truly* alone, as we live within that which by Its very nature provides All That Is and holds us safe and secure in Its very Self. Know that this aura of divine protection and wholeness is truly that in which we live and move and have our being.

The essence of what I have tried to convey in this chapter is the unique relationship that exists between ourselves, our soul/monad and God. This divine relationship at once enfolds us and tests us. It advances us ever on-ward and embraces us right where we are, loving us unconditionally at each step of our evolution. The relationship we have with God is always new and exciting. Therefore, I focused on some of the more common as well as the less common areas into which this divine union may lead us.

In viewing God as the ultimate union, we can know a degree of safety, love and companionship that others can never know — those who see themselves as separate from God or who do not believe that God exists at all. When we feel that our energies are running low or that the fire within is barely a burning ember, all we need do is turn our attention toward God and ask to be filled with the divine fire of which we are but tiny sparks. Before we know it, we will be aflame with the light, love and passion of life itself, for that is the grace of knowing ourselves to be one with the One.

If we are going through a period of loneliness and find that we are seemingly without friends or support, all we need do is turn to God, and we will feel the truth that indeed we can never be truly alone. That by no means implies that we do not prefer to have friends and family about us, but it does state the truth that even in our most seemingly isolated moments, we can bring to mind and heart the joy of knowing our oneness with the One.

When we are in need of love, yet have no lover by our side, we can embrace God as the beloved and know that blessed union wherein lover and beloved are truly one. When we are alone and frightened, we can remember that we are *not* alone and can call forth the experience of divine light, love and protection that comes from God and surrounds us through every moment of our lives.

We also have the vast hosts of planetary ascended masters, cosmic masters, angels and archangels, elohim and positive extraterrestrials we can call forth. In the first five volumes of *The Easy-to-Read Encyclopedia of the Spiritual Path*, I have attempted to make as many of these masters known to you as possible. For some of you, they might seem to be new friends. Others might already have an intimate relationship with many of them. Call upon them, as they are here awaiting our call. But by divine law they must wait until they are invoked into our lives.

As each one of these beings holds a unique position in the planetary and cosmic governments and each holds a specific energy, you might want to consider calling upon one or the other of them depending on the need of the hour. For example, if you are in need of extra strength and protection, Lord Michael is a wonderful being to call upon. If you are seeking to feel more love, you might want to call on Lord Maitreya, Kuthumi or Yogananda. If you are seeking to feel enveloped in the love of the mother, call upon the Mother Mary or other forms of the divine Mother. If you are seeking wisdom, call upon Djwhal Khul, and you are sure to get it, with a good dose of love and levity as well! If you are dealing with health issues, avail yourself of Dr. Lorphan and the team of galactic healers. If you want to open your bhakti, or devotional center, then you can do no better than calling upon Sai Baba.

I have only begun to mention these wonderful beings. If you are not familiar with them and the grace they bring, I suggest that you get acquainted. Many of you are already linked to a specific lineage and know exactly what I am speaking about here. You who are more familiar with or connected to specific masters might want to share your experiences with your friends.

I bring this most important subject to a close with the reminder that in truth, each of us is already in a relationship and that relationship is with God. All other relationships flow out of the stream of this one primary relationship. God, the consummate union, is a part of every other union we have, for ultimately, God is who we are.

# 11

## *Living the Spiritual Life Together*

### Maintaining Your Balance

Cosmic sources tell us that the theme for our universe is courage. The keynote for our planet is harmony through conflict. It is a fact that life on planet Earth is hard. Those of us on the path of ascension are not only dealing with the more mundane aspects of life, but also with the influx of spiritual energies, which have a continual effect on our four-body system. We might find ourselves stuck in traffic, blasted with pollutants and wondering what lesson we are supposed to learn by having a shortage of clients this week, all while trying to process the great currents of spiritual energy we just ran through our system while working with our last client of the day.

Upon our arrival home, we may find it hard enough to deal with ourselves, much less with our mate, who is eagerly awaiting our arrival in order to tell us about an incredible spiritual lecture this evening that we simply cannot miss! Yes, we are deeply in love with our mate, and yes, under different circumstances that lecture sounds most appealing, but this evening it is more than we can bear. How then are we to find the balance?

To begin with, we must first be right with ourselves. This is a time when we need to tip the selfish/selfless balance a little more in our favor. We start by lovingly communicating to our partner how we are feeling, then we take the necessary time for ourselves. If our partner is truly walking the path with us, he or she should have no problem understanding what is going on with us and should support us in taking care of ourselves. Hopefully this is the case, because in any event, we must have that sense of being right with ourselves, and the ideal is to have support in that most crucial area.

Being in a tired and depleted state, perhaps caught between a rock and a hard place, financially speaking, it is hard enough to find that quiet place within ourselves where we can regain our center. Life can be hard, and continuing to live it and maintain it from the highest possible perspective can be challenging. That is why I am calling to your attention the delicate act of balancing this process with yourself and your mate.

Of course, in order to manifest this balance in your relationship, you must first balance it in yourself. This takes work, but it is the work we are here to do. Our sense of personal balance helps create an atmosphere wherein we can find the proper balance in our relationships. So it is crucial for us to honor the need for inner balance as a foundation for creating and maintaining a balanced romantic relationship.

## Balance within the Relationship

In the scenario of the tired mate, the first suggestion I would make to both partners is to try your best to be sensitive to the other's needs. If you have been working on yourselves at all, you should both be able to see where the greatest need lies. Of course, you must both be willing to communicate your needs and preferences in the first place, but I am assuming that you have done this. If it is essential for the exhausted partner to get needed rest, that takes top priority. The disappointment faced in giving up the idea of attending the outside event together would do well to be honored and then replaced with compassionate understanding and the recognition that disappointment stems from attachment rather than the inability to realize your outer objective.

If the outside event is something you feel you need and it is appropriate that you go by yourself or with a friend, then by all means do so. If it is something you must do as a couple or that you choose to do only as a couple, then set the intent to do it at another time. If it is a one-time event, then either go alone or let it go. Being in a relationship involves balancing the needs of the two partners. This will mean compromise and not having everything your way all the time. Since you have committed to one another, however, it follows that you want to be in the relationship and that you accept whatever goes with it. As we are seeking that place of integration and balance within ourselves, we are simply extending that integration and balance to incorporate the couple as well as the two individuals.

At times, living the spiritual life together can seem much harder than living the spiritual life alone. At other times it can seem much easier. Viewing the previous scenario through the lens of living alone, you would find yourself stuck in traffic, blasted with pollutants, wondering what lesson you are supposed to learn by having a shortage of clients this week, trying to process the great currents of spiritual energy you ran through your system while working with your last client of the day, racing home to tend to a vast array of daily chores you were unable to get to because you were at work and having to contend with several telephone calls from excited friends who insist that you simply cannot miss this evening's lecture.

You then might find it much harder to take the respite you so sorely need because the dog needs to be walked, there is no food in the house and so on. Even if you would normally be interested in the lecture, in your exhaustion it would hold little appeal. If you collapsed from exhaustion, you could neither rest adequately nor enjoy the lecture.

The above scenario is slightly exaggerated, with a hint of humor thrown in, so that if you find yourself in the position of one of the partners, you might have a greater appreciation for the other one's predicament and for the part he or she is playing in your life. By no means am I saying that being in a relationship is better than not being in one. If you were going it alone, you would most likely be in a smaller place that did not require a great deal of looking after, or you would hire a housekeeper if you could manage it. You would probably make sure that the refrigerator had the food you liked or else you would have picked up something on the way home.

What I have attempted to demonstrate is that if you are in a relationship, it is not advisable to take your partner for granted, which is a trap almost all of us fall into at one time or another. Or you might resent the five minutes it takes to communicate your point of view or listen to your partner's. You are in a relationship with that particular person because you choose to be, so give the relationship the respect it deserves and learn how to balance as a team. What is the point of being supportive of each other only when you see eye to eye? In that case you might as well be alone.

The trick is to find that place of support and mutual balance even when you don't see eye to eye. By doing this in simple situations, as in the above scenario, you will learn how to manifest this type of balance and mutual support in more crucial moments. You will also be learning how to function in a group body, which all of us must eventually learn to do on our path of evolution. Therefore, why not begin to practice integration and group balance where you are now, with the person you are sharing your life with? You will find that being in a relationship will provide you with ample opportunities to learn the delicate art of balance and integration, and this is how it should be. So take advantage of the love you share as well as the challenges you provide for one another, and you will be walking the path well together.

Understand also that if you are interested in accelerating your spiritual growth, ascension process and total self- realization, there is no quicker path than romantic relationships. This is true because the romantic relationship is the only one guaranteed to press all your buttons — those faulty thought patterns and complexes that need to be cleansed and cleared to realize God.

Romantic relationships, then, are the fast track to God. Anyone can maintain Christ consciousness while living in a cave. The true test of God-realization is demonstrating this state of consciousness in the marketplace, and the ultimate marketplace is living intimately with another human being. Each time you react with negative emotions to your partner's behavior, bless him/her for allowing you the opportunity to pass another spiritual test. In the same vein, you should never leave a relationship until you have learned the lessons from it. Otherwise, you will just continue the same patterns with another person.

In every interaction with your partner the choice is always the same: do I want God or do I want my ego? Do I want harmony and spiritual evolution within the group body, or do I want self-centeredness and narcissism? When you can maintain Christ consciousness while you are immersed in a romantic relationship and fully involved with Earth life, then you have truly achieved self-realization. Achieving a higher light quotient and passing higher initiations are very important, but they are only part of true self-realization. Use your relationship as the ultimate crucible for spiritual growth and be more concerned about learning your own lessons than about being attached to your partner's learning his or hers. When you are right with yourself and right with God, becoming right with your mate becomes a lot easier.

I have seen a great many lightworkers who are at very high levels of initiation and light quotient and have great gifts of channeling, clairvoyance and the like. But in their romantic or professional relationships they are completely dysfunctional. I don't care if you've passed your seven levels of initiation and hold a planetary light quotient of 99 percent; this is *not* God-realization. What difference does it make whether you can channel the masters if in the next moment you indulge in childish ego battles with your mate or business partner?

Many lightworkers are now taking their sixth and seventh initiations, and when they find this out they are very pleased, as they should be. However, their true spiritual work has just begun. Most lightworkers will stay at the seventh initiation until transcendence of the negative ego and inner-child victimization are overcome and right human relationships are mastered.

Achieving initiations and raising our light quotient relate to spiritual development and have very little to do with mental, emotional, physical or psychological development. I was absolutely shocked when I realized the truth of this. Lightworkers must realize that to achieve self-realization at the highest level, there are many levels that must be mastered. These levels are the spiritual, mental, emotional, physical, psychological, professional or service, environmental, leadership and relationship. But the crucial key to self-realization on all levels (and this may surprise you) is the psychological level. This is the foundation upon which your spiritual house rests.

Many lightworkers are highly developed in one or two areas and undeveloped in others. This is not a judgment, but rather a simple statement of fact. True God-realization is mastery of all the above-mentioned levels in an integrated and synthesized fashion. This level of mastery is not easy to attain, for it is far beyond just passing your initiations, which is the first major step to attaining this goal. Lightworkers are often more interested in the ephemeral and esoteric when in truth, what they really need are books like *Soul Psychology* and this volume.

No matter how gifted a person is as a channel, psychic, healer, writer or spiritual teacher, if he has not learned to transcend negative ego, master the subconscious mind, properly parent the inner child, integrate the three minds, balance the four bodies, properly integrate the feminine and masculine, become at cause rather than at effect, become a master instead of a victim, develop self-love and own his personal power in a clear way, he is headed for a fall. His level of initiation, light quotient, leadership abilities, fame and worldly success cannot stop this from happening.

I am emphatic about the importance of getting your psychological house in order and transcending the cancer of the negative ego — the term "cancer" truly is an appropriate term here. The negative ego, if not checked, will contaminate and subtly poison every aspect of your life, including your romantic relationship, which you have spent so much time and energy cultivating like a beautiful garden. This section has been written to give you an opportunity to learn by grace instead of karma. There is no subject about which I feel more passionate. Remember Sai Baba's famous definition of God: "God equals man minus ego."

## Balancing the Extremes

During the course of a long-term romantic relationship, you will inevitably come face to face with some of life's more challenging aspects. There will be times when those in your immediate and extended family are called on to face great health lessons and, ultimately, a time when they make that great transition called death. If it is your choice and destiny, you may face the challenges that go along with birthing and raising children. This brings with it an entire array of potential extreme situations, including the natural ones of their growing up, moving away from home, perhaps marrying and so forth.

You may be put through extreme financial tests, as well as those that spring from career choices and job situations. There is likewise the "test of the light," to which all disciples and initiates are subjected, which primarily deals with all the changes we go through both individually and as a group body when traveling the path of ascension. This includes the incorporation of all the lessons of life through the continually expanding vision of individuals and couples consciously treading the path of initiation and ascension. In this process, old forms are constantly dying and being replaced by new, more refined forms on all levels of existence.

Every situation can either bring the couple closer or see them drift further apart. This has more to do with the choices the couple makes, both individually and collectively, than the nature of any given situation. In the same manner, each situation you are called on to face in life can either bring you closer to God and further along the spiritual path, or it can leave you feeling isolated and disconnected from your path. It is the Hierarchy's hope that individuals and couples will use all the situations they encounter, no matter how difficult, to bring them closer to themselves, each other and God.

Everything going on in your life is a spiritual test giving you the opportunity to remain one with God in your moment-to-moment choices or lose that oneness in realization, but not in truth. Romantic relationships seen from this perspective are secondary to one's spiritual path. This is not to negate the importance of a romantic relationship, but rather to keep one's perspective in regard to one's spiritual path. I think you can see now why half of all marriages end in divorce. People often come together improperly aligned within themselves, with God and with each other.

It is hoped that the truly committed couple will support one another during these trying times and that each person can devote the bulk of his or her time and energy to dealing with the lessons, rather than having to deal with a depressed or upset partner as well. Remember that tests and lessons come to each of us. One person might be stronger in one area, perhaps in the physical body, and weaker in the psychological body. To judge or grow short with one's partner because he/she is dealing with a difficult lesson in one of the four bodies is not expressing unconditional love. I grant you, it is not so easy to keep the love flowing during times of extreme crisis. But is that not the very test of love itself — to remain unconditionally loving during the hard times and ride out the storms together?

If we are in a committed relationship, we must realize that the very nature of that commitment will bring us through many stages in our relationships and put us through many tests. As lessons come to all, if you are currently with a partner going through extreme testing, stop and realize that the difficult lesson could just as easily come to you. Consider how you would want your partner to act with you. You would want to be able to trust at your very core that your partner will indeed ride this out with you. He/she would in turn want to know that you are there in complete support of him/her and the group unit of which you are both a part.

This does not mean that you take on any aspect of your partner's lessons or try to solve them. Rather, your job is to provide a safe and loving atmosphere in which your partner can come to terms with the situation and learn what is needed to transcend it. The point of balance in a situation such as this lies in giving your loving support to your partner while at the same time not get so caught up that you lose your own center in trying to fix his or her situation.

If you are the one going through the major lessons, you in turn do not want to dump on or drain your partner, but keep the space you need in which to heal, accept the love and nurturing he/she offers, and work on deepening your connection with your soul, monad and God. This way you can get to the root of your difficulties, learn the lesson and come out of things closer to God than before. Remember, this principle applies to all extreme financial lessons, environmental lessons, job lessons, psychological lessons, emotional lessons, mental lessons and spiritual transformations.

The couple must reach into their hearts and use such situations to grow closer to one another and to God. It is up to them to choose at every juncture of their lives whether to take the high road or not, and the choice is often not easy. Viewed through the lens of spirit, however, the high road becomes the only viable option, so the choice ultimately is not which road we will take, but which lens we look through. In all honesty, after one glance through the lens of the soul/monad, what choice is there but to continue to view from that lens?

When life is looked at through the lens of the soul, monad and Christ consciousness, adversity is welcomed, not cursed. From one's Christ eyes, the appropriate affirmation in all crises, no matter what form they take, is "Not my will but Thine, and thank you for the lesson." Crises are blessings in disguise that present the opportunity to accelerate your ascension process and realize God at a more expanded level. This attitude, held jointly in a relationship, can transform the most catastrophic-appearing lessons into the most divine moments of intimacy and connection with oneself, God and your partner. As Ram Dass stated so eloquently, "Everything that happens in life is grist for the mill" to create greater love on all levels and greater union with God.

## Affairs vs. Communication

The temptation to have an affair can occur in those who operate out of their lower personalities all the way to initiates or even ascended masters. In the latter case, the two people involved recognize a deep level of spiritual intimacy and are pulled to act this out on the physical plane. It is obvious that this subject needs to be looked at through a variety of lenses.

We need to be clear that we are discussing affairs and not simply the attraction that occurs between single and available people. To have an affair means to do something behind the back of your partner and violate the all-important element of trust. For those not acting solely out of pure lust, the emotional body will be involved to one degree or another, and this is of great significance. If you find yourself getting involved with a person besides your spouse or partner, it is generally because there is an emotional need not being met by your partner. However, it may also include certain physical, mental and even spiritual needs. Thus this common problem is a complex one.

Affairs, or the desire to have them, can be averted if those in a committed romantic relationship keep the channels of communication completely open in regard to this issue. However, if the couple simply waits for the issue of an affair to surface instead of remaining in communication about their relationship as a whole, it will be much more difficult. By that time, many thwarted desires or painful wounds will have had time to fester and grow. Therefore, it is recommended that all couples remain open and willing to communicate their needs when those needs arise. This prevents a buildup of resentments that might trigger involvement with another person and open a Pandora's box. I am not suggesting that you weigh your relationship down with continuous harping on the subject of your relationship, but that you pay close attention to the needs of both yourself and your mate that arise in the relationship and that you set aside time to discuss these matters.

For example, if you have a much greater need than your partner for the physical display of affections, such as hugging, holding hands, cuddling, kissing each other hello and good-bye, these needs are as valid to discuss as the need for more sexual interaction. In relationships, one partner will generally be of a more generous nature in the physical display of affection, and if you are that partner and end up feeling neglected, please bring it to your partner's attention. Often the less expressive partner will have no idea they are not giving you what you want or need. A little communication on your part and a willingness for both of you to find a happy medium can work as preventive medicine. A little communication, particularly in physical matters, often goes a very long way.

For some reason, people are often more willing to communicate over other issues than those relating to sexual intimacy and expression of affection. However, communication in this area is a must. During the course of a committed relationship, our needs are bound to change. Perhaps at the beginning of the romance, both partners desired a high level of sexual intimacy. But later, one partner often moves away from sexual desire to a greater degree than the other partner. This does not mean that the feelings of love have diminished, but simply that the focus of the relationship has now expanded to include wider vistas and responsibilities.

If we do not communicate with our partners, the partner with the greater sexual urge may feel rejected and the partner with the lesser need will feel put upon. That one will either pull away completely or indulge the other partner resentfully. Then expressions of affection that might otherwise be forthcoming, such as cuddling, massaging, hello kisses and the like, might be completely withdrawn out of fear that this will be misinterpreted by the other partner, who is waiting for any encouragement to initiate sex.

What we are talking about here is a complete lack of communication, which leads to inappropriate behavior and greater and greater confusion and conflict. The avoidance of a discussion on this matter can provide fertile ground for an extra-marital affair. However, discussing these varying needs from a place of unconditional love, calm and openness can help bring the couple closer than ever.

What I am driving at here is that communication is the key to keeping a relationship committed. Without this communication, frustrations and resentments can easily develop, which can lead one or both of the partners to stray, seeking to have their needs met. This might lead to their drifting apart. Preventing this involves a willingness to work together on all issues.

An affair can result from lack of communication and frustration in many areas of the relationship. Then a person begins to feel unheard, feeling a disinterest from the partner in any number of possible scenarios. He is left feeling isolated, alone and unappreciated, and seeks to bond with another in order to feel that sense of communication, interest and appreciation. What then occurs is the affair.

So you can see how vital communication is to every aspect of your relationship. The opposite of communication is isolation, and the seeming solution to isolation is an affair. Of course this is no solution at all, for it breaks the most sacred bond of trust between the couple. This creates a host of other problems that touch so deeply to the core that often couples can never fully come to terms with the fact that the affair has occurred. Then a separation or divorce ensues. This is not inevitable, but it is most often the case. Therefore, keep up the preventive medicine of open, loving, honest and spiritually attuned communication on whatever subjects require that communication.

## Stopping an Affair at the Mental Level

The manifestation of everything begins with the mind. In the case of sexual encounters, one generally begins to look at a certain person in a sexual light and then proceeds to carry that forward into the realm of personal fantasy. The fantasy often grows into obsession, and the mental pictures of the sexual encounter grow to such a height that having sex is basically a done deal. Of course, with potential affairs there are two people doing this with each other as well as in their own minds. The little looks and glances exchanged between them will only serve to bring the sexual act into manifestation all the more quickly.

We can stop it, however, before it gets to that point. This is in our power as cocreators with God. There are ways not to let this type of temptation get the better of you. Granted, this is not always easy; in fact, it would be appropriate to say that this is almost always quite difficult, but it can be done by simply working at the dissipation of the thought form that holds the other person in a sexual and sensual light. If you are both lightworkers, you can discuss this and agree to see each other as brothers and sisters of spirit.

Make a pact not to give each other those little telling looks that are in effect saying, "I want you, I desire you, I must have you" — looks that come in the twinkling of an eye, or rather a blast of sexual energy that comes through the eyes at lightning speed. When you are away from one another, keep watch that you do not revert back to the pattern of lustful fantasizing over each other. Rather, keep affirming for as long as necessary, *"We are brothers and sisters, sons and daughters of God, and it is in this light that I hold my sister (or brother)."* Feel free to call on the masters' help, for they have had human form and know the intense energy involved. You may even look upon one another as aspects of the divine Mother or Father, which in truth you are.

The other thing that is important is to avoid perpetuating an affair of the heart. By this I am referring to a secret affair that is not sexually acted out, but that contains much sexual energy, finding expression in the emotional, secretive encounters between the two of you. This type of affair often wreaks more havoc on your already committed romantic relationship than a physical affair, for it emotionally pulls you away from your partner and breaks the line of open and honest communication that should be finding expression within your committed relationship. It perpetuates the avoidance of the real issues that you and your mate should be dealing with, gives your heart into the keeping of the other person and keeps your sexual desires, thoughts and emotions focused on your secret partner. One could say there are physical affairs, mental affairs and emotional affairs, and all three types should be nipped in the bud when they begin to manifest.

I am not saying that it is inappropriate to have an appreciation of the human form and to acknowledge the pleasing looks of a person of the opposite sex. This is not about putting blinders on, but about choosing how we will interact with those we find attractive. We can be attracted to others on a variety of levels—physically, emotionally, mentally and spiritually. The point is to keep your relationship with your partner the top priority and refrain from feeding the desires that might spring up regarding other people. There is a fine line here that must not be crossed on the physical, etheric, energetic, emotional or mental plane. This is the true and full meaning of commitment and integrity in a primary romantic relationship.

You and your partner need to know that you come first on each other's list. The trust factor is of the utmost importance. Know that the power lies within you to transform thoughts of another into thoughts of brotherly love and friendship. If there is an emotional bond, keep it open and not a secret from your partner. It is fine to have separate friends, but in a case like the one just described, you would do much better to have a friendship that includes your mate as well. For there would still be a high risk of falling into a secret affair of the heart or an actual affair.

In times when there is a strong physical attraction between you and someone else, use the affirmation given above to help you keep your thoughts turned elsewhere. Remember, the mind is the gate through which all things must pass in order to find physical manifestation. Therefore, be the keeper of the gate, and simply do not let the mind get the better of you by indulging in fantasies. Use your personal power and the sword of discrimination and clear thinking to choose which direction these thoughts will take.

You *do* have the ability to stop them from self-perpetuating and, with the power of divine intent, to transform them into their highest spiritual counterpart. With the simple adjustment of your thought process, that which was lust can be turned into brotherly/sisterly love. And that which held the threat of secrecy can be brought into the light of honesty, inclusiveness and purity.

The key to transcending temptation is to understand that what manifests in life is what we focus our attention on. Ideally, your conscious mind should keep its attention on the ideals of the higher self and God. When temptation arises, simply shift your attention in the initial stages before the energy, feelings and thought forms gain too much momentum and force. As *A Course in Miracles* says, "Be vigilant for God and His kingdom."

## Affairs and Soul/Monadic Connections

There can be a desire to have an affair when two closely linked souls meet and feel their spiritual bond. This situation is of a very different nature than lustful attraction or affairs that arise from a communication gap. This type of attraction, however, should not be indulged in when one or both people are in a committed relationship. But since many of us are now connecting with others in our monad, this type of situation warrants some discussion.

When two highly evolved beings begin to work together on the outer planes, there is a strong electrical current that flows between them. This is actually how it should be, since what we are dealing with at this level is the freely flowing God force moving through all our lower bodies, including the physical. This is what the masters want, because this empowers the service work these beings came in to do. However, when two people within this group who have had close ties as partners come into contact, there is often a desire to express the dynamic energies flowing between them in a sexual fashion — to rebond physically.

If these people were single at the time of their meeting, destiny would have assigned them a different pathway and they could freely explore the past ties through to the present, giving total expression to all levels of the energies they carry. But if these people are already in committed romantic relationships with people of like caliber whom they have chosen to be their mates for this present lifetime, they would do well to understand the nature of their attraction but definitely not act on it in the form of an affair.

The energies between two monad mates can be great indeed, and the temptation can be great to act on what seems quite natural. But it is *not* the thing to do. Rather, the two can talk together about it and see how they might use this energy in their service work in the present lifetime and let it go at that. Unless you feel beyond the shadow of a doubt that *this* is the person you are truly meant to be with, do not act out your feelings sexually. The point is to understand what you are feeling and then get back to the work at hand.

If by some strange quirk of fate you are indeed meant to reconnect with this person in a physical and romantic manner, then know that you must first disconnect from the person with whom you are currently involved. This situation can and does occur, but it is quite rare. If it is the case, a secret affair is obviously not the answer. This situation would need to be dealt with in an honest and above-board manner. As you more deeply connect with your higher group body, understand some of the feelings that might arise and proceed with due caution.

## Affairs of the Lower Nature

I would like to make one further point. There are affairs that occur from lust, which is no longer at play within the initiate. This is what is known as the meat-market syndrome and is generally found in bars, strip clubs and the like, where people gather in an attempt to hook up with someone and try to forget themselves with alcoholic beverages and acts of sex that stem from a purely lustful nature. The reason I bring this up is to caution all disciples and initiates to steer clear of such places and the people who frequent them.

This may seem quite obvious, but there is an underlying element that most are not aware of. Sometimes, because of certain social or business obligations, disciples, initiates and even ascended masters in body might find themselves associating with people carrying these frequencies. Then one of two things can occur. The first is the most common response, in which initiates find themselves immediately repulsed by such energies and pull away. But the second thing that can happen is that the initiate is so filled with divine, all-embracing love that he or she may temporarily interpret the lower energies of such people as the energy of pure love that he or she carries. If she is in a particularly vulnerable spot, she may gravitate to such an inappropriate person, especially if she has work to do learning this aspect of discernment. In the case of the single person, it is just such an encounter that leads to highly inappropriate relationships.

In a case where the lightworker is married and not rightly communicating his or her true issues with his partner, he might find himself swayed by the strong energy of the lustful person. He might filter it through his own love channel and seemingly convert it into something it most definitely is not. Please be aware of the tremendous power of love that you on the path of initiation hold, and do not let yourselves falter. Always go to the Source, as in God and your monad, and also the source of your committed relationship to work through all difficulties. In this way you cannot deceive yourself that what is wrong is right or that which is of the lower nature is of the higher, and you will remain in integrity with yourself, God and your relationship.

Affairs are not the solution, but the doorway to new and more difficult problems. They are an attempt by the negative ego to avoid facing issues, and there is no way this can be done. We must continually face ourselves at every level and turn of the spiral. The ultimate issue is you and your relationship with yourself. If you are in a committed romantic relationship, then *be* in that relationship; use it as a couple and individually to grow closer to oneself, God, the masters and each other. This is living the spiritual life together.

## Living Together

When I asked the Hierarchy their viewpoint, they told me that they are very much in favor of people living together before making the commitment of marriage. This is because they regard the union of two people in a relationship of commitment and unconditional love as sacred. So they would prefer that couples get to know each other well before actually getting married. This is not a point they insist on, for it all depends on the particular couple and their choices. But they tell me that living together first, even for a little while, can be of great value in specific areas.

First of all, the Hierarchy takes marriage quite seriously and would prefer that couples who make this commitment to each other really mean it. A period of living together can help the two people become accustomed to the many aspects of daily life together. This brings in many factors totally excluded from the dating arena and gives them a dose of hard reality from which to view their relationship. It is far easier to be in love when one is not exposed to another's dirty laundry, both literally and figuratively, and this can be and is avoided during the dating process. But it cannot be avoided when living together and sharing the same household.

The Hierarchy feels that it is best to know for sure what we are getting into. If the choice is not made to live together first, the couple is encouraged to become as actively involved in each other's daily lives as possible before marriage. This would be ideal for all couples, since it would involve sharing responsibilities and finances (not necessarily equally, but how it would be if they were married), listening to details of each other's day and staying in close communication the way they would want to if they were married. This would help the couple get to know the habits, mood swings, give and take, and all-around patterns of daily living with each other and prevent many surprises that come to couples who do not know each other intimately prior to marriage. This would also relegate the sexual passion to a more realistic place. It would not be the primary focus, but would be shared along with all the other aspects of their lives.

In regard to sex before marriage, the Hierarchy is not against this at all. What they do not support is casual sex and all the ramifications that have already been discussed. However, in a relationship between two committed people, they feel that the better the couple can get to know each other before marriage, the more realistically they will enter the marriage and the better the chance that the marriage will last. Sometimes couples are compatible in almost every area but the sexual one, and this would leave the couple in utter frustration. The better prepared we are, the more we will be able to keep our marriages thriving in as healthy a way as possible.

The main gist of what the masters are saying is that once a commitment is made, either through traditional marriage or the couple's own personal vows of commitment, they would like people to view that commitment as sacred, holding it in unconditional love, trust and loyalty. They feel that it is therefore crucial that each couple get to know each other as completely and realistically as possible before entering into such a commitment.

I also asked the Hierarchy about their view on open marriages. They said that they are against them because ultimately it does not work. Although it may seem to work, it is usually for the benefit of the partner who has a hard time making a commitment. The other partner might go along with it until the "open" idea of the marriage is actually acted on. Then the partner who reluctantly went along with the idea feels nearly as betrayed as if he/she had found out he had been cheated on. The same feelings of insecurity, hurt, anger and jealousy arise. Interestingly enough, if the partner who first initiated the idea of the open marriage finds out that his mate has had sex with someone else, either before or afterward, the same feelings of hurt, betrayal, anger, jealousy and insecurity often arise within him. It is really a no-win situation that might sound good initially, but which falls flat on its face when acted on. This is another example of the negative ego trying to find ways to justify inappropriate behavior and exploit unresolved issues.

This can also be seen when one of the partners (usually, but not always, the male) expresses the idea of having a threesome. The man is apt to select a close friend of the woman in an attempt to convince her of the harmless fun that the three of them could have together. "Anything once," they say, "right?" *No*, the masters tell us. Wrong! The result is usually embarrassment and/or jealousy, plain and simple, and what was once a wonderful friendship is thrown off kilter, at least for a time. This is not the proper bonding of three friends. And it is the misuse of sexual energy if the situation ever gets to that stage.

Since the situation invariably ends with embarrassment on the part of someone, the couple and the friend are left to deal with a situation that should never have occurred in the first place. If you have been involved in such a situation, please understand that there is no judgment here, only observation. If you escaped any of the above outcomes, consider yourself lucky. But by no means consider yourself judged. The masters impart their higher vision of things as guideposts. We are always left with freedom of choice, and they never judge our choices. However, their input serves to guide us away from behavior patterns that lead to difficulties so that we may more lightly tread the pathway home.

Sexuality is most wonderful and sacred. It is meant for two people to share in a loving and committed relationship. It should be kept within that sacred venue as a physical expression of God's love between a couple in love. Please don't let the negative ego, with all its unresolved issues, try to tell you that sex is anything less than this. In the same vein, do not let the negative ego make you ashamed of the sexual aspect of yourself. Sometimes lightworkers feel they are straying from the path even when they have sex with their mates. In extreme cases, certain lightworkers feel that the desire alone to have a mate or partner in life keeps them from honoring their union with God. This is simply not true.

Living together, loving together, sharing sexual intimacy as well as daily life with the proper person—all of these are some of God's greatest gifts to us. Again, this path will not apply to everyone, for each person is a path unto himself. However, the union between two people, when it also includes God, is a most wonderful thing. There is no way you can reach God except through your own inner ascension process, and there is no way that being in a relationship can keep you from the very path that you yourself *are*.

The only danger lies in getting sidetracked for a while and getting caught up with each other to the exclusion of your spiritual evolution. But that is something that we all have total control over. So by all means love, and love to the fullest. Simply keep your relationship with yourself and God first. If you continue your spiritual practices and include your partner in some joint spiritual practices, you will not be in any danger whatsoever of getting off track with your true intent and purpose of ascension and God-realization.

## The Traditional Way

The Hierarchy wants to emphasize that they by no means disapprove of the tradition of waiting until you are actually married to share sexual intimacy. In fact, this demonstrates a type of commitment and a view that the vital fluids are sacred, which is very rare in today's world. People who choose this path have already demonstrated a rare form of commitment and self-control. This is not at all discouraged, but looked upon with great admiration.

To those couples, what must be kept sacred, after the marriage has taken place, is the full commitment to their love. This will allow them to face the ups and downs of daily living without being thrown off balance once the daily challenges appear. The partners who have lived together before getting married have already faced the mundane, and they know what they are getting into to a greater degree. Those who wait until they are officially married before living together must be aware of the challenges that day-to-day life together will bring. This prenuptial awareness will help them avoid being overwhelmed by life together, and they can more easily take in stride the changes that come along.

Again, the more involved you become in the daily realities of each other's lives, the more quickly and easily you will be able to blend your lives. One example of this would be to be honest with your partner regarding your financial needs and how you use money. Don't try to disguise your spending habits, only to have these habits come as a big surprise, especially if you are an avid shopper! Another example is if you have a weekly night out with friends, and you want to keep this up after marriage. You need to discuss this with your partner to avoid any feelings of abandonment on his or her part.

The more you know about each other, the less room you will have for confusion and misunderstanding, and you will have a healthier start as newlyweds. This is really what the masters are saying when they say they are in favor of couples living together before a major commitment. In other words, the sooner things are out in the open between a couple, the better. This allows a more gradual adjustment and acceptance.

We need to be watchful not to enter into a marriage trying to maintain a pretense in *any* area. Honesty is not only the best policy, it is truly the *only* policy if a relationship is going to serve both people. To enter into a marriage while hiding certain parts of ourselves will surely lead to disaster. We each need the freedom to be who we are, and our partners deserve to know us as we are. If they cannot truly accept us, we need to give serious thought to whether or not they are the right partner for us. But neither of us can know this unless who and what we are is expressed and dealt with, and this goes for both partners.

At the other extreme, we don't want to get into a pattern of neurotic honesty in which there exists a faulty belief that everything must be shared and nothing is to be kept sacred (just between yourself and God). From the Hierarchy's point of view, in some cases certain things are better left unsaid. However, do not take this to an extreme, for open communication is the best policy.

Communication should unfold as the relationship progresses so that false illusions about ourselves are kept to a minimum. No doubt if we are starry-eyed in love, some illusions will remain in the earlier stages, but this head-over-heels-in-love factor is a great cushion with which to expose some of our quirks. Once the stars start to dim and the light of daily reality begins to dawn, the more we have shared with each other about ourselves, the better it will be. So begin open and honest communication at the earliest possible phase of your relationship. If you make this one of the foundations of your relationship, the healthier, happier and more securely lasting will be your partnership.

## Prenuptial Agreements

The subject of prenuptial agreements is quite complicated and multi-faceted, so I specifically asked the masters for their viewpoint. They do have a strong preference, and they proceeded to communicate this.

While they are not totally against prenuptial agreements, such agreements definitely are not their first choice. They said that this is because a prenuptial agreement is basically a predivorce agreement. Thus it carries within it the implied prophecy of eventual separation and an underlying attitude that speaks of a less-than-total commitment. The prenuptial agreement brings into the union of marriage an attitude of separateness. This can leave the person who has fewer material assets feeling that there is almost an inevitable likelihood of abandonment. It also leaves that person with the feeling that this agreement has been made because the other person is of more value simply because he or she is the one with more money and other material assets.

The Hierarchy would like to see people who join in marriage really love and care for one another and look upon that union as a holy union of two becoming one group body within the vaster body of God. From their perspective, the prenuptial agreement serves to reduce this spiritual union of souls into one based on possessions and separateness. Again, the very term "prenuptial agreement" presupposes separation and divorce rather than affirming commitment and unity. This is why the masters are not in favor of it.

They go on to say, however, that they understand the complexities within which we, as a race, are functioning in today's world. The fact is that there are many divorces, and all too often the worst comes out of people at these times. Although the masters are not in the habit of telling people what they should or should not do, they say that if partners feel more comfortable with this sort of agreement, they should follow their own inner guidance and needs. For some, it will indeed save much arguing in the eventuality of a divorce, and the less discord, the better. Also, sometimes these agreements relate to inheritance by children from previous unions, and clarity about this may be important in order to avoid future misunderstandings. The important thing is that couples enter into a union with whole-hearted love and commitment.

## The Hierarchy's View of Multiple Spouses

According to the Hierarchy, having one wife — or one husband, for that matter — is quite sufficient. In fact, they have gone on to paraphrase Jesus by stating, "The challenges of one romantic relationship is sufficient unto itself." They do want to address this point, because various cultures throughout the ages have allowed or urged males to have several wives at once.

They have said that during different times in history, this practice was thought of as a necessary practicality. This was sometimes the case when there was a shortage of men because large numbers of them had been killed in battle. Other cultures viewed polygamy as the most practical way to run a household. In many cultures this involved tending flocks and other things of similar nature.

Even in situations where this type of arrangement seemed to be the practical solution to many daily problems, it frequently created a constant energy of jealousy and competition among the wives — who was the favorite, who held the most power by virtue of being the eldest, who held the most appeal by virtue of being the youngest and most attractive, and so forth. This feeling among the wives was the same whether they were tending sheep or were part of the great dynasties that also practiced plural marriage. In the United States, the Mormons practiced polygamy openly until near the end of the nineteenth century. In 1890, the Mormon Church ordered that this practice cease.

Polygamy still exists today in certain cultures and in isolated situations in the United States. It is much more inappropriate today than in the past, for it is in direct conflict with the new energies of equality, balance and the manifestation of the mother principle on the Earth. We are moving away from the domination of patriarchal values into an era of balance between the masculine and feminine and an honoring of the mother. In addition, any plural marital arrangement is not the equal union of two people involved in a committed and loving relationship, but rather an indulgence of the negative egos of the men of that culture to the detriment of the women.

With all due respect to other cultures and the various needs that were present during certain periods of history, the masters tell me that it was in fact a matter of satisfying these needs from a male viewpoint only. In actuality, this practice allowed the negative-ego needs of a man to prevail and be indulged.

There is a related topic that the masters want to discuss, for it deals with a potentially very damaging situation. They wish to warn all lightworkers to be aware that similar situations are springing up in our midst. As most of you know, there is a certain type of spiritual leader who attempts to play on the feminine energy by convincing his female followers that they are divinely endowed. Such a leader further attempts to persuade every woman with whom he wants to have sex that she should feel honored and comply with his wishes with no hesitation whatsoever.

This, of course, is a gross distortion of the use of sacred energies, and is a manipulation of the most damaging nature. It is to be avoided at all costs, yet it is going on even as you are reading this book. It is more common than most of us might suspect. The masters wish to make you aware of these practices, as some of these leaders are so smooth in their approach that even advanced lightworkers can buy into their program before becoming aware of what is really going on. To be forewarned is to be forearmed, so make sure that you use your discernment when listening to anyone's teachings. Certainly when asked to participate in anything that feels the least bit suspicious to you, listen to that inner voice and retreat with haste.

Remember always that the ascension process involves integrity with ourselves first. Sometimes we are called on to be highly discriminating in order to know when our integrity is being infringed. Never do anything that goes against your grain. It is far wiser to err on the part of caution than to participate in something you are unsure of. This is equally applicable to men and women. We are all attempting to climb the heights, but we must also pay heed to the depths and to all possible pitfalls.

Any path that separates or fragments us from self or instills guilt or seeks to control is not sanctioned by the Hierarchy. The true path of ascension guides us to unity with self, and our true path calls us to maintain an attitude of utmost integrity and respect for every person. All else is manipulation and should be avoided like the plague!

## The Effect of AIDS and other Sexually Transmitted Diseases

Needless to say, the effect that AIDS has had on the way people interact sexually has been great indeed. While a part of the population seems to be living in a state of denial, the fact remains that with the introduction of the AIDS virus into our culture, there has been a vast swing away from the free-love attitude of the sixties and seventies. The attitude that sex was becoming more and more common, even for preteens, has given way to that of "I may be paying for this lovemaking with my very life."

This concern actually began with herpes, as people were told that there was no cure for it but only a possibility of controlling it to some degree. Caution then began. Herpes, and ultimately AIDS, turned the tide of the sexual revolution rather quickly, although there are still some who choose a state of denial. Yet fear and concern haunt everyone these days; even those who seem to deny it by their actions, hold that fear in their hearts.

From one important perspective, this causes us all to pause and reflect on the way we were indulging in sex in the not-too-distant past. Sex was never meant to be a source of casual diversion and entertainment, and this is now being driven home to us in a less-than-pleasant way. We were always meant to come back to this awareness, though not in such a harsh and deadly manner as the AIDS virus has done. I have dealt with the nature of AIDS in *Hidden Mysteries*, so I am not going to focus on that here. The point is that AIDS is a fact, and it is up to us what we do with that reality. We need to look at the lessons that can be learned from observing our responses both to AIDS and other sexually transmitted diseases.

The first aspect I would like to look at is the pendulum swing. What we had before the sexual revolution of the sixties and seventies was a sexually uptight and inhibited society. Even couples who were married and intimate on almost every other level often had a hard time being open about sexuality. Women were not encouraged to speak of their menstrual cycle, but were forced instead to come up with some coy and inappropriate phrase in order to convey to their partner that they were in their menstrual cycle and/or were experiencing pain as a result of it. PMS was considered to be "all in your head." So women were left alone, without anyone to discuss their "supposed" mental or emotional problems with.

Sex usually occurred only in the dark and was hardly ever discussed even between the most intimate of married couples, so it isn't hard to understand how, in that atmosphere of such extreme repression, the pendulum would take such a dramatic swing in the opposite direction. Hence, in the sixties and seventies we had the era of free love and all it entailed. Because pendulums, always seeking their point of greatest balance, will swing to and fro until that point of balance is found, the next great swing originated in our concern about sexually transmitted diseases, with herpes at the fore until AIDS made all other such diseases insignificant by comparison.

Now the pendulum is once again seeking a point of balance, so we must take the best of the lessons current situations and conditions can offer. I am not saying that AIDS is here by divine intent in order to teach us these lessons, but we may as well learn from what has manifested before us.

One point worth noting is that at first, humanity tried to use AIDS as a vehicle for further separation and discrimination. It was first blamed on the gay population because AIDS first took hold in the gay community. Some people even went so far as to say that homosexuals were being punished by God through this horrible disease. Of course, they did not realize at that point that AIDS is a disease of the blood, and the act of sex between two men made them more vulnerable to the transmission of this disease. The gay and lesbian community was attacked horribly and quite unjustly — an attack that attempted to keep "them" separate from "us."

Then AIDS was found to be more in evidence in the black and poorer communities, and we had yet another them versus us type of situation. I am left wondering how long humanity as a whole will continue looking for scapegoats instead of realizing that humanity is all one whole.

Eventually, of course, it was learned that AIDS, though sexually transmitted, can also be transmitted through infected blood. The ultimate effect, though, was to make everyone aware that there are no scapegoats and that humanity as a whole must deal with this disease together. This, the Hierarchy states, is a far better situation than if AIDS were confined to certain portions of the population, for it has helped bring people together.

People once again are being forced to look at the specialness of sex and the intimacy it is meant to express between two loving, caring and committed people. However, this also brings up the question of just how committed we are and how important a role intercourse has when compared to the unconditional expression of love itself.

I often wonder at the dilemma that two people find themselves in when one partner is diagnosed with AIDS, not as the result of cheating but from a previous relationship or a transfusion of infected blood. What happens to the love that has been shared between them and to the commitment? Because there is so much fear surrounding the terrible effects of AIDS, only the strongest and most soul/monadic-based relationships are able to survive this extreme test. It is one of the hardest tests of our times, yet viewed through the soul/monadic lens, it can be one of our greatest opportunities.

By no means am I saying this with a cavalier attitude. The stamina and level of love and commitment *must* be strong if one is to see one's mate through a positive HIV diagnosis, yet a great opportunity is there. Quite often the illness itself will take years to manifest, if at all, and there are various alternative health treatments that can outwit its manifestation altogether. But one must be utterly and totally committed, because one's basic instinct is to run from danger or what one perceives as potential danger.

I am not advising anyone to follow anything other than their own inner guidance, but I would suggest that we take time in meditation to see just what our highest and clearest guidance is. It is most important in any challenging situation that we do not simply react. So take time to connect in meditation with your soul and monad; journal and commune with the various aspects of yourself, the masters and God before taking any action. This guidance is for all extreme situations, for the question is ultimately the same: "Will I react out of my fear-based negative ego, or will I act from the love and wisdom of my own I Am Presence?"

In regard to AIDS, all of us can go within and see where we are still reacting with fear and prejudice, then work to replace this with love, wisdom and compassion. If we use each situation to learn, to grow in awareness and understanding and to reach toward God for our decisions, everything can support the outworking of the divine plan. If we have the strength and courage to ask what can be learned here and what is for the highest good in this situation, then everything serves as our teacher and propels us upward on our path of ascension. This is my prayer for us all.

## Celibacy and Marriage

The masters recently told me that there are rare cases in which celibate marriages are appropriate. This is not for the average initiate or even for most people who have passed their seventh initiation while in body, but it does have a place among the few.

One such example is the case of Lahiri Mahasaya, who was very advanced spiritually. He was a direct disciple of Babaji and was instrumental in the founding of the Self-Realization Fellowship. Yogananda, in *Autobiography of a Yogi*, relates how one night Mahasaya's wife awoke to find him levitating in a corner of their room. After that she called him her guru and became an official disciple of kriya yoga and the teachings Mahasaya imparted. It is obvious that this was not a typical marriage. The two of them lived lives of such devotion to God that sex simply was not part of their focus.

However, this is not commonplace and is not recommended. Certainly one partner should never try to enforce this, because the other would feel rejected and would miss the special bond of sexual intimacy. But, because the spiritual acceleration is so great at this time, what happened in the case of Lahiri Mahasaya might well happen to other couples. If you are in a committed relationship and this shift honestly takes place within *both* of you, then by all means follow that energy. But this by no means implies that you are taking the vow of celibacy for a lifetime. You are simply honoring certain frequencies at that time.

In this instance, the Hierarchy's advice to married couples about having sex at least once a month would obviously not apply. Some couples might even find that they desire to marry with the understanding that a basically celibate relationship is to ensue. An initial physical bonding is recommended even here, but of course each couple must decide what is right for them. The times are bringing forth such rapid development that the Hierarchy foresees an increase in celibate marriages.

The masters wish to reiterate that this is not something either to seek out or to strive for but something that might arise out of the combination of various frequencies functioning at this particular time. The couple must also be open-minded about shifting to a more normal relationship if the energies shift back again. This must be agreed on in advance by both partners. The masters felt that it was important to mention this so that if you belong to this rare group of couples, you need not think anything is wrong with you.

It is important that a decision to be celibate does not come out of a psychological disturbance, wherein celibacy is used as an excuse to avoid facing sexual issues. Although celibacy is not the goal of any aspect of the ascension process, it might be the effect of certain energies at play. If there is a committed love between the couple and a joint appreciation of the unique process at hand, there is no need for the couple to refrain from honoring this unique and rare calling.

## Releasing All Judgments

We have been dealing with extremely sensitive topics, and it is important not to feel any guilt or shame over past or present actions. It is equally important that you do not pass even the subtlest judgment on your partner. One of the subjects we have discussed at length was the importance of being faithful to one's partner and not engaging in affairs on any level. However, perhaps you have been involved in an affair or even now find yourself caught in that dilemma. It is important that you do not drag yourself down with feelings of shame and guilt. What we are attempting to convey, with this and other topics, is the *ideal* toward which to move in order to live a life in harmony with oneself and God.

We have pointed out the pitfalls of having an affair and have given guidelines that can stop this process before it has the power to engulf you. But if out of confusion or loneliness within your relationship you have found that having affairs has brought you solace of some sort, all we ask you to do is to look at healthier, more productive ways to handle things. Please do not compound an already complex situation with feelings of guilt and shame. Compassion and forgiveness of oneself and others are key attributes for progress upon the path of ascension.

There might have been certain other periods in your life when you felt outside the mainstream and confused about your heightened sensitivities. You might have frequented bars in an attempt to escape the depth of feelings and energies you were connecting with but did not understand. Many masters in the making have little understanding of the process or nature of the spiritual path. Some might be found sitting alone in a bar, searching for answers or a way to numb certain energy frequencies. It is important that you release all judgments of yourself for such actions. It is also important to let go of condemning yourself for times when you have judged, or were prejudiced against, certain individuals or groups.

There are many phases and ways of dealing with things that we go through on our path homeward. At each step we need to learn the lessons from the situation, be willing to move forward and hold an attitude of total compassion and forgiveness. As Yogananda once said, "A saint is a sinner who never gave up."

All of us have our own points of weakness and our areas of strength, so we need great compassion for both ourselves and our partners. If your partner is stuck in a place that seems obviously limiting to you, simply be there to support him or her so that she can more easily get beyond that stage. Mistakes are part of the learning process and are to be expected. In fact, what might be a mistake for one person could well be the school of accelerated learning for another. We must learn to let go of all judgments as we continue on our paths of evolution and ascension into the light.

# 12

## *The Golden Keys to Effective Romantic Relationships*

The last chapter in this book is meant to synthesize and summarize what I consider to be the 166 golden keys to effective romantic relationships. This chapter might be considered "the Cliff notes of romantic relationships" from the perspective of the soul, monad and Spiritual Hierarchy. Here are reviewed a number of the major keys from throughout the book for making your relationship work, and additional "golden nuggets" have been added. In this chapter I attempt to condense this vast subject into an easy-to-read and practical compendium.

### 1. Unconditional Love

Personality-level relationships function on a premise of conditional love. Soul and monadic level romantic relationships strive to be unconditionally loving at all times. From the perspective of the soul and monad, it is never acceptable to attack your partner. It is important to be honest, but this is always done in an unconditionally loving and respectful manner no matter how bad the misbehavior of your partner is. In truth, each person is the eternal Self, and all ideally are related to from this vantage point.

### 2. Relationship to Self and to God

The most important relationship in your life is not your relationship to your spouse or partner, your children, the ascended masters or God. The single most important factor in your life for making your relationships work is your relationship to *yourself*. If you are wrong with yourself, you will be wrong with God and your partner. If you are run by your emotional body, your inner child, your negative ego and your subconscious mind, how can you possibly be right with another person?

In my counseling practice of over 15 years, whenever I would see a couple for relationship counseling, I would see them together only once. Then I would do individual work to get them right with themselves before I would see them together again. In my professional experience, 80 percent of the problems were cleared up by getting each person into their personal power, self-mastery, self-love, proper parenting of their inner child and the conscious creating of their own reality. The second most important relationship in your life is your relationship to God. If these two relationships aren't right, your romantic relationship will have problems.

## 3. Forgiveness.

This includes self-forgiveness and forgiveness of your partner. Jesus said, "Do unto others as you would have others do unto you," As *A Course in Miracles* says, "Forgiveness is the key to happiness." Lack of forgiveness hurts self much more than it hurts others. Everything that happens in life is a lesson, a challenge and an opportunity to grow. Mistakes can be turned into gold by learning from them!

## 4. Preferences, Not Attachments

Learn to have preferences instead of attachments and addictions in your relationships. Buddha said that all suffering comes from your attachments. A preference is the attitude that if you don't get what you seek, you are still happy. With attachments and addictions, if you don't get what you want, you lose your happiness and inner peace and usually you get upset and angry. These negative emotions are caused by one's own faulty attitude.

## 5. Self-Actualization

Learn to develop centered, whole relationships and not father/daughter, mother/son relationships. When each one is right with self and right with God, the couple bonds as two self-actualized, independent people. When one is not right with oneself or right with God, one ends up seeking wholeness in another person instead of within one's own being. There is no judgment in this, for we have all done this in past lives and this life. All is forgiven, but as one evolves, one's romantic relationships need to change.

## 6. Communication

What may be the most important key of all is communication. Virginia Satir, the famous marriage/family counselor, said, "Communication is to a relationship what breathing is to living." It can't get much clearer than that! Where the lines of communication are not open, the relationship is doomed to failure. When the lines of communication *are* open, anything can be worked out. People who communicate effectively make mountains into molehills. People who don't communicate effectively make molehills into mountains!

## 7. Commitment

Being committed is keeping one's spiritual vows to your partner on all levels. It is also a commitment to communicate when things are bothering you and not to stuff things away. Commitment deals with holding up your end of the partnership on all levels. It is a commitment to love and help your partner as well as yourself to become actualized to your highest potentials.

### 8.  The Need to Be Right

The key question is always, "Do you want harmony, or do you want to be right?" You cannot have both. The need to be right is run by the negative ego. Set the example of admitting you are wrong and have made mistakes. This example will inspire your partner to do the same, and even if it doesn't, you are doing it for yourself and God anyway. Never forget that God and the ascended masters listen to your every word! This is especially true of high-level disciples and initiates.

### 9.  Communicating through Ego

Never communicate when you are caught up by your negative ego or in excessive anger. Make this agreement with your partner. When the negative ego is engaged, you are not right with yourself or right with God. In this mode, communication will only end up hurting and scarring your partner. You will end up feeling guilty later for what you said when you were too overidentified with your emotional body. It would be better to go off by yourself and cool down, meditate and journal.

It is always better to communicate about heavy things in a calm, rational, loving manner. When I started doing this in my relationship, we were able to improve our relationship as much as 80 percent from this simple insight. Usually when we would come back and communicate after cooling down, we would resolve things in short order. We would both set a spiritual example upon resuming communication, for we would both realize that we were off center, and this would inspire both of us to be as Christ-like as possible.

### 10. Anger

Anger is ego, and don't be deluded into thinking it isn't. When your buttons get pushed and anger arises, it can be dealt with in your relationship in one of two ways. One is intrapsychically and one is extrapsychically. The intrapsychic method is to resolve the issue in your mind or journal and/or do attitudinal healing work. Catharsis on occasion may be also appropriate.

The extrapsychic method is to express and communicate your feelings to your partner, but this must be done in a loving way. There is no such thing as righteous anger. The negative ego will tell you there is, but there is not. The true definition of anger is "loss of control and an attempt to regain it." Negative anger is transformed into positive anger by using it as an energy source channeled in a proper direction. Tough love and being a spiritual warrior is one example. Energy is transformed in a positive direction.

### 11. Primary vs. Secondary Communication

Primary communication is where you communicate from a state of absolute egolessness. Secondary communication, which is also an essential tool to have at your disposal, is to communicate your negative emotions, which are triggered by the negative ego, in a loving way. We all have to use this secondary communication method at times, for no one on this planet is clear all the time. The third form of communication, which is the wrong one, is to take out your negative emotions on another person. If you find yourself doing this, major work on yourself is needed.

### 12. Arguments

Arguing is a manifestation of the negative ego and should be stopped the second it starts. It is much more important in life to maintain oneness and love. The question here is, "Do you want to argue, or do you want oneness?"

### 13. The Difference between Spiritual Discernment, Observation, Judgment and Criticism

It is never appropriate to judge or criticize your partner — or anyone else, for that matter. It is fine and necessary to have observations and spiritual discernments, for they are loving. Judgment and criticism are not. It is not meant that you should not see or think. The key is in having an observation or spiritual discernment about your partner and knowing whether or not to share it.

One of the most important keys in a relationship is knowing when to talk and when to be silent. You are not your partner's guru or spiritual teacher. It is much more important for you to be concerned with learning your own lessons than being concerned with your partner's. When it is appropriate to share some feedback with your partner, you can say something like, "Honey, I have an observation and spiritual discernment I would like to share with you if you are open to hearing it." If they don't want to hear it, then keep your mouth shut.

It was a big relief to me when I realized that I didn't have to be my wife's teacher. Being a psychologist and spiritual teacher, I see a great many things, but I don't need to share everything. When it is appropriate to share, say it once and then let it go. We all know that nagging and harping do not work.

### 14. Timing

The inner child wants to express everything instantly, for it wants instant gratification and instant release. This is not always the best move and can lead to disastrous consequences. Every communication should be expressed in the proper tao, or moment. The same communication expressed in the same way can produce positive or negative results, depending on whether the proper timing was taken into consideration.

### 15. Honesty

Spiritual honesty in a mature form is different than inner-child honesty. A child may blurt out everything with no self-control or discernment. This can be hurtful and inappropriate. Many people think that this is what honesty means. This is not honesty; it is oral diarrhea. Spiritual honesty, in its mature form, is communicating what is appropriate in a loving, respectful manner. Some things in life are better left unsaid. Some things are between oneself and God. Some things are better dealt with in your journal. Go within and soul-search as to what your true motivation is for wanting to say something.

### 16. Praying for Help

When you pray to God, the Holy Spirit, Sai Baba and/or the ascended masters for help in your relationship when things are going wrong or you are at an impasse, God and the God force can undo energetically a lot of blocks and help move things along.

### 17. When Divorce is the Answer

Divorce is not always a bad thing. Sometimes it is the right choice. Many times in my counseling practice, my function has been to help people get divorced rather than bring them back together. One should not leave a relationship too soon, but neither should one hang on long past the time when it no longer serves those involved. Life is too precious. But the other key here is never to leave a relationship until you learn its lessons. Otherwise you are destined to repeat the same lessons with a new partner!

### 18. Putting Your Spiritual Path First

So often in my counseling practice I would see very spiritual people get involved in new relationships, get comfortable in their relationship and discontinue their focus on their spiritual development. They were very committed to the spiritual path as long as they were single, but somehow when they got into a relationship they began to let go of it. We must all put our relationship on the altar before God and our spiritual path. If we don't, life will bring us challenges in an attempt to get us to straighten out our misaligned priorities.

### 19. Invulnerability

This is one of the most important qualities to develop to make your relationship work. It is the understanding that you create your own reality and your own emotions. Neither your partner nor anyone else causes these. Just because you are married or in a committed relationship doesn't mean that the relationship or marriage causes your emotions. The development of invulnerability means that no outside person or situation can take away your inner peace and joy unless you choose to allow this to happen.

Every person is emotionally vulnerable in this regard. We must each develop a strong psychological immune system. In actuality, there is no such thing as a contagious physical disease; there are only people with low physical resistance. The same is true on the psychological level. When your partner is irritable, moody or angry, you don't have to take on his or her emotional state. Have compassion but do not allow yourself to absorb his emotions. Your job is to stay centered and help bring your partner up, rather than allow him to bring you down.

The same applies to feelings of sadness, depression and grief. You can try to help where this is appropriate. But these are your partner's emotions, not yours. When it is aimed at you, you can choose to practice humility and turn the other cheek. Or you can communicate your spiritual observations to your partner in a loving way and your preference that they not do this. As *A Course in Miracles* says, "An attack is a call for love." Defensiveness and retaliation are not appropriate responses. The ideal romantic relationship deals with the transcendence of negative ego.

## 20. Maintaining the Romance

There is a common belief that there is an inevitable loss of romance in all marriages. I am here to say that this is not true. The romance, the passion, the spark, can be kept going indefinitely. However, to achieve this takes conscious work so that bad habits are not allowed to grow like weeds in your relationship garden. When issues of having children, money pressures or job pressures enter in, even more consciousness is needed so that the spark of romance is not diminished.

In a relationship, it is often the little things that make all the difference, such as writing little loving notes, making a loving phone call, bringing flowers or buying a little gift for no special reason, and creating special times for romantic intimacy. In my relationship we created a date night that we always kept. We might meditate together or go for a walk together.

Creating a time once a week for taking care of business, both personal and work-related, works well. To maintain romance, one must become a master of priorities and time management. In the busy life of modern society, all lessons of life must be appropriately balanced. The romance factor must not be put on the bottom of the priority list.

## 21. Sexuality

This is quite a complex issue, and in *Soul Psychology* I have attempted to address it in great detail. What is crucial here is to create the time for this important part of your relationship. Each couple will differ in terms of what this means. Higher-level initiates may not have sexual relationships as often as younger disciples, although there is no hard and fast rule. Ascending couples may be interested in tantric sexuality for the purposes of enjoyment and raising the sexual energy. With tantric sex, the couple uses sexual involvement as a type of meditation.

Couples must find a selfish/selfless balance in terms of the sexual relationship so that both partners' needs are met. Both must ask for what they want and be willing to teach their partner. Often relationships get into sexual habits and ruts that become rather unexciting after a while, and both parties must be willing to experiment a little and, perhaps, take chances. It is essential that both parties be willing to initiate sexual involvement, for this should not be only the man's job. Both partners should try to serve one another's needs first while enjoying the sexual interaction. Communication in this area, as in all areas of life, is the key.

During one phase of my life when sexual expression was not much of a priority and I was more interested in raising the energy, I asked Djwhal Khul's opinion about this. He said this was often the case with couples on the path of ascension, and that this was okay. But he said that couples should not go more than three months without sexual contact, for there is a certain kind of bonding and connection that needs to be maintained.

I am not saying that couples should not have sex as much as they want. I am trying to show here an extreme in couples who are not sexually focused. With sexuality, as with all things, balance, moderation and integration in other areas of one's life must be maintained. It is another form of communication and an expression of love. Sexual expression is appropriate when it serves the higher self and not the lower or carnal self. Sexuality is appropriate when it is loving, supportive and pleasurable to both partners. Sexuality is appropriate in terms of that which creates intimacy and love.

## 22. Finding Your Mate

The key to finding a spiritual, romantic relationship, a twin flame or a soulmate in this regard is to not *need* one and to be perfectly happy and whole in your relationship to yourself and God. The second key here is to pray to God and the masters for help in making this happen. The third key is to put one's entire energies into one's spiritual path and service work. Surrender your prayer into God's hands. Just forget about it and know that it will manifest when the time is right.

Your total commitment to God, your spiritual path and your service work will attract a spiritual mate who has an equal commitment in his or her own life. This will show up when the time is right. Your prayer preference has been stated, and if it is meant to be, it will happen. If it isn't meant to be, then you will be so happy and fulfilled in your relationship to your higher self, God, the masters and your service work that it will not matter. There are some on the spiritual path who do much better being single, which is much better than being with the wrong person. I think you can all agree.

### 23. Ending a Relationship

You should never end a relationship until you have learned the lessons of that relationship. Otherwise you are destined to relive the same lessons in a new relationship. It is also essential that we on the spiritual path work out our relationship issues with our parents and all past relationships. Otherwise these relationships will be projected onto our current relationship.

### 24. Balance in Selfishness/Selflessness

The issue of maintaining an appropriate selfish/selfless balance is a very important lesson in relationships. Women often tend to be too selfless, although this can also be true of men. This lesson speaks to the importance of having appropriate boundaries and knowing how to say no and not feel guilty. It also speaks to knowing how to say yes decisively and not feel resentful. In every relationship there is a time to be spiritually self*ish* and a time to be spiritually self*less* and a time for compromise. There is a time to look at the intensity of the feelings of both partners and make decisions that take this important factor into account. Awareness and balance are the keys.

### 25. Balance in Self-Identity and Couple Identity

Each person has an independent identity. In a couple relationship, there is also a group body formed on the etheric, emotional, mental and spiritual level. This is why your partner's suffering is as much a concern to you as your own. It is important to avoid symbiosis and codependency. One should not take on the pain of the other, but compassion and concern are natural and appropriate responses. The act of getting married is the commitment to this bond. The key is to maintain a balance where you are neither too independent or too immersed in the group body.

### 26. Complementation

Complementation is different from codependent, father/daughter or mother/son relationships. Every person has strengths and weaknesses. When two people come together, it is usually because they are totally alike or totally different and therefore they complement each other well. This can apply to certain sun signs or certain types of ray configurations. It applies to one being more of a mystic and the other being more of an occultist. It applies to one being more of a mental type and the other more of an emotional type. Maybe one operates more from the heart and the other the third eye. These types of complements are wonderful.

One person might be more socially adept and the other a better meditator. One person may be more right brained and the other more left brained. One may access information more through listening and the other through seeing. The list of possibilities is endless. It is important to become aware of how you and your partner complement each other, This creates richness and a greater wholeness in life. Your partner becomes your teacher. The goal is for each partner to integrate what the other has to offer. Relationships that are opposite in nature are sometimes more difficult, but they also offer enormous opportunities for spiritual growth.

### 27. Relationship as Spiritual Training

Romantic relationships are the ultimate teachers for spiritual growth and self-realization. There is no better way to become self-realized than to be in a marriage and/or committed romantic relationship. The romantic relationship is guaranteed to bring up all, and I mean all, of your stuff. Any dysfunctional pattern or complex in your subconscious mind that is not apparent is guaranteed to be triggered. Anyone can be spiritual living in a cave, in a monastery or in the Himalayas. The true test of being spiritual is living in the marketplace. If you can practice the presence of God in your romantic relationship, you can do it anywhere. Romantic relationships are the ultimate teaching tool if you use them in that way.

As I look back over my relationship history, I see each woman I was involved with as a spiritual training course, as was I for them. I have always used my relationships for this purpose, and I mean this in a very positive sense. Each partner had different spiritual gifts, which I took advantage of for spiritual growth. And I functioned in a similar manner for them. Even when these relationships ended, we both felt good about each other, for we appreciated what we had gained.

Each romantic relationship or friendship helps bring to the surface certain disowned selves that we need to own. These might be called undeveloped parts of ourselves. If, in every relationship and friendship, these are owned and integrated through allowing oneself to learn from that person, over time enormous wholeness is achieved. This is also why those with a diverse relationship history have the opportunity for great learning and growth. Each relationship and friendship is like a spiritual workshop. There is also much spiritual growth and beauty that comes from being with one person for a whole lifetime. One is not better than another; it is just a matter of learning from the life experiences and destiny that unfold for us.

### 28. Trust

Trust is a key component of every healthy relationship. If trust is broken in a relationship, the chances of that relationship working are greatly decreased. This is why issues such as adultery are so serious. Having an affair breaks the bond of trust, and it is often impossible to get it back.

In my counseling practice, I have sometimes been able to patch relationships back together by the use of a relationship contract. It is like a new set of personal and spiritual vows, with God and the masters serving as witnesses when appropriate. The spiritual contract serves as a vehicle to reestablish the trust factor. New commitments are written out on paper. In reality it is like a new spiritual marriage contract.

### 29. Understanding Your Types

I have spoken of the four-body system in regard to relationships in which one is the emotional type and the other the more mental type. This can also be seen in the heavenly and earthly balance. Usually one person is a little more heavenly, spiritual or etheric and the other more grounded and earthy. This, of course, encompasses the fire, air, Earth and water types, or mental, emotional, intuitive and sensation function type. It is a helpful exercise to look at your type and tendency and then see your partner's. It is extremely important not to get locked into your particular lens and to be open to learning from your partner's lens. The ideal is to strive for the greatest possible sense of wholeness. This is a great strength, and it increases in magnitude when having a partner. There is a greater sense of wholeness present when our relationship tendencies are understood and integrated with our partner's. Over time both partners become more whole in the process.

### 30. Ego Battles

What do you do when ego battles take place? This occurs in every relationship at times, and no one should be ashamed of this. I have found one tool to be extremely effective. We would sit down on the sofa and do a short meditation to connect with our monads. We would hold hands and do this and totally connect to spirit. Then we would begin talking from our connection to this higher place.

Another method would be to read some passages from sacred scriptures. The attainment of spirit is what helps transcend the negative ego. One might also call in the Holy Spirit for help, for the Holy Spirit is the answer to all delusions of the negative ego. I cannot recommend these techniques more strongly. Whenever something heavy or difficult would come up, we would both do this. In less difficult discussions it would not be necessary. We saved it for the heavier processing.

### 31. Staying Current

Don't let things build up too much. It must be understood here that it is possible to communicate too little, and it is also possible to communicate too much. I have seen some couples who spend all their time processing.

They don't know how to let go of things and have fun. Sometimes simply enjoying each other is the best medicine. The reverse of this is holding things in too much, which then causes what I call the Mt. Vesuvius method of communication—the volcanic eruption. Couples need to learn to stay on top of things.

One time I asked my grandparents, who had been married for over 50 years, what their secret was for their lasting marriage. My grandmother said something I thought was extremely wise. She said that the key to the success in their marriage was that she would never allow herself and my grandfather to go to bed angry. She would always force communication to clear things before they went to sleep. This is a good piece of wisdom for us all. The issue of staying current in your communication is like weeding your garden every day instead of waiting to do it once a week or once a month.

## 32. Feedback

Feedback should only be given if it is asked for. It is not your job to point out all of your partner's lessons. In my relationships, I would see my partner, for example, eating foods that were not good for her, or in bad combinations, which went against my beliefs. It might have been appropriate to mention this one time, but after that, my lesson was to keep my mouth shut. It was none of my business. In reverse, there were certain pieces of feedback I was not interested in hearing from my wife. Once was okay, maybe even twice, but after that I did not want to hear it anymore.

It is very important that both partners understand and respect this right. The same is true on the psychological level. I would see a great many things going on, but I am not my wife's counselor and she is not mine. Even though I am a psychologist and spiritual teacher by trade, I did not feel a need to be this in my relationships, which made the relationships work much better. I see many lightworkers who often cannot make this separation. Lightworkers should be much more concerned with working on themselves than working on their partners.

## 33. The Homemaker Role

The homemaker in a relationship is usually the woman, but sometimes these roles are reversed. It must be understood from a spiritual perspective that being a homemaker and/or raising children is one of the most noble of all professions. The woman, in truth, is the guru and spiritual teacher for the children. What can be more noble than this? Everything is energy, and one profession or form of work is no better than another. In every relationship there must be an equal exchange. How this is worked out does not matter, but each person must carry his or her weight.

### 34. Independent Activities

It is very important in every relationship that both partners have independent lives apart from each other. It is true that sometimes a little absence makes the heart grow fonder. There is danger in becoming too symbiotic, or joined at the hip. In a mature relationship, it is totally permissible and appropriate for each person to have separate friends with whom they spend time. There are friends you see together and friends you see separately. There are some spiritual practices you might do together and some you do separately. It is very important to allow this space in a balanced way.

### 35. Self-Worth

A feeling of self-worth is essential in a relationship. If you do not love yourself and allow yourself to receive love from God, then you will seek it from your partner and other people. This will create neediness, victim consciousness and a smothering of the other person. We have all heard it said that we cannot love others if we do not love ourselves. The same applies to self-worth. If you don't get it from within yourself, you will be driven to find constant approval from other people, including your partner. But if you don't feel worthy inside, no amount of external recognition can fill the void.

### 36. Counseling

If you are having serious problems, seek professional help. If you have plumbing problems, you call a plumber. If you can't find a library book, ask the librarian for help. If you have electrical problems, you call an electrician. If you are having marriage problems, go see a marriage counselor. This is an act of strength, not an act of weakness. Sometimes a third objective party is needed to facilitate getting through a certain block.

### 37. Praying for Your Partner

What do you do when your partner won't take feedback on some very important issue? What I recommend is to pray about it and put it into God's hands. It is also possible to do affirmations for your partner as well as visualizations or treatments for them without their knowledge. I have also recommended this in the case where one partner was very spiritual and the other wasn't. Outer-plane work was not appropriate, but inner-plane work was. Patience, persistent effort and nonattachment can often bring great dividends.

### 38. A Nonspiritual Mate

What do you do if your partner is not spiritual? This might sound like a strange statement to those who could not imagine being in a relationship with a nonspiritual partner. I could never do this myself, but there are many lightworkers who find themselves in this situation. My answer here might surprise you. I do not necessarily recommend breaking up. This is a choice each person must make. Sometimes the person, usually the man, is providing material and financial contribution that is very important to the overall picture, and this should not be immediately thrown out as unimportant.

It is not essential for all people to be involved with their twin flame or soulmate. People can seek soulmate relationships with friends to fill this need. Understand that even if you found a soulmate or twin flame, it doesn't mean that you would get along with the person on a personality level. You might be totally connected on a spiritual level, but sometimes more-spiritual mates do not have their acts together on a financial and practical level, which can create many problems. I am not recommending seeking nonspiritual relationships but simply saying that the whole picture must be considered.

### 39. Seeing the Best

It is of the highest importance in your relationship to be a love-finder and not a faultfinder. This is similar to being optimistic instead of pessimistic. What you see is governed by your thinking and interpretation and is not necessarily the truth. We see through the lens of the programming from all our past lives and this life. Seek to see the best in your partner. Seek to build up your partner. You will see what you look for, and what you focus on is what you will see.

### 40. Homosexuality

As I have stated, from the perspective of the ascended masters, there is absolutely no judgment regarding homosexuality. What Gods looks at is the quality of the relationship and the level of love that exists. Everything I am saying in this book is applicable to *all* relationships.

### 41. Harmlessness

Cultivate the quality of harmlessness. It is important to set the example that no matter what happens, no matter how serious a mistake your partner makes, you will be unceasingly harmless in your response. Mistakes need to be forgiven. Mistakes must be dealt with honestly, but not in a way that attacks the person.

### 42. Setting an Example

In my past relationships, I would always try to set a Christ-like example when fights or ego battles would occur. In most of my relationships, this would inspire my partner to follow suit. Often my partner's example would also inspire me to be as God-like as possible. This give and take could become very inspiring and would set a precedent for the entire relationship that was both fulfilling and exhilarating.

I have been in some long-term relationships in which the person I was with was not quite as clear, and she would stay stuck in her ego and not fol-

low suit. As long as I was in this relationship I took the approach of not caring, for all that was truly important to me was that I stayed right with myself
and right with God. If my partner wasn't willing to take full Christ-like responsibility, then this was her karma and was something she would have to
work out between herself and God. This gets back again to the importance
of focusing on your own lessons above all else. This last example, if not corrected over time, will probably lead to the ending of that relationship.

### 43. Differences of Opinion

Differing opinions and perceptions are inevitable and appropriate in all
relationships. Even the ascended masters in their council meetings don't
always agree, although consensus is ultimately achieved. Everyone thinks
differently, so of course relationship partners will have different perceptions at times. It would be boring if this weren't so. When this happens in
your relationship, it is important to honor your partner's opinion and perception as well as your own. The key is to agree to disagree without creating
any separation.

When the negative ego is involved, differences of opinion lead to arguments and separation. Make it okay for you not to be clones of each other.
This leads to a win-win in all situations, never a win-lose. It leads to an "I'm
okay, you're okay" philosophy and a philosophy of diversity within unity.
The attitude in your relationship should be love and oneness at all times. In
reality, the whole purpose of the relationship has been to serve as a forum in
which to practice staying in love and oneness. It has been a forum set up by
God to test your abilities to remain in Christ consciousness rather than negative-ego consciousness.

### 44. Listening

It is absolutely essential to learn to listen to your partner before needing to come up with your own opinions and thoughts on the issues you are
dealing with. The lesson here is truly to listen and hear what your partner
has to say. Listening has a lot to do with caring. Never forget that your partner is God visiting you in physical form. Aren't you interested in what God
has to say? You are also God visiting your partner in physical form, and that
is why you need to be true to yourself. This is why you must listen and have
compassion as well as follow the adage, "Above all else, to thine own self be
true."

### 45. Bad Moods

If you don't have anything positive to say, don't say anything. If you are
in a bad mood, explain this to your partner and try not to take it out on
him/her. If you are not right with yourself, take some space. If you want help
from your partner, ask for what you want, be it a hug, being held or what-

ever. I will say here also that PMS is not a legitimate excuse for being moody or bitchy. It is true that the hormones and emotions are kicked up at this time, so more mastery is needed. We are each God and not victims of anything. If I offered you a million dollars to remain in a good mood for two days, you could do it. I am not saying it would be easy, but you could do it if you were motivated enough and/or your life depended on it.

### 46. The Opposite Sex

From the point of view of a high-level initiate, there is nothing wrong with enjoying the beauty of the opposite sex on a physical level as long as the soul is seen also. Each man and woman is a God and Goddess. The spirit should be acknowledged first, and then the physical beauty can be enjoyed and appreciated. Seeing spirit first is the great equalizer. It keeps the heart and crown open. It acknowledges each person as God regardless of the attractiveness or unattractiveness of the physical vehicle.

It is important not to lust after another or commit adultery mentally, for it is as bad to think it as to do it. From a spiritual orientation, sexual fantasy must be watched and monitored very closely, for as you know, everything we think and visualize affects the other person. The higher you go in your initiation process, the more powerful is the effect of your thinking and visualizing. To commit adultery in your mind is not right. Consistency of commitment must be maintained on all levels: physical, emotional, mental and spiritual. Djwhal Khul has said that pornography is of the lower self and negative ego, and as you evolve, it is transcended.

### 47. The Sexual Bond

Understand that every sexual union and sharing of fluids between two people creates a bond for life that cannot be broken. It can be broken in a psychological sense, but not in a spiritual sense. The sharing of fluids in this matter creates a cord of energy that connects you with that person. This is one of the reasons why the masters teach the example of creating sacredness in the expression of sexuality. Do you really want etheric telephone lines with thousands of people?

But do not judge yourself about this. The lesson is to be such a light in this world that your light will not allow you to be victimized by these cords, but rather uplift all others with whom you are connected, even if you never physically see them.

### 48. Jealousy

Jealousy stems from not being right with oneself. It stems from the contamination of insecurity within oneself, which leads to feelings of ownership of another and competition with known or unknown competitors. It also demonstrates a lack of trust. Jealousy is a psychological cancer and should be exterminated. It does not exist in people who bond completely from the Christ consciousness. There is no judgment if it arises; it is simply a sign that attitudinal healing is needed within oneself and in the relationship.

### 49. Letting Go

"Love develops from letting go, not from holding on." Holding too tightly to love kills it. Preferences should be stated and then let go of. If something is meant to be, it will come back to you, and if it is not meant to be, then let it go. A bond based on this truth is the most powerful and long-lasting, for it is free of all coercion.

### 50. Understanding Your Purpose in Relationship

Understand why you get involved in a romantic relationship in the first place. The true spiritual reasons to become romantically bonded are to share love, to accelerate your spiritual growth and to have more joy on your spiritual path. This is not to say that single people cannot have equal joy, but most people are more the bonding type. Yet I would certainly have to say that beings such as Jesus, Paramahansa Yogananda and Sai Baba were or are quite joyous on their own.

### 51. Loneliness vs. Being Alone

Understand the difference between loneliness and being alone. Loneliness develops when one is not right with oneself and God, so that one seeks wholeness outside oneself. Being alone can be a very exhilarating state of being. This is not to say that the single person may not at times have a preference to be with people. But this is a *preference*, not an attachment or addiction. If it is a need, attachment or addiction, it will manifest in feelings of loneliness. The single person who is right with self, who enjoys his/her own company and is one with God, is never alone.

### 52. Defensiveness

There is the need for both partners to let go of ego sensitivity. There are two levels to this lesson. One is to let go of hypersensitivity in general and learn to let things roll off like water off a duck's back. This is learning to respond instead of react. The second part of this lesson deals with each person learning to develop a strong sense of self in terms of personal power, self-love, self-worth and self-concept, so that the negative ego does not interpret things as rejection and hurt when none has been intended.

People who are very ego sensitive will get defensive and insulted by just about anything you say to them no matter how lovingly it is presented. Those who are very ego sensitive need to be communicated to with extra love until they can transcend this character flaw. Be aware of this in your own relationships. The more right with yourself and God you become, the less touchy you are. Ego sensitivity is caused by past-life and current life lessons that have not been resolved on a subconscious and conscious level.

### 53. The Inner Child

It is important to deal with your own inner child and your partner's inner child appropriately. If you don't learn to parent your own inner child properly, there will be the need to have your partner parent it for you. On the reverse side of the coin, it is important to be aware of your partner's inner child. Using this term in your communication can be a very helpful tool. It is a loving and nonjudgmental term that we can all relate to.

Normally we think of dealing with our own inner child, but we don't necessarily think about the inner child of other people in our communication with them. An expression to your partner about the concern for their inner child's needs will be received in a very open and loving manner. We are trying to get the higher self, conscious mind and inner child in proper alignment. The Huna teachings from Hawaii call the higher self the aumakua. Aumakua is defined as the utterly trustworthy parental self. We are meant to parent our inner child just as the aumakua parents us in this utterly trustworthy manner.

### 54. The Right to Say No

A woman and a man have the right to say no. There should be no obligation to have sex if you really don't feel like it. There is a selfish/selfless balance in this area that must be considered, however. Both partners should be able to say no and not feel guilty if they are not in the mood. The man and woman must learn not to pout or punish if their needs are not met. This is childish behavior.

Sexual energy is very strong, but mastery in service of God must be stronger. One must not allow oneself to get attached to having sex. If this is the case, anger and pouting will result. If one has to have a release, one can masturbate, and there is certainly nothing wrong with this. The higher one goes in the initiation process, the more sacred the use of sexual energy becomes. This is why when someone is sick or has chronic health lessons it is best to have sex less frequently to save and conserve the person's energies. This energy can then be used for healing. It takes a lot of energy for the body to make sperm, for example. To constantly expend it in an overindulgent way will deplete one's health over time. Be moderate and balanced in your sexual practices.

### 55. Taking Your Partner for Granted

This is something that often occurs in marriages over time. It is very important to maintain the specialness of your relationship. When this specialness begins to dissipate, make a conscious effort to do things to redevelop it — for example, loving notes, special candlelight dinners, unexpected presents, romantic weekend getaways and so on. Be creative!

### 56. Involved Detachment

There are three types of bonding patterns. One is being too attached and addicted to another person. The second is the opposite, which is to be too detached, which is also not good. The ideal is to have what can be called involved detachment. We all must be involved with life and people, or what is the use of living and being incarnated? The key is to be fully involved with life, yet simultaneously detached. This is similar to being in this world but not of it. Another way to put it would be to bond out of preference rather than addiction.

### 57. Giving and Receiving Love

Often people are good at giving and not receiving. Or in some cases a person may be good at receiving and not giving. This can be played out in one's sexual relationship and in the relationship in general. Ideally, balance should be striven for to achieve a mature, satisfying relationship.

### 58. Sexual Stereotypes

Let go of masculine and feminine stereotypes in your relationship. Women, of course, have been typed as emotional, passive, receptive, intuitive and nonassertive. Men are meant to be more macho, stoic, assertive, goal-oriented and mental. This must all be let go of because it is part of the old patterning that is ingrained in the consciousness of humanity. Men and women are different — that is a fact. To think that they are exactly the same is illusion. But our goal is to blend, in a balanced way, the inner male and female. This is one of the keys to the ascension process.

### 59. Money

This can be a complex issue. In my opinion the best way to deal with money, if this is truly a life-mate relationship, is to pool the money. Each person could have a separate bank account if needed, or money could be drawn out of one account. Usually one person is better at dealing with money than the other. There is nothing wrong with this. However, both people should have a working knowledge of finances. Often in father/daughter relationships, for example, the man will control the money and keep everything secret, and this is not good.

No one plans to get divorced, but it happens. Women often don't have the first clue about the family finances. I suggest a business meeting or financial meeting once a week, or at least once a month, to go over everything. I recommend setting up a budget on paper together. Some couples have separate money and separate bank accounts. I am not saying that this is wrong, but it is a statement and symbol about the relationship. Its meaning should be examined very closely.

The next thing that comes to mind is the legal financial agreement called a prenuptial agreement. This is nothing I would personally be involved with, for it seems to start the relationship off on a bad note. I would not say it is inherently wrong. In some cases, this might be a consideration. If someone has had many divorces and is not good at romantic relationships, this might need to be considered.

## 60. Causes of Divorce

There are many reasons why people get divorced so much in our society. The first reason is that people often get married at a very young age, before they have had a chance to develop themselves and get right with both themselves and God. Young people often get married before they have really opened to their spiritual life. Without the proper integration of spiritual life, romantic relationships are destined for a very rocky road. First marriages are often personality-level marriages and not soul marriages.

In regard to young marriages, most young people have not learned to properly parent their own inner child. They have not learned to control their negative ego or master their emotions and desires. Nor have they learned to control and reprogram the subconscious mind or to even think properly. How can a romantic relationship work effectively if these lessons are not mastered to some degree?

The second reason for divorce is that marriage is hard, and it takes a lot of work and psychological and spiritual development to make a harmonious union.

The third reason is the effect that children, financial pressures, work pressures and the stresses of modern-day society have on the relationship. We live in such a complex society that it is hard to balance everything.

The fourth reason for so many failed marriages is that we are not trained to make a romantic relationship work. We are taught math, science and history; however, we are not taught in school or church the principles of being right with oneself, right with God and right in our human relationships. The result is that people go into marriages completely ill-equipped to deal with all the lessons that come down the pike.

The fifth reason is that people often get married out of emotional impulse and the honeymoon syndrome without really knowing the person. They don't spend enough time dating and even possibly living together first to see how things work once the honeymoon is over.

The sixth reason is that people change. Not all people are meant to be together forever. As people evolve, they switch from the personality ray to the soul ray and finally to the monadic ray. Each shifting of rays brings a major transformation in the consciousness. Thus people may evolve out of a relationship. This is the different-elevator phenomenon.

The speed at which evolution is moving now also impacts the above. People are going through initiations in one year that in the past took many years or a whole lifetime. Humanity is going through a period of what I can only call *hypertime*. The process of change and transformation is so speeded up that this planet will go through more growth in the 40-year period from 1988 to the year 2028 than in the past 3.1 billion years. Most people are ill-equipped to deal psychologically with this time warp. It is like a cyclone, and those who are not centered are flung to the outside of the cyclone rather than being in the center where all is still. This wreaks havoc on relationships.

These are just some of the factors that cause divorce. I want to repeat here that divorce is not a bad thing. Sometimes it is the best thing in a particular situation. Whether it is positive or negative really depends on each relationship and the psychodynamics involved.

### 61. Ascended-Master Relationships

Understand how the romantic relationships of ascended masters differ from romantic relationships on Earth. On one level they continue as they always have. Ascended-master romantic relationships are totally focused on God and one's mutual spiritual path.

There are also relationships that are totally focused on service. They are often what might be called mission-mate relationships. People in this type of relationship are right with self and right with God first, and they see their mutual relationship as third in priority to the first two. This does not take away from the love between the two, but actually *adds* to it. It is important to understand that romantic relationships evolve just as individuals evolve.

Ascended-master relationships are bonded out of the monadic ray, not out of the personality or soul-level rays. Ascended-master relationships still have lessons to work out, and the partners need to communicate as they always have. Their relationship garden still needs to be weeded as it always has. What has been achieved, however, is a much higher level of maturity and oneness with God.

### 62. Unfolding the Divine Plan

Allowing your partner to unfold his or her part of the divine plan as you unfold yours is necessary, but you also need to unfold your *mutual* part of the divine plan together. It is essential in life to develop self-mastery and self-control. One must learn, however, to let go of all need to control and manipulate others.

### 63. The Savior Complex

I have seen this often in my past counseling practice where women are bonded in their relationship to save the man. They are often in the relationship because they see the man's potential, but they are not willing to see reality as it exists. There is nothing wrong with wanting to help another, but to bond in a marriage to try to save someone is setting yourself up for trouble.

### 64. Asking/Demanding

Understand the difference between asking and demanding. Only a child or a dictator demands. A spiritually mature person makes loving, preferential requests rather than giving orders.

### 65. Enjoying Your Partner's Growth

Cultivate the feeling of joy and happiness in seeing your partner evolve and flower into his or her full God-being. This requires a consciousness of separation and the letting go of all competition, jealousy and envy.

### 66. Fake It Until You Make It

This means to hold to the highest spiritual ideals even when you have not yet arrived at fully integrating those ideals. So even if you don't feel loving, force yourself to be loving and respectful. This is true honesty. Honesty is not indulging your negative ego, an imbalanced inner child who has a hissy fit and takes it out on your partner. True honesty is holding to your spiritual ideals even when the subconscious mind is not cooperating. Who is in control, the conscious mind as a tool of the higher self, or the subconscious mind? Fake it until you make it, and soon the spiritual pattern of relationships will become programmed into your subconscious mind and into your relationship pattern with your spouse.

### 67. Abandonment

The feeling of abandonment develops out of improper bonding, where one has bonded with another out of a lack of feeling whole. One seeks wholeness in another instead of finding wholeness within one's relationship to self and God. When we seek fulfillment through another and that person leaves, we feel abandoned. The path that results can be overwhelming. But when we have worked through it, it will be possible to see the truth of the improper bond from a perspective of renewed strength and clarity. This knowledge can then be used to avoid improper bonding in the future. If one is truly whole within oneself and God, one will never feel abandoned.

### 68. Rejection

In truth there is no such thing. Feeling rejected is the negative ego's interpretation of a breakup, rather than the interpretation of the Holy Spirit and the Christ consciousness. The negative ego always interprets everything in a win-lose manner. The Christ consciousness interprets everything in a win-win manner. The Holy Spirit says there is no such thing as rejection; there are simply relationships that are not meant to be.

If someone does not want to be with you, it is not that you are a bad person or that something is wrong with you. The feelings of rejection are connected to an attachment and addiction to that person caused by improper bonding. The truth is that the relationship is not meant to be and your God-selves have other plans for each of you. If you can look at the situation in this way, you can stay out of judgment and blame for yourself and the other person. Rejection will occur only if there has been an unequal sense of power in the relationship. In life we often want things and might more appropriately call this *needing things*. There might be a far better person for you just around the corner if you can surrender to God's wisdom in the matter.

### 69. Breaking Up

When relationships *do* break up, end them with total love, forgiveness and nonjudgment. If you don't, you will have to reincarnate with that person or another like that one in a future life. If you forgive and end in unconditional love and your partner doesn't, you are freed from the karma, but your partner who is holding a grudge will have to reincarnate in a future life with someone similar to you who did not learn the lesson. For you to be freed, you do not need your partner to learn the lesson. You only have to learn your own lessons.

### 70. Attacks and Hurt Feelings

When dealing with feelings of being hurt, it is important to understand that in truth you cannot be hurt, for you are God, and you cause your own reality and your own emotions. You are not a victim. So be clear that your partner did not hurt you. You hurt yourself by allowing his/her attack to penetrate your emotional field and body. As we become grounded in this understanding, when our partner or others attack us, we will see it with more detachment and the attack will not push our buttons. We will see that it's their stuff, and we will not take it personally. We will have a strong psychological immune system. We will recognize that an attack is a call for love.

We will respond instead of react. We will not catch their psychological disease. If we get hurt and defensive, we have caught the disease. Djwhal Khul has referred to the need for divine indifference. Other schools of spiritual thought have referred to this as detached objectivity, or being the witness. In this state, when our partner is attacking us, we are able to observe the situation as if it were a movie and are not engaged by or reactive to what is happening. This is the consciousness of living in the eternal self.

When we do respond, it is then in a loving, even-minded way. The appropriate response might be, "I see that you are angry, and I would be happy to discuss this situation with you. However, it is my preference to do this in a loving manner." Once your partner realizes that he/she is angry or in attack mode, he is then likely to calm down. If he doesn't, you should politely and lovingly remove yourself physically from the conversation. Set the boundary that you will engage only in a loving and respectful conversation. Since you are responding in a loving way and not counterattacking, you will have learned your lesson, and you are setting an example for the relationship. You are here to set a Christ-like example.

## 71. Grief

When a loved one dies, grief is normal and appropriate. It can also apply to the death of a relationship. What is important to consider here is that the degree of one's grief and the length of one's grieving process will be determined by the nature of the bonding pattern and the degree of spiritual enlightenment. If one is in a codependent rather than a healthy interdependent relationship, the grieving process will be far more intense.

If the one who has lost a partner does not believe in God or in an afterlife and reincarnation, then the grieving process will be much more painful. In India, when people die they celebrate, for everyone realizes the soul has been freed and that there is no such thing as death. You view things from a much different vantage point when you realize that the person who has died is alive and attending the funeral and that they have simply changed dimensions. This eases the emotional sense of loss, for in reality there *is* none. All that one is really grieving for is the loss of the physical vehicle. You will see the person again in dreams, meditation and when you make *your* transition, if the love bond is truly there.

In appropriate grieving you honor the person you shared so much time with and you miss their presence on the physical plane, even though you feel and know their presence spiritually, mentally, etherically and emotionally. Some may be so filled with the spiritual reality of the presence of the person that they may not grieve at all. Others will grieve for a short period. In a sense, one is really grieving for oneself, not for the other person. The other person is probably extremely happy to have gone through the tunnel and merged with the light, and that person will be waiting for you to join him/her when your mission is over. Love is the strongest force in the universe, and all loved ones will be seen again if that is your desire. We are all immortal and eternal beings regardless of our level of evolution.

## 72. Disappointment

Deal with your feelings of disappointment. It must be understood that disappointment stems from attachment and addiction. It gets back to the lesson of needing to have only strong preferences. Happiness needs to be inside, not based on what another person does. There is nothing wrong with having strong preferences, but the nature of a preference is that you are happy whatever the outcome.

Disappointment is a sign of having expectations, which are the same as addictions and attachments. Again, this is the ideal. If you can't shake it by the process of attitudinal healing within self, then share it with your partner in this secondary communication method. You can share your preferences by saying something like, "It would have been my preference if you would have called me to tell me that you were running late." This way you do not lose your inner peace or happiness, but your message is still communicated about the person's inappropriate behavior, and it is done in a loving way.

## 73. Deciding to Pursue a Relationship

How one knows if a relationship is really worthwhile to continue. First, you should never make such a decision when you are emotionally triggered. When you have calmed down and are more objective, you must consider if the person you are involved with meets enough of your preferences. No person on planet Earth or in the infinite universe will meet all your preferences, but they *will* have to meet enough of them to make the relationship worthwhile. If you are in conflict about such a matter, I recommend that you make a list on a piece of paper. First, list all the reasons why you want to remain in this relationship, then list why you want to get out. These lists are like the defense attorney for the relationship and the prosecuting attorney against the relationship. You are the judge sitting on the bench listening objectively to both arguments.

I have realized from my past relationships that each woman I was involved with offered me certain unique things. Certain relationships earlier in my life were highly sexual, and that was one component. Other factors were love, the ability to communicate, similar interests, enjoyment, general compatibility, similar philosophies, emotional, mental and spiritual compatibility, social development, channeling or healing abilities, clairvoyance, mission-mate compatibility, professional compatibility and social compatibility. Each person was developed in some of these areas and a little less compatible in others. No one will meet all of your preferences, nor will we meet all preferences of our partner. There are always areas that need more development. If this weren't the case we would not be here on Earth.

It is very important to be aware of what you are getting and what you are not getting to see if the relationship meets enough of your preferences to make it worthwhile. It might be worthwhile for many years, then after ten or twenty years it might not. There are no hard and fast rules on this. This is an exercise you can do just between you and God. It will give you a very realistic look at your reality and the choices you are making.

### 74. Journal-Writing for Clarification

Journal-write about the rocky areas in your relationship before you talk about them. Be clear in yourself and your relationship to God first, then communicate and share with your partner. I have found this to be very helpful in the past. In one of my past relationships, when this wasn't done, we would humorously call our discussion "journal-writing on each other."

### 75. Punctuality

Often one partner is very punctual and the other runs on a nonlinear time clock, to put it politely. One should never make a commitment on any level that one does not plan to keep. If you don't like to keep commitments, don't make them in the first place. But I would also say that punctual people need to be a little more flexible and patient as long as the basic time commitment is kept. Those who do not do well with time commitments must allow plenty of time to prepare for them. It is important to remember that other people are involved, not just yourself. Once the pattern is perceived this way, appropriate adjustments and communication need to be made so that this is not a recurring conflict.

### 76. The Relationship Function

People who have been single for a long time or who grew up with parents who were quite dysfunctional in their relationships often have not developed a relationship function. For example, when making social plans, part of having a relationship function is to ask your partner first. Having a relationship function includes calling when you are running late, communicating that you are in a bad mood instead of taking it out on your partner and remembering birthdays and other special occasions.

Often people get married but are still living like two single people. Developing a relationship function has to do with recognizing that you are now living as a team in a group body as well as living as an individual. This group body must be considered in all your major decisions.

### 77. Violence

In a nut shell, neither psychic nor physical violence is acceptable, *period*. It should *never* be tolerated. It should be clearly stated in the beginning of the relationship that violence of any kind is unacceptable, and that if it occurs, it is immediately grounds for terminating the relationship. Forgiveness is important, but as Jesus said to the prostitute, "You are forgiven, but go and sin no more" [John 8:11]. If a partner cannot learn this lesson, then out of self-respect you need to leave or separate. Violence in any form is unacceptable because unconditional love and respect need to be the guiding principles of every relationship.

## 78. Staying Present

Watch that you don't go on automatic pilot. It is important to remain vigilant for God and God's kingdom. It is easy to let down and sometimes say things you don't really mean out of mental fatigue or just running off at the mouth. A true master remains vigilant at all times and never lets down, even for an instant, his or her attunement to God in thought, word and deed. God and the ascended masters hear and watch everything, and everything is written into the soul records.

## 79. Short Vacations

It is important to take a romantic vacation every once in a while, even if it is just for the weekend. This will do wonders for a relationship. It is often hard to maintain the spark, romance and passion in the daily grind of Earth life. Even, and especially, when you have children, short vacations away need to be arranged.

## 80. Money Problems

Money problems are lessons, so work together to solve them. Pray together every day and do affirmations and visualizations together. The burden is easier to carry if two carry it rather than one. Each person may have different responsibilities in turning the lessons around, but the feeling of teamwork will be of great help. Read *Golden Keys to Ascension and Healing: Revelations of Sai Baba and the Ascended Masters* and the chapter on manifestation in *Soul Psychology.*

## 81. Giving Up Too Quickly

I sometimes saw in my counseling practice that people were often quick to talk about breaking up at the first sign of an argument or disagreement. This is childish and should be stopped if you have this pattern. Make an agreement and a spiritual vow not to speak of breaking up unless you really mean it, and it should be only after all other options have been attempted. It is amazing how a simple agreement like this can sometimes make an enormous difference in the relationship.

## 82. Self-Righteousness

Don't fall into the pattern of self-righteousness. It is always important to speak in "I" messages, such as "I feel" or "I think" and not to speak for another. It is also essential to state everything as your personal opinion or perception instead of self-righteously stating that this is the way it is.

Every person is entitled to his/her personal opinion about things even if it is an ignorant or unconscious one. To be self-righteous is to not allow people to have their own beliefs and opinions. Often the things we are self-righteous about tend to be wrong in the future, and then we eat crow. As the biblical proverb says, "Pride goeth before...a fall" [Prov. 16:18]. It is always better to state everything as your personal opinion, perception, observation or preference.

### 83. Equal Power

There is a need to maintain an equality of power in the relationship. The fact that someone makes more money than a partner does not give him or her the right to wield more power. Personal power is an inherent spiritual and psychological quality, and it has nothing to do with anything outside of oneself.

### 84. Separate Social Activities

It is important to have a social life beyond your relationship with your partner. So that you do not become too enmeshed with each other, it is important to have a social life both with each other and separate from each other.

### 85. The Family as a System

Understand the concept of the family system, which says that any changes in one aspect of the family system affects the entire family. For example, let's say you have two children. When the romantic relationship with your partner becomes more self-actualized, this has a very positive effect on the children, even on an energetic and psychodynamic level. Every positive change you make in your relationship to yourself and God has a positive effect on the entire family system. The family is a group body also. What affects one, affects the entire family unit. This is an important concept to acknowledge and realize. Often the problems that children have are resolved as the marriage is put back into proper order.

### 86. Mind-Reading

Do not expect your partner to be a mind-reader. If you do not communicate what is going on with you and what you want, it is not fair to expect your partner to be able to fulfill your wants and needs. This is one of the most common problems I have seen in the relationship counseling work I have done.

### 87. Confrontation

There is egotistical confrontation, which is not positive, and there is spiritual confrontation, which *is* positive. Egotistical confrontation deals with ego battles and arguments. Spiritual confrontation is when you do not hold things in but openly, honestly and lovingly address issues that need to be dealt with, even if at first this triggers some sensitive and emotionally charged situations.

It is human nature for most people to be afraid to confront some of the deeper issues that need to be confronted. The solution is to listen to your

God nature rather than your human nature. Having a spiritual, if slightly confrontational, open and loving conversation is much better than carrying a silent resentment and talking and gossiping behind your partner's back. There are sins of commission and omission on the spiritual path. To not communicate on these sensitive issues when communication is needed is a sin of omission.

### 88. Partner as Cheerleader

Be a cheerleader for each other in the process of evolution and self-actualization. The spiritual path is hard enough on Earth, so to have one's partner cheering you on is a wonderful gift. In the ideal marriage your partner is really your best friend as well as your lover.

### 89. Open Marriage

I asked the ascended masters about this and they were very firmly against it. An open marriage allows you to be married and also sleep with other partners. I was told that it creates jealousy, competition and separation, and that it is a product of the negative-ego distortion of reality.

### 90. A Balanced Life

It is important to balance your career, family roles and spiritual life. This is not the easiest thing to achieve. No matter how imbalanced you or your marriage becomes, the mistakes you make can always be corrected. Adjustments can be made if you are both willing to communicate. There will be phases in life where one aspect might be somewhat more emphasized than another. This is okay so long as balance is maintained in the larger context. The more that family, career and spiritual life can be integrated and blended, the better.

### 91. Taking Time for Yourself

To have a healthy relationship, you need to take time for yourself, which might consist of journal-writing, meditating or doing nothing. This is essential in developing and maintaining a right relationship with yourself. Enough time must also be designated for one's relationship and one's family, as stated in Key 90. The key to effective living is balance. Balancing the care of one's physical body, one's mental and emotional well-being, one's spiritual life, relationship, family, career, social life and service work is no small task. All must be prioritized and kept in proper balance. This is the life of a self-realized being.

### 92. Affection

Affection is different from sexual contact. Cultivate being affectionate with your partner. This means hugging, kissing, touching, love pats and just holding. This is totally separate from sexual activity.

Affection when connected with sexuality is a part of the foreplay and afterplay aspect of the sexual process and is very important for both women and men. However, there is a great need for the mutual expression of affection and touching quite apart from sexual contact. This can be very tender and nurturing and is an important part of making one's partner feel loved and special.

Sometimes in marriages we lose things that were important to us in the beginning. If the daily expression of affection is one of those things, now is a good time to begin expressing more affection and nonsexual touching to your partner.

### 93. Optimism and Positivity

Focus on what is good in your relationship and not what is bad. Are you looking at the donut or the hole? Is the glass of water half empty or half full? It all depends on your perception. Focus on the victories and express gratitude for what you have. Negative elements can always be found if you look for them, and one little negative thought can destroy a perfectly beautiful moment, a day or even a life. So it is of the highest importance in making a marriage work that positivity and optimism be cultivated continually and unceasingly!

### 94. Progress Checks

Make regular progress checks of your relationship growth with your partner. You don't want to do this *too* much, however, or it would be like planting a seed and continually digging it up to see if it is growing. On the other hand, lack of introspection and examination can allow weeds to grow that could become vines which might strangle the relationship.

### 95. Advice

Be careful how much advice you give your partner. In some marriages this can be more of a sensitive point than in others. Certainly, give advice only if it is appropriate and if your partner is open to receiving it. You are not your partner's therapist or formal teacher; you are an equal partner.

### 96. Logic and Emotion

Both people in a relationship need to learn to balance and integrate logic and emotion. This might also be stated as balancing the head and the heart. Usually one partner leans more in one direction than the other. There must be an appreciation for the other person's perspective. When people see primarily through different aspects of their being, this can create a rocky relationship if this is not understood and respected. In the ideal state, both individuals work to integrate themselves.

## 97. Holding a Grudge

Never punish each other. This is childish behavior, like holding a grudge. The lesson is to communicate what is bothering you, or let go of it inwardly. The key is never to get stuck in the twilight zone or sit on the fence. Either communicate or attitudinally heal it, but don't stay in the middle and hold a grudge.

## 98. Calling Time-Out

Call time-out if the conversation you are having becomes too uncomfortable and unproductive. This can be very useful in providing time for both of you to become calmer and more centered. Maybe a twenty-minute break can be taken to allow for personal processing.

## 99. Cleanliness and Order

Often one partner is neater than the other in terms of the home environment. The careless one clearly needs to be more responsible, and the neater person needs to relax and give a little so that the issue does not gnaw at their inner peace. It must also be understood that there is such a thing as inner cleanliness within one's mind, emotions, and spirit.

Ideally, all levels are kept clean and in order. Communication is needed in this area as to what is expected by both parties and what chores need to be done. Lists should be made so there are no misunderstandings. Once lists and agreements are made, each person needs to stick to his/her commitment as an aspect of integrity. On the whole, if people know what is expected and it is made simple and clear, a habit can be formed that facilitates getting things done.

## 100. Sharing Dreams

A lovely practice to cultivate is sharing dreams every morning. Dreams obviously reflect our inner realities, and this can be a very fruitful way of connecting, creating intimacy and learning to blend inner and outer realities together.

## 101. Relationship Appointments

Make relationship appointments when unresolved issues come up. Knowing that relationship appointments will be made when things aren't going well helps keep both partners on their toes. The tendency of human nature is to go into automatic pilot and go unconscious. Carl Jung said man's greatest sin is his indolence or laziness. Making a relationship work is both an art and a science. It doesn't just happen; it must be constantly worked on.

This is the same when you develop a right relationship to yourself. It doesn't just happen; it is something you develop over time and constantly monitor. Continual adjustments must be made to maintain equilibrium and balance. There is a center point or tao that one ideally strives to maintain — a state of balance, inner peace, joy, unconditional love and oneness. When imbalance sets in on any level, be it within oneself, one's relationship to God, or one's family or career, adjustments must be made to bring things back into the tao — back into harmony and balance.

## 102. The Blame Game

Let go of the blame game. The concept of blame is of the negative ego. It is based in judgment rather than love. Blame is used to make people wrong and make them feel bad. It should be released completely from your relationship and your reality. It is a wonderful thing to be in a relationship and know you will be loved and supported no matter how much you screw up and that you will give this same consideration to your partner.

## 103. Inner and Outer Union

Those looking for your soulmate or twin flame must first understand that your ultimate soulmate is your own higher self and I Am Presence or monad. This is the true union and marriage you are seeking. You will never truly realize the outer union until union with your higher self and spirit are achieved.

Once these inner marriages are complete and whole, it is possible to attract and magnetize the ideal spiritual mate. Do not get caught up in trying to find the other half of your soul or soul extension from your oversoul or monad. If this happens, it happens, but it is nothing to look for. As I have said earlier, even if you meet such a person, you might not be harmonious on either a psychological or a personality level.

What is most important is not these esoteric factors, but finding the right person for you at this time. This could be someone you have been involved with or married to in past lives, but perhaps not. These are all interesting esoteric points. It is most important that you find the person who really fits your present life. That person then becomes a soulmate if you can communicate and connect with him or her on a soul level; or a monadic mate if you can communicate on that level; or a mission mate when you blend and harmonize your service work together. In other words, *you* create all this by how you build your relationship in the present moment.

## 104. Factors in Relationship

Understand how and why people connect in relationships and the importance of keeping priorities clear. The first thing people usually look at is physical attractiveness. Physical appearance is one factor in a relationship but by no means the most important one. If the person is physically attractive but has little else to recommend him/her, then looks obviously do not mean much.

I believe that the most important factor in relationship bonding is the spiritual, and that many people reading this book will share my view. If your spiritual path is the most important thing in your life and you and your partner are not spiritually compatible, you will not have the support you seek for the most important aspect of your life. It is not necessary that your partner have the same beliefs or the same forms of spiritual expression, but it is important that the spiritual path should be a top priority in your partner's life.

If the person isn't working to grow spiritually, then the negative ego is likely to be operating to quite an extent. In most cases, the person will not have evolved to the place of coming from unconditional love and the entire bonding pattern will be off kilter. If you are just starting a relationship, take a look at this aspect first. If God and your spiritual path are what are most important in your life, why would you get involved with someone who doesn't share this? I would rather be alone and single. This is setting yourself up for a karmic relationship.

The second thing to look at in your bonding pattern is the mental level. Do you share similar goals, beliefs, ideals, and philosophies? Do both of you desire marriage? Do both of you agree on whether or not you want children? Mental simpatico, I believe, is the second biggest factor.

The third biggest factor is love. Is there a strong love between you, a real heart connection? Are you emotionally compatible? Do you feel warmth and an emotional comfort when you are with the person? Love and emotional compatibility are key bonding factors in any successful relationship.

The fourth aspect to look at is the energetic or etheric aspect. Is there chemistry? Is there electricity? When you come together, is there an increase in energy and vital force? Do your batteries get charged up when you spend time together, or do they get depleted?

The fifth factor is the physical level. One aspect of this is physical looks. Is there an attraction? However, it is important to understand that one's perception can change. In looking back at my life, I don't believe that any of the women with whom I developed long-term relationships were ones to whom I initially felt a high degree of physical attraction. What happened in each case was that when I spent time with the woman, things changed. Once I had the opportunity to feel her energy and spirit and share in a mutual exchange of feelings and thoughts, I became extremely physically attracted.

This is a very important concept to understand. We don't just see with our eyes, we also see with our minds and all our chakras. In my case, these became very passionate and highly sexual relationships, as well as deeply spiritual. At that point, I couldn't understand how I could not have been attracted to this person in the beginning. So the physical level cannot be separated from the other aspects of a relationship, for our perceptions of a person's beauty shift as we get to know that person on a deeper level.

The sixth aspect to consider is the material one. This relates to the amount of money the person has and the type of job or if he or she *has* a job. It also relates to how functional a person is in the day-to-day practical skills of living on Earth. The material level is the least important level to me, for I would rather have true love than money any time. But the material level should not be discounted as totally *un*important. Love alone is not always enough to make a relationship work. Love is wonderful and essential, but you also need money to buy food. There are practical aspects to life that must be considered, or life can become extremely stressful and unpleasant.

One's bonding with another can be looked at through these different lenses and bonding patterns. People will differ as to the degree of importance they place on the various aspects, and this is fine.

### 105. Delightful Surprises

Do nice, unexpected things, such as bringing flowers or buying a gift for no reason. Take your spouse on a special unexpected date. Cook dinner when it is unexpected. Create a romantic dinner with candles and all the rest as a surprise. Doing these special things from the heart goes a long way toward nurturing a relationship.

### 106. Attractiveness

Look nice for your partner. This may have to do with having good habits of personal hygiene, being clean, putting on nice clothes occasionally. At times it might mean wearing more sexy clothes, especially when planning a sexual liaison. We sometimes fall into bad habits in this regard, and this is something for us all to be conscious of.

### 107. Planning Romantic Time

This is the issue of whether sexual involvement should be planned in advance. I personally don't see anything wrong with this. With the busy lives we all live, sometimes we almost *have* to create time. This is not to say that when the moment arrives, if either party is not in the mood, there is any obligation. What is important to understand, though, is that one can help oneself to be in the mood by proper preparation. For example, maybe taking a hot bath and getting all dressed up, putting on music and lighting candles might help enhance one's mood. Perhaps a back rub and massage, incense or aromatherapy will create the mood. I personally think that planning romantic time is very nice. It is also nice, however, to be spontaneous.

### 108. Noting Your Biorhythms

Be aware of each partner's biorhythms. This deals with such things as one's sleep habits and whether one is a morning or a night person. This applies to timing your communication and sexual encounters. Some people like to get sexually involved before bed, others in the morning, and still others in the middle of the night. Communicate about this and see if your biorhythms are on the same wavelength as your partner's.

Some adjustments must be made if the partner's biorhythms are different. For example, I like to get up in the morning, jump in the shower and start working. I don't like lying around in bed. So although I am a morning person in regard to work, I am more of a night person in terms of leisure time. Flexibility is the key here.

### 109. Affectionate Greetings

The simple habit of regularly kissing your partner hello and good-bye might sound like a little thing, but it is the little things that often build positive relationships and facilitate the continual flow of love energy. You will want to explore and develop other habits and structures that help keep the flow of love, passion and connection going as well.

### 110. Resolving Disconnection

When you feel disconnected from your partner, there are two approaches. First, see if it can be resolved within yourself by examining what thoughts and/or judgments might be causing it. The other approach is to share this with your partner, saying something like, "I am feeling a little disconnected from you, and I don't like the feeling. I am sharing this in the hope that we can become closer. How are you feeling? Do you have any sense of what caused us to get a little disconnected?"

In my experience, sharing this and having a loving discussion about it usually dissipates it rather quickly. This feeling of disconnection happens in every relationship at times. It is hard enough to stay totally connected to oneself and God all the time, let alone another human being.

### 111. Go the Extra Mile

Be willing to go the extra mile for your partner. This example set by either partner, and ideally both partners, will do wonders for the relationship. An example of this might be your spouse wanting a little treat or ice cream or healthy cookie at night while watching television and your being willing to go to the market to get that for him/her, even though you are comfortable and it is cold outside. Your loving example will inspire the best in your partner.

### 112. Courtesies

Be courteous to your partner. Just because you have been together for a long time doesn't mean the common courtesies of life should be cast aside. Being courteous and considerate can go a long way in creating love and positive energy. Like warm touching and other displays of affection, little courtesies and special considerate acts go a long way toward creating a bond of closeness and harmony in a relationship.

### 113. Issues Will Arise

Self-actualized, ascended marriages are not free of conflict. Mature marriages are characterized by expert communication and a striving for wholeness, but there are always decisions to make and issues to resolve.

### 114. Your Current Reasons for Relationship

Examine why you are really staying in your relationship. It is important to be honest. Is it out of true love? Is it out of practicality? Is it for the children? Is it because you are afraid to be on your own? Is it for financial reasons? Is it out of insecurity? Is it for spiritual reasons? Is it for sexual reasons? Is it because you don't feel you will ever meet anyone else? Is it because you are afraid you will be lonely? Is it because you don't want to get back into the dating scene? Is it because you are comfortable? There is no judgment in any of this. Even if some of these are your reasons, it doesn't mean you have to leave your marriage.

### 115. Imperfection

There are no perfect people in the world, including you. We are all perfect on an essence level, but not on a realization level. Finding an ideal mate is not the easiest thing in the world to do. Your partner does not have to be the reincarnation of Jesus Christ or the Virgin Mary in order for you to have a very fulfilling life, even with all of his or her faults and yours.

### 116. Leaving

Let go of the thought and feeling that the grass is greener on the other side. This is not always the case. Leaving a relationship is a very big decision and should not be made lightly or impulsively. Make sure all other means of resolution have been exhausted. When they have been, have the courage to leave and trust in God.

### 117. Outside Interests

Don't make your partner the whole focus of your life. There is a book titled, *Women Who Love Too Much*. Focusing so completely on your partner is not so much loving too much as being too attached and codependent. It happens when you make your partner the whole focus of your life. Your relationship to your partner becomes idol worship. Anything you put before God is an idol. When you neglect your relationship to yourself and God, things become very unbalanced because your mature relationship to yourself and God is the foundation on which all healthy relationships are built.

### 118. Using Anger to Control

Don't use anger as a manipulative tool to control your partner. This happens when a person gets angry and loses control, then lashes out to assert control over another. If your partner starts getting angry in this way, stop the conversation and tell him or her that if she is not willing to speak in a loving and respectful manner, you are not willing to communicate with her. Also affirm to yourself that you will not be intimidated by such tactics. Of course, if the situation appears to be getting out of hand, remove yourself from it. If this is characteristic of your relationship, seek outside counseling for this serious problem.

### 119. Express Love Verbally

Be willing to express your feelings of love at all times. Say the words, "I love you," as often as you feel inspired to do so. Many problems in a relationship stem from one partner not feeling loved. Expressions of love and affection nurture and strengthen a relationship and build positive feelings and harmony.

### 120. Your Other Aspects in Sexual Activity

This golden key again has to do with sexuality. Too often I see couples too much in their feeling body around sexuality. In others words, the emotional body guides whether sexual involvement can take place. The emotional body is certainly the most important body involved with this process, but it is not the only factor to be considered. Let's say that you have not had sex for a while and your husband has not been getting his needs met. His needs should be taken into consideration as well as yours.

In any given moment where the potential for sexual involvement is present, you may be able to go either way. You need to understand that it should not be just your own feelings that determine this. Your will can be exercised to help yourself get in the mood. Once the decision is made to have sexual involvement, put your will behind it and make it mutually satisfying. If you choose to have sex, make it great sex or don't have it at all.

Too many couples I see are indecisive and don't stand behind their decision to have sex with their physical, etheric, emotional, mental and spiritual bodies. Be decisive and make it work. Sometimes you might choose to have sex out of consideration for your spouse, and there is absolutely nothing wrong with this. Other times you might choose to be spiritually selfish, and there is nothing wrong with that, either. And still other times you might do just what you feel like doing. If you wait to be in the mood to have sex, you can end up waiting for months for the right moment.

### 121. Letting Down Your Work/Social Persona

Every person needs to let down a little after a long day at work or after obligatory socializing. But it is important not to let down with your spouse to the point of allowing your lower self and negative ego to run you. For example, one person might be wonderful at work and a social butterfly at the party you just went to, but the minute he or she gets home she gets into a bad mood. This is unacceptable behavior and is nothing more than laziness and self-indulgence.

Couples often have problems because they allow themselves to let down too much. As long as they are forced by outside structures to be centered, they are. When they get home and no one is forcing them to be kind and pleasant, they aren't. This is nothing more than psychological and spiritual laziness. Ideally you should treat your spouse like you would a guest visiting from out of town. We lose the excitement and passion in our relationships if we become lazy in terms of our relationship habits. I admit this takes energy, but who said God-realization was easy? The fact is that this kind of demonstration will become a positive habit after practicing it for twenty-one days, and it won't take much energy after that.

## 122. Outside Relationships

Every couple has relationships with extended family and friends. There can be friction in these relationships with parents and in-laws, and one simple remedy is to not insist that your spouse join you for family visits. In some family systems it is better if they don't.

It is important that couples present a unified front to children, to the extended family and to the outside world. It is also important that confidentiality be honored. A partner should never reveal to others the sacred sharings of his or her partner. We are speaking here of developing self-control and honoring your group body of two.

## 123. Morning Mood-Setting

Try to set a loving mood as early in the day as possible. It must be understood that love is not simply a feeling. It is, first of all, divine energy from God. Its expression relates both to attitude and an aspect of will. I have learned to have effective romantic relationships because I make them work. I will settle for nothing less. I will keep working until we are there. Once we are, I do not allow that feeling to leave. If it does, I will make all the corrections, communications and attitudinal adjustments that are needed to get us back in that loving place. Weeds don't grow, because I don't allow them to and because I take the attitude of being vigilant. When they do start to grow, I pick them out as soon as possible.

## 124. Increasing Your Desire

Improve your sexual desire for your mate. When it needs to be fired up, visualize a time when you were head over heels in love with him or her and/or having your best sex. This will prime the engine, so to speak. It does work! Use your will and mind power and don't run on autopilot or be run only by your feelings of the moment.

## 125. Discretion

Communicate as much as possible with your spouse and be discreet about whom you discuss your relationship with. Every person has a friend or friends who are confidants, and that is fine. The key is not to share with others what is most appropriately shared only with your partner.

## 126. Affairs

Having an affair is morally and spiritually wrong because it is breaking a commitment and you are being dishonest. Someone will get hurt if the truth is known. Even if your partner never knows, it hurts the bonding and trust of the partnership. The lesson here is not to be in the twilight zone. Either make the relationship work or get out of it. To have an affair is to stay dishonestly in the middle. A triangle is being formed and bad karma is being created.

## 127. Mixed Marriages

Interfaith or interracial marriages, from the perspective of the ascended masters, are wonderful. The more blending and integration that occurs between the people on Earth, the more the thought forms of separation are healed. One problem is the foundation of all other problems: feeling you are separated from God. This leads to feelings of unworthiness and being an object of judgment by others, for these are two sides of the same coin.

There are many paths back to God, so do not let the different forms of religion create any lack of love or separation. The most important thing is that your partner believes in God. Everyone is the eternal Self regardless of skin color, so to make a fuss over it perpetuates egotism and thought forms of separation.

## 128. Weekly Sharing

Allow room for yourself and your mate to talk things out and have a catharsis or "be his/her journal-writing pad." There are so many lessons in life we have to deal with on so many levels that we are constantly processing reality to retain our proper perspective and inner peace. I remember many years ago in one of my first long-term relationships, we used to go out every Friday evening and have a glass of wine or a bottle of mineral water and process reality for that week. It was a kind of journal-writing, but we would do it together out loud, which created a nice feeling of intimacy. It became a weekly ritual for many years.

### 129. Honoring Feelings

Honor your spouse's feelings no matter what they might be. The important thing is first to listen and honor the feelings. Later there might be a loving, respectful discussion about what attitudes and beliefs might be causing those feelings. It is important to honor feelings but also to be responsible for the beliefs that are causing them. Both are important.

### 130. Keeping Silent or Speaking

Holding back communication because you don't want to hurt your mate is a noble thought and at times it might be appropriate. At other times, however, it might hurt them more not to share. Often when too much is held back, disconnection and resentment build. When communication is given in a loving, respectful, nonattached manner, you are not hurting anyone. Often it is the egosensitivity of your partner that is causing him/her to feel hurt.

When communicating about sensitive issues, it is of the utmost importance to qualify your communication with extra love and kindness. This is appropriate. Say some nice things first to soften the feedback and give only constructive criticism where it is appropriate and really necessary and when your partner really wants it. If it is just going to create a fight, why give it? Often people give feedback more for themselves than for the true and selfless benefit of their partner. Examine your motivations.

### 131. Thanks and Appreciation

Remember to thank your partner for the kind things he/she does. This might also be stated as showing appreciation for those acts of kindness and love. If you give positive reinforcement for such acts, they are more likely to occur again. This is another part of not taking each other for granted.

### 132. Pray for Success

Pray every day for God's help in making your marriage work. The law of life is that God is not allowed to help unless you ask, but if you do make such a simple request, you will be amazed at the results.

### 133. Visualization for Rough Periods

When you are going through a rough period in your marriage, every night before bed visualize in your mind's eye the two of you getting along and being very close. Do this for two or three minutes each night before drifting off to sleep. You will be amazed at the transformation your subconscious mind will enact for you.

### 134. After a Fight

After a fight, call in the ascended masters, the healing angels and the Holy Spirit. Ask them to undo energetically all the negative energy in yourself and your partner. These spiritual forces will transmute and clear away all the negative energy and replace it with core love.

### 135. Special Days

Remember birthdays, anniversaries and Valentine's Day. Try to do special things for your partner all year long, but especially make a big fuss on these days. This will go a long way to build good feelings that will help you during times of stormy weather.

### 136. Consistent Thoughtfulness

Follow all acts of kindness by your partner with a reciprocal act of kindness within a week or so. Keep your acts of kindness and love coming even if your partner isn't focused on this. In other words, you don't want to *need* your partner to do something for you; you want to be self-motivated. However, if your partner is responding, be sure to respond in kind shortly afterward. This is the opposite of weeding your relationship garden — you are planting flowers there.

### 137. One Rose

Bring home a single rose. A rose, as we all know, is the flower of love. One little rose, different in color throughout the year, will make your partner putty in your hands!

### 138. Back and Foot Rubs

Another way to make your partner putty in your hands is to volunteer a back or foot rub. If you always want to give to him or her, very soon he/she will want to give to you.

### 139. Touching

The simple action of touching is powerful. For instance, if you are watching television, you can gently put your hand on your partner's leg or shoulder or hand. The simple act of being physically in contact has great emotional and symbolic significance and comfort. These simple little things help to make a relationship work. They combine to build a bond of love, enjoyment and unity.

### 140. Regular Arcturian Clearing

Call the Lord of Arcturus and the Arcturians to anchor for you and your spouse the liquid-crystal technology and the golden cylinder to remove all alien implants, negative elementals and imbalanced energies. I would recommend doing this once every two weeks. If necessary, do it once a week. With their advanced technology, the Arcturians will remove these dense energies from your field. This is what might be called preventive medicine for your relationship.

Living in this earthly world, with all the challenges and lessons we must face, we all pick up debris in our energy fields. It is very important to do this clearing work on a regular basis, for chaotic energies in our field can bleed over and create contamination in the marriage and with oneself. If you have pets, do this for them as well. If you are clear and your partner isn't, you can get recontaminated, so ask for this for both of you. If possible, ask your partner's permission. If permission is not given, do it privately, asking for permission from their higher self and surrendering the prayer request to God. You will be doing a great service for your partner.

### 141. A Burning-Pot Clearing

Occasionally do a burning pot in your bedroom, living room and whole house. This is done by putting a quarter cup of Epsom salts in a pan with one-third cup of rubbing alcohol. Place a mat of some kind on the floor to protect it, then light the mixture. This will burn up all negative energy in the atmosphere in the house. The cleaner you keep your individual fields and the metaphysical atmosphere of your house, the better you will get along. Especially do this if you have just had a fight. Invite your partner to join you in this process, for it is a symbolic act as well.

### 142. Demonstrating Your Marriage's High Priority

Demonstrate to your spouse that he/she is at the top of your priority page. As time goes on, the marriage often falls lower and lower on the list of priorities. Don't let this happen. It really is nothing more than keeping this intent and demonstrating it. These simple acts in your relationship take little time or energy, but they can make all the difference in the world.

### 143. Random Acts

Keep surprising your spouse with random acts of kindness, love and small gifts. If you make up your mind you are going to cultivate and maintain love, it will happen. If it doesn't, you are with the wrong partner. Listen closely to the things your spouse says to you. For example, you might be walking in the mall and he/she might innocently comment about wanting something, not really thinking he would ever get it. Make a note to yourself, and at some appropriate occasion get it for him. Doing such things shows that you care, that you are listening to him, that what he wants is important to you. If you try, this will inspire your spouse to try. This demonstrates that with all the lessons and stresses of life, you are not forgetting him/her.

### 144. Compliments

Tell your spouse how nice he/she looks when she gets dressed up — and, for that matter, anytime you feel inspired. Make a habit of complimenting her. Everyone likes a compliment. Make it your job to help him/her build self-esteem and feelings of self-love. Don't be afraid to spoil your partner a little.

### 145. Asking for What You Want

Be sure to ask your partner for what you want. In other words, you are doing all these nice things for them, and there may be things you would like them to do for you. One of the most important principles of an effective relationship is to ask. You can ask to be touched more. You can ask for more expressions of appreciation. State your request as a loving preference. Ask and you shall receive. When you are being so nice to your spouse, he/she will likely respond in kind.

Most couples receive what they are given instead of seeing that by asking, they can stimulate the giving process. You are not attached, so if they don't do what you ask, you are still happy. If it is given, it will be given to you freely out of their own free choice. Your lack of manipulation in terms of the way you state it, and your lack of neediness, breed love. People do not like to give to people who are clinging vines. They do like to give to people who are strong and loving and clear.

Your positive demonstration and your clear, preferential requests for what you want will create and build a flow of love energy that fills you fully. Your giving will fill you full of love, and the reciprocation from your partner, both spontaneously and by your asking, will fill you full of love. Do you see how in life everything is a matter of just making adjustments? Keep making adjustments in your relationship by demonstrating love and asking for what you want until your romantic relationship comes perfectly back into the tao.

### 146. The Top of Your Priority List

Tell your spouse that he/she is at the top of your priority page right next to being right with yourself and right with God and that you will be demonstrating this by your actions from now on. Ask her to join you in this commitment.

### 147. Repeating Your Marriage Vows

Consider repeating your marriage vows. This can be a private ceremony you do yourself or a spiritual marriage or ceremony with a minister or rabbi. This ceremony will be the rebirth or renewal of your marriage vows in the light of the Christ consciousness. It will be a commitment to demonstrate a soul/monadic-level or ascended-master romantic relationship.

### 148. Using This Book Together

This golden key may be one of the most important of all. Ask your partner to read this book as a personal favor to you. Go through these golden keys and make a checklist of the ones you want to practice. Then hang it on your bulletin board and go over it every morning for a minute or two. Maybe you can even read the book together and discuss the keys as you read.

### 149. Balancing Power with Sensitivity

Demonstrate a balance between personal power and sensitivity and keep your ideal a masculine/feminine balance. This applies to both men and women. A woman likes a man who is strong, but one who can also be very loving and sensitive. This combination is the greatest sexual aphrodisiac. I know this from personal experience. A woman who is loving and sensitive but not in touch with her power tends to be childlike. This can be a turn-on and attractive for a little while, but it eventually gets old. A man who is strong but not sensitive cannot connect on an intimate level. A man who is sensitive but has no power is also a turn-off.

### 150. Openness with Power/Sensitivity

One of the golden keys I learned early on in my romantic involvements was to be powerful in my romantic and sexual advances. I would always be sensitive, but when I wanted to kiss a woman I would not be shy about it. If I wanted to make love with a woman, I would tell her and not mince words. Women like this. Speaking from a man's perspective, men like this openness and expression of personal power (with sensitivity) as well.

### 151. Experimentation

This applies to the dating process as well as marriage. Dating is clearly an experiment of sorts. You go out with someone you don't know very well. You are checking things out. Don't be afraid to experiment. In other words, touch the other person on the hand or leg while conversing and see how that makes you feel and how it makes them feel. As you get to know him/her better, you might experiment and kiss them, just to see how it feels. Be powerful about it. Look at it as an experiment. Ask him/her to dance and see how *that* feels. People are often too shy and sensitive to do this. If you wait until you feel like it or when it feels totally comfortable, it might never happen. Sometimes such an experiment might not work, but that is good information.

This concept of experimentation also applies sexually, when you get to that point. In a committed relationship and marriage, be willing to experiment sexually and try different things. It is too easy to get into the same sexual pattern every time. Ask your partner if he/she is willing to experiment. Get some of the sex manuals or books on tantric sexuality and try some of the different positions and tantric meditations. When you are through, talk about it with your partner. What did you like and what didn't you like? Make mental notes about what worked and what didn't. Over time you will build up a rich arsenal of lovemaking knowledge. Your partner wants to be sexually fulfilled as much as you do. If you think of this process as experimenting, there is no judgment when something doesn't work. The most important thing is that you communicate with each other to monitor what is working and what is not for both partners.

## 152. Independence vs. Neediness

Don't fall into neediness, dependency and a clinging-vine mentality. Both should make it clear that they are fully capable of being on their own if they have to, though this is not their preference. Knowing that your partner can make it on his/her own without you and you without him makes both partners be on their toes and not take the other for granted. It also prevents the resentment that comes from overdependence.

## 153. Compromise

Sometimes in relationships you have to do things you don't want to do, but you can accept them and have a positive attitude about it. You might have to go over to the in-laws for Christmas dinner and perhaps you don't feel like it. Forget about your feelings — feelings are not your god. The Yiddish word, mensch, is good here. A mensch is a good person or solid citizen who always does what is right. Sometimes what is right to do is something you don't feel like doing. Your spouse might want to go on vacation and you really don't want to. At some point you will probably feel it is best to just bite the bullet and go.

Once you make the choice to meet a specific need of your partner, keep a positive attitude and have a good time. Do not let feelings be your god. Feelings are often created by the negative ego with its selfish perspective. Being in a relationship involves compromise. You can't always do exactly what you want. If you are not willing to compromise, and if you are not willing to do what your partner wants to do at least part of the time, you have no business being in a relationship. Maybe a single life is best for you.

## 154. Sharing Personal Feelings and Secrets

In our society men are often taught to be silent, to be macho and never cry. Women are trained to be the exact opposite. They love to share feelings and their innermost secrets. Men clearly need to open up more. Women, on the other hand, often need more masculine energy in terms of learning to be more impersonal and having a greater mastery of their emotions and desire bodies.

In terms of relationships, there needs to be an open flow of sharing one's inner reality. What is the purpose of a relationship if you are not willing to do this? This is the main reason for having a full-time romantic partner. He/she is someone with whom you can share your deepest feelings and thoughts and feel safe in doing so. This builds intimacy and closeness. Men need to let down their barriers and do this more. Women are good teachers here.

## 155. Standards of Beauty

Both men and women should let go of societal norms about beauty. Physical beauty is not what *Playboy* magazine and our media make it out to be. For a while Twiggy was the rage — I thought she looked emaciated. In the 1600s the Rubenesque woman was the rage. The thin models of our time would have been considered completely unattractive. So beauty is in the eye of the beholder. I was programmed like everyone else. I soon learned, however, to appreciate the Rubenesque woman. It is very important for both men and women—for themselves and their relationship—to let go of society's standards of glamour and beauty.

### 156. Consideration
There is a great need to be thoughtful and considerate. So much in a relationship has to do with transcending selfishness. If you are going to run an errand, ask your spouse if there is anything he/she needs. The little things you can do for each other are endless, so be creative and inventive.

Act like a gentleman and a gentlewoman. When one is first dating, we all act like perfect gentlepeople. After marriage, we let go of many of these noble qualities. The list is endless here too, such as opening the car door for your wife, helping her on with her coat and lifting heavier objects. Some may call this sexist; I call it being considerate. In the reverse, there are things women can do in a more feminine frame of reference. It may have to do with cooking and serving meals or creating a lovely home, bringing her husband his slippers, unfolding or making the bed. Some of these may seem like silly examples, but it is a principle I am talking about here, one I think is important.

### 157. Dividing Chores
Everyone has certain chores they hate and certain chores they don't mind. Be creative. For example, I don't mind doing the dishes, vacuuming or taking out the trash, but I hate dusting, washing and waxing the floor and watering the plants. Work out a fair division of responsibilities that both people are comfortable with.

### 158. A Relationship Prayer
Someone turned me onto the following relationship prayer that you can say before bed, either together or privately.

Lord, help us remember that our love for each other
reflects your love for us.
May we empower one another to fulfill our purpose in life.
May our love be an example for our children and a model for all.
May our experience as a couple give us a preview
of the oneness we will experience someday.
Help us to see that everything is either love or a call for love.
Help us to celebrate our similarities and honor our differences.
Help us to accept our limitations and utilize our talents.
Thank you for this opportunity, this life
and for my loving partner.
Amen

### 159. Spiritual Tests

Every conflict you overcome in your marriage deepens and strengthens the bond. Every fight and conflict is a spiritual test of your love for each other. Do not bail out of a relationship at the first spiritual test. Bailing out is easy. Hanging in there and processing all lessons is the true test of maturity in a relationship.

### 160. Frequency of Sex

There is no hard, fast rule about the frequency of sexual involvement. Some people have a higher libido than others. There are other factors such as one's spiritual focus, priorities, job, stress level and physical health. Obviously, when you first become deeply involved, your desire for sexual contact will be relatively high, and this is appropriate for the bonding process. The frequency will also change during different phases of the marriage. Some compromise might be needed.

It is also possible to have sexual involvement without either one having an orgasm. In some sexual involvement the man or the woman might not feel like having an orgasm but can still pleasure the partner. As long as this doesn't become a regular habit, this is appropriate. In a christed relationship, your partner's needs are just as important, or even more important, than your own. Great pleasure is received from meeting your partner's needs.

### 161. Willingness to Show Desire

Do not be afraid to demonstrate and show passion and desire for your partner. Also, do not be afraid to enjoy sexuality to the fullest. I speak here of that ascended-master consciousness or Christ consciousness not being in conflict with sexual pleasure. God would have us feel pleasure and give pleasure to our partner. Giving pleasure is an aspect of love. Being passionate is not antithetical to spirituality.

The key here is to demonstrate higher-self, not lower-self passion. Higher-self passion is like animal passion blended with unconditional love, caring, intimacy and respect. Lower-self passion is just a pornographic movie for sex with no caring, no love or intimacy; it is just a physical act. When one truly understands the spiritual path, one sees that it is the path of integration and that one can integrate the best of both worlds.

### 162. Play Days

Institute a play day once or twice a month. It is an entire day given to just enjoying life together.

### 163. Foreplay

It is very important for men to realize that women have a slower sexual response buildup time than men. Men need to learn to be more process-oriented instead of goal-oriented. When one approaches sexual involvement with the attitude of being more concerned with serving your partner first rather than yourself, this comes into greater balance and harmony.

### 164. Afterplay

In Gregory Godek's book, *The Portable Romantic*, he quotes a woman named Sally who says, "A man's attention to foreplay indicates his knowledge of sex. But his attention to afterplay indicates his knowledge of love."

### 165. Your Relationship with Self

To be sure to bond in your relationship out of preference, wholeness, oneness, personal power, strength, self-love, self-worth and being right with oneself and God. It is at that moment when you are ready and able to live your life in fullness without a partner that you find one. The ideal is for two wholes, or two self-realized God-beings, to blend. If you seek your completeness in a partner instead of within yourself, you are setting yourself up for karma. Often people think what they need is a relationship partner, but more often than not what they really need is to develop a relationship with themselves and God.

### 166. Developing a Right Relationship to Self and God

The final golden key in making your romantic relationship work is to do everything in your power to help yourself and your partner develop a right relationship to self and a right relationship to God. The more your partner is right with self and with God, the more your relationship is going to work. Make a lifestyle of mutual spiritual growth. Go to workshops and seminars and support each other in counseling if needed. Occasionally you might want to see a high-level channel.

I would recommend that you and your partner read *Soul Psychology*. This book is extremely helpful for developing a right relationship to oneself. On the spiritual level, I would recommend reading, *The Complete Ascension Manual, Beyond Ascension* and *Golden Keys to Ascension and Healing: Revelations of Sai Baba and the Ascended Masters*.

The more you and your partner fill your lives with God, the better your relationship will be. The higher you go on the personality, soul, monadic and self-actualization scale, the more self-realized you and your relationship will become.

# *Special Thank Yous*

At this time, I would like to give a special Thank You to another wonderful spiritual sister, Mary Rosales, for her devoted and selfless computer work, which has allowed the logistical aspect of putting this book together to occur with lightning speed.

I would like to acknowledge Michael Day for his outstanding editing help. His joy, love, enthusiasm, skill and devotion to his work are greatly appreciated.

I would also like to give a special Thanks to Marti Elana Peace for her skillful editing.

# *About the Author*

Dr. Joshua David Stone has a Ph.D. in transpersonal psychology and is also a licensed marriage, family and child counselor in Los Angeles, California. On a spiritual level he anchors what is called the "Melchizedek Synthesis Light Academy & Ashram", which is an integrated inner and outer plane ashram representing all paths to GOD. Serving as a spokesperson for the Planetary Ascension movement, Dr. Stone's spiritual lineage is directly linked to Djwhal Khul, Sananda, Kuthumi, Lord Maitreya, Lord Melchizedek, the Mahatma and Metatron. He also feels a very close connection with the Divine Mother, Lord Buddha as well as a deep devotion to Sathya Sai Baba.

Reverend Janna Shelley Parker is a long time initiate of the Ascended Master Djwhal Khul and past student of Hilda Charlton. Rev. Parker currently works as Dr. Stone's personal assistant in the Melchizedek Synthesis Light Ashram in Los Angeles, California serving Lord Melchizedek, the Mahatma, Metatron, Sai Baba, Lord Buddha, Lord Maitreya and Djwhal Khul. She teaches Yoga, journal channeling, and is a writer of poetry and song lyrics.

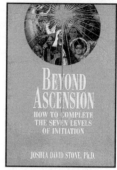

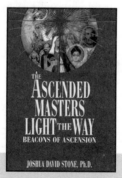
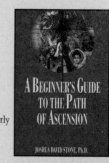

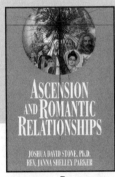

# Book ◆ 15

Joshua David Stone PhD

## *Encyclopedia of the Spiritual Path*

# HOW TO BE FINANCIALLY SUCCESSFUL: A SPIRITUAL PERSPECTIVE

As one of the most successful businessmen of the New Age movement, Dr. Stone has written an easily digestible book full of tools and advice for achieving prosperity. This book conveys esoteric secrets of the universe that, if mastered, can lead to maximum manifestation results.

- Keys to Prosperity Consciousness from the Soul's Perspective
- How to Develop the Midas Touch
- The Seven Keys to Releasing Fear and Worry
- How to Master the Twelve Levels of Integrated Spiritual Power in Life
- Integration of the Seven Rays and Spiritual Leadership
- How to Program the Subconscious Mind for Success in Business

$14⁹⁵   SOFTCOVER 235 P.
ISBN 1-891824-55-4

LIGHT TECHNOLOGY PUBLISHING • 928-526-1345 • 800-450-0985
Or use our online bookstore: www.lighttechnology.com

# BRIAN GRATTAN

## MAHATMA I & II
### *The I AM Presence*

Awaken and realize that all of humankind will create their "body for ascension," whether they accomplish this now or later, and that this is not the exclusive domain of Christ or Buddha or the many others who have ascended—*this is your birthright*. When humans lift the veils of their unworthiness and recognize that they are the sons of God, that there is divine equality and that no one is greater than another, then you will have begun your journey in the way that it was intended. The *Mahatma* is for those who are motivated to search for the answers that can respond to their mental and spiritual bodies. No matter how contrary your current beliefs, this book contains methods for creating your spiritual lightbody for ascension and also explains your eternal journey in a way never before available to humankind.

$19^{95}$ SOFTCOVER 480 P.
ISBN 0-929385-77-2

## Chapter Titles:

- Introduction by Vywamus
- The Journey of the Mahatma from Source to Earth
- The Spiritual Initiation through the Mahatma
- What Is Channeling?
- Evolution of a Third-Dimensional Planet
- The Rays, Chakras and Initiations
- Conversations with Barbara Waller
- Transformation through Evolution
- Patterns
- Time and Patience

- Mahatma on Channeling
- Conversation Between the Personality (Brian) and Mahatma (the I AM Presence)
- Mastery
- The Tenth Ray
- Integrating Unlimitedness
- The Etheric and Spiritual Ascensions
- The Cosmic Heart
- Mahatma as the I AM Presence
- So What Does the Personality Think of All of This?

## TITLES ON TAPE
### by Brian Grattan

BASEL SEMINAR
10 TAPE SET (AUDIO CASSETTE), English with German translation . . . . . . . . . $35.00

EASTER SEMINAR
7 TAPE SET (AUDIO CASSETTE), English with German translation . . . . . . . . . $59.95

SEATTLE SEMINAR
12 TAPE SET (AUDIO CASSETTE) . . . . . . . . . . . . . . . . . . . . . . . . . $79.95
Twelve one-hour audio tapes from the Seattle Seminar, October 27–30, 1994. These twelve powerful hours of meditations lead to total spiritual transformation by recoding your two-strand DNA to function in positive mutation.

# CHARLES KLOTSCHE

## COLOR MEDICINE
### *The Secrets of Color Vibrational Healing*

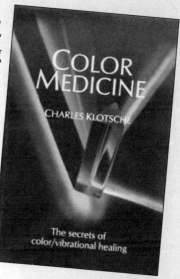

A new dimension in holistic healing, *Color Medicine* provides a powerful technique for treating specific imbalances and strengthening the immune system. By combining aura-attuned chromatherapy with harmonious sounds, tissue salts and hydrochromatherapy, the forty-ninth vibrational technique was developed. A breakthrough, yet as old as recorded medicine, it utilizes subtle energy vibrations similar to those found in the visible spectrum. A textbook and how-to handbook, this book encompasses an encyclopedia of fascinating information, charts, diagrams and tables as well as methods of treatment and technical advice. Whether you are a holistic practitioner or merely curious, this book marks a new frontier in the world of alternative healing.

$11⁹⁵ SOFTCOVER 114 P.
ISBN 0-929385-27-6

## Chapter Titles:

- Does Color Medicine Really Heal?
- Color Physics: The Scientific Explanation of Color Medicine, or Vibrational Therapy
- Color Energetics: How Color Medicine Works with the Subtle Energy Fields of the Body
- Color Harmonics: The Twelve Healing Colors and Their Use
- Color Practice: Materials and Practical Techniques for Applying Color Medicine
- Color Schedule Application: Determining the Appropriate Color(s) for Relieving/Healing the 123 Major Illnesses
- Color Medicine Schedules for 123 Specific Human Disorders
- Quick-Reference Checklist for Color Tonation
- Suggested Readings

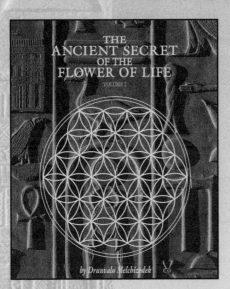

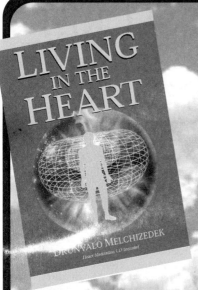

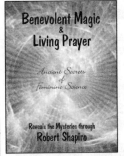

# This School Called Planet Earth

## DR. JAMES MARTIN PEEBLES AS CHANNELED BY
## TRANCE MEDIUM SUMMER BACON

$16^{95}$ SOFTCOVER 323 P.
ISBN 1-891824-54-6

"If I could but lift one robin unto its nest again, I shall not have lived in vain." This is truth, my dear friends. There is a purpose to your life, and you will find it before you leave the Earth, without question. There's no way you can escape yourselves. Some have come here to finish karmic relationships. Some have come here to discover that there is beauty in ugliness and vice versa. Some have come here in an exploration of abundance and what this means. On and on the lessons go! The planet Earth is a canvas, you are the paintbrush and your heart is the paint with which you color the planet—with your words, with your hands, with your heart, with your hugs and with your kisses. God bless you, indeed!

—Dr. James Martin Peebles

### Chapter Titles:

- You Wear a Coat of Many Colors
- A Collection of Wisdom
- Earth Changes
- Living in Rapture
- A Day of Play
- Seasons of the Soul
- The Tip of the Iceberg
- The Many Faces of Abuse
- Healing the Pain of Yesterday
- Love Everlasting
- Creating Intimacy with Life

---

# Pathways & Parables
## for a Changing World

PRETTY FLOWER
THROUGH
MIRIANDRA ROTA

This book is about practical solutions called pathways. Have you ever asked Pretty Flower a question only to have her answer begin with, "Once upon a time . . ."? At the end of her parable, did you ever find yourself saying, "Huh?" and then, "Oh, yes!" It's easy, simple. That's what the parables are all about: a shift in consciousness, spiritual awakenings galore. But don't let me keep you a moment longer from these easy pathways, delightful parables and simple solutions for your powerful living!

—Miriandra Rota

Interwoven within your story, dear beloved ones, is the truth of who you are. Interwoven within the fabric of your being are the encodings that contain all knowing and the capability to venture forth in the fulfillment of your heart's yearning. And within your heart's yearning resides your beloved innocence, which holds the wisdom you seek while creating your story. Blessed are you.

—Pretty Flower

$19^{95}$ SOFTCOVER 380 P.
ISBN 1-891824-53-8

### Chapter Titles:

- We Are All Journeyers
- Truth Does Burst Forth!
- Ripples in the Timeline
- Friendship and Truth
- The Light Within
- The Energy of Completion
- The Spring of All Springs
- Fulfillment of the Dream

LIGHT TECHNOLOGY PUBLISHING
928-526-1345 • 800-450-0985
Or use our online bookstore:
www.lighttechnology.com

Visit our online bookstore: www.lighttechnology.com

# THE EXPLORER RACE SERIES

## ZOOSH AND HIS FRIENDS THROUGH ROBERT SHAPIRO

*THE SERIES: Humans—creators-in-training—have a purpose and destiny so heartwarmingly, profoundly glorious that it is almost unbelievable from our present dimensional perspective. Humans are great lightbeings from beyond this creation, gaining experience in dense physicality. This truth about the great human genetic experiment of the Explorer Race and the mechanics of creation is being revealed for the first time by Zoosh and his friends through superchannel Robert Shapiro. These books read like adventure stories as we follow the clues from this creation that we live in out to the Council of Creators and beyond.*

### ❶ THE EXPLORER RACE

You individuals reading this are truly a result of the genetic experiment on Earth. You are beings who uphold the principles of the Explorer Race. The information in this book is designed to show you who you are and give you an evolutionary understanding of your past that will help you now. The key to empowerment in these days is to not know everything about your past, but to know what will help you now. Your number-one function right now is your status of Creator apprentice, which you have achieved through years and lifetimes of sweat. You are constantly being given responsibilities by the Creator that would normally be things that Creator would do. The responsibility and the destiny of the Explorer Race is not only to explore, but to create. 574 P. $25.00 ISBN 0-929385-38-1

### ❷ ETs and the EXPLORER RACE

In this book, Robert channels Joopah, a Zeta Reticulan now in the ninth dimension who continues the story of the great experiment—the Explorer Race—from the perspective of his civilization. The Zetas would have been humanity's future selves had not humanity re-created the past and changed the future. 237 P. $14.95 ISBN 0-929385-79-9

### ❸ EXPLORER RACE: ORIGINS and the NEXT 50 YEARS

This volume has so much information about who we are and where we came from—the source of male and female beings, the war of the sexes, the beginning of the linear mind, feelings, the origin of souls—it is a treasure trove. In addition, there is a section that relates to our near future—how the rise of global corporations and politics affects our future, how to use benevolent magic as a force of creation and how we will go out to the stars and affect other civilizations. Astounding information. 339 P. $14.95 ISBN 0-929385-95-0

### ❹ EXPLORER RACE: CREATORS and FRIENDS
### The MECHANICS of CREATION

Now that you have a greater understanding of who you are in the larger sense, it is necessary to remind you of where you came from, the true magnificence of your being. You must understand that you are creators-in-training, and yet you were once a portion of Creator. One could certainly say, without being magnanimous, that you are still a portion of Creator, yet you are training for the individual responsibility of being a creator, to give your Creator a coffee break. This book will allow you to understand the vaster qualities and help you remember the nature of the desires that drive any creator, the responsibilities to which a creator must answer, the reaction a creator must have to consequences and the ultimate reward of any creator. 435 P. $19.95 ISBN 1-891824-01-5

### ❺ EXPLORER RACE: PARTICLE PERSONALITIES

All around you in every moment you are surrounded by the most magical and mystical beings. They are too small for you to see as single individuals, but in groups you know them as the physical matter of your daily life. Particles who might be considered either atoms or portions of atoms consciously view the vast spectrum of reality yet also have a sense of personal memory like your own linear memory. These particles remember where they have been and what they have done in their infinitely long lives. Some of the particles we hear from are Gold, Mountain Lion, Liquid Light, Uranium, the Great Pyramid's Capstone, This Orb's Boundary, Ice and Ninth-Dimensional Fire. 237 P. $14.95 ISBN 0-929385-97-7

### ❻ EXPLORER RACE and BEYOND

With a better idea of how creation works, we go back to the Creator's advisers and receive deeper and more profound explanations of the roots of the Explorer Race. The liquid Domain and the Double Diamond portal share lessons given to the roots on their way to meet the Creator of this universe, and finally the roots speak of their origins and their incomprehensibly long journey here. 360 P. $14.95 ISBN 1-891824-06-6

## ZOOSH AND HIS FRIENDS THROUGH ROBERT SHAPIRO

### ❼ EXPLORER RACE: The COUNCIL of CREATORS

The thirteen core members of the Council of Creators discuss their adventures in coming to awareness of themselves and their journeys on the way to the Council on this level. They discuss the advice and oversight they offer to all creators, including the Creator of this local universe. These beings are wise, witty and joyous, and their stories of Love's Creation create an expansion of our concepts as we realize that we live in an expanded, multiple-level reality. 237 P. $14.95 ISBN 1-891824-13-9

### ❽ EXPLORER RACE and ISIS

This is an amazing book! It has priestess training, Shamanic training, Isis's adventures with Explorer Race beings—before Earth and on Earth—and an incredibly expanded explanation of the dynamics of the Explorer Race. Isis is the prototypal loving, nurturing, guiding feminine being, the focus of feminine energy. She has the ability to expand limited thinking without making people with limited beliefs feel uncomfortable. She is a fantastic storyteller, and all of her stories are teaching stories. If you care about who you are, why you are here, where you are going and what life is all about—pick up this book. You won't lay it down until you are through, and then you will want more. 317 P. $14.95 ISBN 1-891824-11-2

### ❾ EXPLORER RACE and JESUS

The core personality of that being known on the Earth as Jesus, along with his students and friends, describes with clarity and love his life and teaching two thousand years ago. He states that his teaching is for all people of all races in all countries. Jesus announces here for the first time that he and two others, Buddha and Mohammed, will return to Earth from their place of being in the near future, and a fourth being, a child already born now on Earth, will become a teacher and prepare humanity for their return. So heartwarming and interesting, you won't want to put it down. 354 P. $16.95 ISBN 1-891824-14-7

### ❿ EXPLORER RACE: Earth History and Lost Civilization

Speaks of Many Truths and Zoosh, through Robert Shapiro, explain that planet Earth, the only water planet in this solar system, is on loan from Sirius as a home and school for humanity, the Explorer Race. Earth's recorded history goes back only a few thousand years, its archaeological history a few thousand more. Now this book opens up as if a light was on in the darkness, and we see the incredible panorama of brave souls coming from other planets to settle on different parts of Earth. We watch the origins of tribal groups and the rise and fall of civilizations, and we can begin to understand the source of the wondrous diversity of plants, animals and humans that we enjoy here on beautiful Mother Earth. 310 P. $14.95 ISBN 1-891824-20-1

### ⓫ EXPLORER RACE: ET VISITORS SPEAK

Even as you are searching the sky for extraterrestrials and their spaceships, ETs are here on planet Earth—they are stranded, visiting, exploring, studying the culture, healing the Earth of trauma brought on by irresponsible mining or researching the history of Christianity over the past two thousand years. Some are in human guise, and some are in spirit form. Some look like what we call animals as they come from the species' home planet and interact with their fellow beings—those beings that we have labeled cats or cows or elephants. Some are brilliant cosmic mathematicians with a sense of humor; they are presently living here as penguins. Some are fledgling diplomats training for future postings on Earth when we have ET embassies here. In this book, these fascinating beings share their thoughts, origins and purposes for being here. 350 P. $14.95 ISBN 1-891824-28-7

### ⓬ EXPLORER RACE: Techniques for GENERATING SAFETY

Wouldn't you like to generate safety so you could go wherever you need to go and do whatever you need to do in a benevolent, safe and loving way for yourself? Learn safety as a radiated environment that will allow you to gently take the step into the new timeline, into a benevolent future and away from a negative past. 208 P. $9.95 ISBN 1-891824-26-0

# SHINING THE LIGHT SERIES

## ZOOSH AND OTHERS THROUGH ROBERT SHAPIRO

The Shining the Light series exposes the malevolent, controlling and manipulating actions of the sinister secret government (SSG) as they attempt to keep humans from accessing soul and spiritual functions and ascending into the fourth dimension and beyond. For many years you have all wondered, "What stops wonderful goals from being accomplished even if everyone is in favor of them?" These books will attempt to explain the invisible network and give you tangible things you can do to improve the quality of life for yourself and others and to gently but firmly dissolve the stranglehold on your societies by this sinister invisible network that we choose to call in these books the sinister secret government.

### SHINING THE LIGHT I
### THE BATTLE BEGINS!
SOFTCOVER 193 P. $12⁹⁵ ISBN 0-929385-66-7

Despite official denial and tactics of derision, active minds are demanding the truth. This truth is stranger than all the fictions about ETs, alien bases and the sinister secret government. The revelations are shocking and enlightening. A crashed UFO leads to information on: ✦ The sinister secret government's time-travel spacecraft ✦ Renegade ETs mining on the moon ✦ The U.S. peace-avatar president ✦ The prime directive—now ✦ Underground alien bases and populations ✦ Ancient Pleiadian warships ✦ Many more startling facts!

### SHINING THE LIGHT II
### THE BATTLE CONTINUES
SOFTCOVER 418 P. $14⁹⁵ ISBN 0-929385-70-5

Current status of the sinister secret government and those who want to usurp its power. Actual cosmic photographs of hidden crafts, beings and events. Photon Belt "Doctor" comes to save Mother Earth. The truth becomes even stranger as the story of alien involvement in Earth history continues. ✦ Update on humanity ✦ The light is returning home ✦ The sinister secret government is back in Sedona ✦ Zoosh explains the sightings ✦ Nineteen time-space anomalies ✦ Contactee children ✦ Bringing the babies home ✦ Sinister secret government moves entrance to underground base ✦ Xpotaz-sinister secret government shootout over Grand Canyon ✦ The face of God: Robert Meyer's photos explained ✦ The Creator and his friends ✦ Cosmic holograms (photos) ✦ The new vortex ✦ And more!

### SHINING THE LIGHT III
### HUMANITY GETS A SECOND CHANCE
SOFTCOVER 460 P. $14⁹⁵ ISBN 0-929385-71-3

The focus is on humanity as we begin to learn to render the sinister secret government powerless by being the light that we are. Earth becomes a member of the Council of Planets and the universe time-shifts to preserve the Explorer Race. ✦ Ninth-dimensional Mars ✦ The null zone ✦ ET helicopter pilots ✦ Sonic mapping ✦ Material masters ✦ Time collapses ✦ Exploding plane ✦ Cosmic photographs ✦ The Photon Belt ✦ And more!

### SHINING THE LIGHT IV
### HUMANITY'S GREATEST CHALLENGE
SOFTCOVER 557 P. $14⁹⁵ ISBN 0-929385-93-4

Includes information on Hale-Bopp, SSG, all updates since Volume III and material on the uncreating of Hitler in 1993. ✦ Negative Sirians coming to the third dimension ✦ The express bus to creatorship ✦ The poison HAARP project ✦ Luciferian traits and critical mass ✦ ETs in Brazil ✦ Comet brings lightbeing-filled vehicle bigger than Earth ✦ Sinister secret government under control of beings from the alternate negative future.

### SHINING THE LIGHT V
### HUMANITY IS GOING TO MAKE IT!
SOFTCOVER 460 P. $14⁹⁵ ISBN 1-891824-00-7

Zoosh and others blast the cover off past events and hidden forces at work on this planet and reveal opportunities for immense growth and power. This is a pivotal time as the secrets and mysteries that have so long bewildered humanity are at last illuminated by the light of truth. ✦ Revelations about Area 51 by a rocket scientist ✦ A 75-year-long Zeta restructuring of the past ✦ Cloning: the new ethics forum ✦ Recent UFO activity in the skies ✦ The first humans and the original dark side, our shadow ✦ Angels: guides in training (30% of humans are angels) ✦ Using manifestation powers to avert man-made disasters ✦ The angel of Roswell ✦ Symbiotic spacecraft engines and faster-than-light travel ✦ The true purpose of the Mayans ✦ The SSG downs military planes ✦ The SSG realizes they need customers, not slaves ✦ Grid lines rising above the planet ✦ Homework for changing your past.

# The Amethyst Light

## by Djwhal Khul through Violet Starre

**P**erhaps you are thumbing through the pages of this little book, wondering if it contains the insights you are looking for. Who is Ascended Master Djwhal Khul? Will this book be useful to you? Will it help you to understand metaphysics and present time in Earth history? Will it help you in life?

I was a Tibetan Buddhist monk. I ran a monastery. In that life I focused on meditation, study, simple chores and teaching. The contemplative life helps to raise consciousness and provides a testing ground for how well principles have been learned. In my Tibetan incarnation I sought my true Buddha nature to demonstrate compassion for all sentient beings and to break free of reincarnation and join the Noble Ones. I write not as a man incarnated on Earth, but as a member of the spiritual hierarchy, for the benefit of. Join me in this work.

**$14**⁹⁵  Softcover 128 P.
ISBN 1-891824-41-4

# The Diamond Light

## by Djwhal Khul through Violet Starre

**T**his book presents esoteric teachings similar to those given to Alice A. Bailey between the two great world wars and offers them in short, concise and simple form. The original teachings from the Master Djwhal Khul were presented in lengthy volumes that were difficult to understand without a deep background in Theosophy, founded by Madame Blavatsky in the late 19th century. The Master wishes now to offer a short, clear and accessible text for the general New Age reader. The Master is one member of a planetary council of spiritual beings who exist within another dimension and guide the spiritual destiny of this planet and its life forms. Although this spiritual government exists, it does not interfere with the free will of humanity but occasionally sends such teachers to guide us.

The Master is accessible to all and does not reserve his communication only for the most advanced souls. He is available to those who most desperately need him, who feel as if they are struggling to survive in the modern world without a message of hope. That message can be found here.

**LIGHT TECHNOLOGY PUBLISHING**

Call us at
1-800-450-0985
or log on to
www.lighttechnology.com

**$14**⁹⁵  Softcover 154 P.
ISBN 1-891824-25-2

# CROP CIRCLES REVEALED

## LANGUAGE OF THE LIGHT SYMBOLS

BARBARA LAMB, MS, MFL
JUDITH K. MOORE

$25⁰⁰

SOFTCOVER 308 P.
ISBN 1-891824-32-5

W elcome to the world of crop circles, one of the most **TANTALIZING** phenomena in our world today. It is difficult not to be captivated by their beauty and complexity and by the questions and issues they provoke, including one that becomes more pressing everyday—what other **INTELLIGENT** life forms are out there trying to communicate with us? What are their intentions? What is the communication system between them, the Earth and humanity? Unlock the secret keys for the emergence of a new world of peace, freedom, healing and unconditional love. We are being assisted with energy as never before to **REGENERATE** ourselves and our ailing planet. Reactivate and discover your invaluable gifts and divine mission. Awaken your DNA and empower yourself! This comprehensive document reveals the deep mysteries of the crop circle phenomenon. Scientific analysis of the hoaxing controversy and high-level spiritual transmissions are combined in one masterful presentation for your use and interpretation.

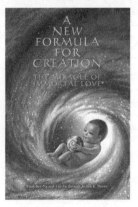

# A NEW FORMULA FOR CREATION

## Laiolin and the Council of Abboraha
### through Judith K. Moore

"What do I think? Wow! It's definitely a mind-expanding experience. I can only imagine how it must have stretched Judith during the 'birthing' process. Perhaps the holographic message within this book will finally generate the 'critical mass' necessary to elevate human thinking above the egocentric mind control still so prevalent today. One way or another, a new age is dawning! This book admirably reminds us that that dawning extends far beyond just the refreshment of our patient little Mother Earth."

—Dr. Edwin M. Young

$16⁹⁵  Softcover 214 P.
ISBN 1-891824-57-0

- Enak-Kee-Na Speaks
- Sacred Geometry and the Nature of Creation
- Expanded Understanding of DNA
- Raqui-Sha-Ma Hears Her Story
- Solstice 2001: The Time Portal Opens

- The Saturnian Empire
- The Enshroudment of Isha
- Isha, The Unified Field
- Masters of Dimensions Project the Distortion
- I AM ENAK-KEE-NA

# TOOLS FOR TRANSFORMATION

## VYWAMUS channeled by Janet McClure

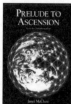

### PRELUDE TO ASCENSION
**Tools for Transformation**
*Janet McClure channeling Djwhal Khul, Vywamus & others*

Your four bodies, the Tibetan Lessons series, the Twelve Rays, the Cosmic Walk-in and others. All previously unpublished channelings by Janet McClure.

**$29.95, SOFTCOVER 850 P. • ISBN 0-929385-54-3**

---

### THE SOURCE ADVENTURE

Life is discovery, and this book is a journey of discovery "to learn, to grow, to recognize the opportunities—to be aware." It asks the big question, "Why are you here?" and leads the reader to examine the most significant questions of a lifetime.

**$11.95, SOFTCOVER 157 P. • ISBN 0-929385-06-3**

---

### SCOPES OF DIMENSIONS

Vywamus explains the process of exploring and experiencing the dimensions. He teaches an integrated way to utilize the combined strengths of each dimension. It is a how-to guidebook for living in the multidimensional reality that is our true evolutionary path.

**$11.95, SOFTCOVER 176 P. • ISBN 0-929385-09-8**

---

### AHA! THE REALIZATION BOOK
#### (with Lillian Harben)

If you are mirroring your life in a way that is not desirable, this book can help you locate murky areas and make them "suddenly . . . crystal clear." Readers will discover an exciting step-by-step path to changing and evolving their lives.

**$11.95, SOFTCOVER 120 P. • ISBN 0-929385-14-4**

---

### SANAT KUMARA
**Training a Planetary Logos**

How was the beauty of this world created? The answer is in the story of Earth's Logos, the great being Sanat Kumara. It is a journey through his eyes as he learns the real-life lessons of training along the path of mastery.

**$11.95, SOFTCOVER 179 P. • ISBN 0-929385-17-9**

---

### LIGHT TECHNIQUES
#### That Trigger Transformation

Expanding the heart center, launching your light, releasing the destructive focus, weaving a garment of light, light alignment and more, this book is a wonderfully effective tool for using light to transcend. Beautiful guidance!

**$11.95, SOFTCOVER 145 P. • ISBN 0-929385-00-4**

# Forever Numerology

## Includes Master Numbers 11–99!

## by Lynn Buess

$17⁹⁵ Softcover 290 p. ISBN 1-891824-65-1

In *Forever Numerology*, Lynn Buess again takes a gigantic leap for numerology with extraordinary new insights and methods of interpretation. This volume will define new standards for years to come. You will be swept through transcendent realms of light and awareness, even as Buess's solid psychological base and down-to-earth reality keep you centered right here in the present moment.

Having practiced for decades as a psychotherapist, Buess has uncovered deeply repressed blocks and negative unconscious complexes in many of his clients. In this book, he works some of his insights for recognizing dysfunction into the interpretation of numerology in the hopes of awakening new seekers to the dark side of the self. Once you recognize this dark side, you have the possibility of working it out of your life. The interpretations and experiences presented in this book are given through the symbolic wisdom of numbers.

Truly, no complete volume can be written on any subject; however, this book comes closer than ever to portraying the evolution of consciousness through the symbology of numbers. It will be of help in your journey through life and in your search for the meaning of numbers.

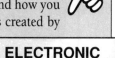